IN ONE PLACE

*THE NATURAL HISTORY
OF A GEORGIA FARMER*

by

MILTON N. HOPKINS, JR.

INTRODUCTION
by

JANISSE RAY

*Best Wishes
Milton Hopkins
3-19-'02*

THE SALTMARSH PRESS, INC.

In One Place: The Natural History of a Georgia Farmer
Copyright © 2001 by Milton N.Hopkins Jr.
Published by THE SALTMARSH PRESS, INC
P.O. Box 20032 St Simons Island Ga 31522

Library of Congress Catalogue in Publication Data:

Hopkins, Milton N.
    In One Place: the natural history of a Georgia Farmer/by Milton N. Hopkins ; introduction by Janisse Ray..
    p. cm.
ISBN: 0-9666365-5-4 (alk. paper)
1. Farm life—Georgia—Fitzgerald 2. Hopkins, Milton N. 3. Natural history—Georgia—Fitzgerald. 4. Fitzgerald (Ga.)—Social life and customs. I. Title.
S521.5.G4H66 2001
630'.9758'852—dc21

Typeset by: Jesse Howard
Cover by: Mike Brooks
Printed in The United States By: McNaughton and Gunn, Inc.

For My Grandchildren

And

Great-Grandchildren

And For

Donna Raiford Hopkins

1962-1968

ACKNOWLEDGEMENTS

I began to write down these stories many years ago for my amusement and in the hope that my children and grandchildren might find something of interest in them. The people I have described here are real people whom I knew and trusted. I often agonize over not having listened more closely to my elders; their tales were so interesting they would put mine to shame.

Many friends have jogged my memory in recalling for me conversations, dates and experiences, particularly those I had 'appeared' in and long forgotten.

Early field observations from 1938 on in the company of Robert A. Norris gave me much insight into the natural world and continue to do so.

Frankie Snow has enhanced my understanding of botany and has been a field trip partner for many years.

Son Bubba Hopkins has keen eyes and an uncanny ability to ride by fields and spot the movements of animals and birds, which I would have overlooked. He contributed to the farm's bird list with first recordings of the painted bunting, the scissor-tail flycatcher and the golden eagle.

Thanks also to Willard Andrew, Wilson Baker, Clyde Connell, Herman Coolidge, Jim Cottingham, John and Nell Crenshaw, Ken George, T.P. Haines, Fred Hancock, Katy Hopkins, Donnie Hopkins, Jack Hopkins, James Kilgo, Brooke Meanly, Bruce Means, Philip Murton, Leon and Julie Neel, Eugene P. Odum, Richard Parks, Frank Parris, Franklin Ray, Carol Ruckdeschel, Betty Stewart, John Stokes, Bob Shoop, Chris Trowell, Emil and Lois Urban, Carol and Darrell Weeks, Angus and Eloise Gholson, Mary Andrew, Jack Paulk and David Wilcox.

I am indebted to Janisse Ray for her early encouragement, which has meant much to me. Thanks to Saltmarsh Press, Margaret Birney and Victor Howard for their editing expertise, and for seeing some potential in these tales.

INTRODUCTION
By
JANISSE RAY

What feels like a hundred years ago but was really only seven or eight, I pulled up in front of the renovated railroad depot where Milton Hopkins lives on his farm in southern Georgia, near the ghost town of Osierfield. Milton had been recommended to me on two accounts: he was native to my homeland and he was, as I wished to be, a naturalist.

On these same accounts, we also differed greatly. Milton was a far more knowledgeable naturalist than I, having studied with the father of ecology, Eugene Odum, and having lived many of his sixty and more years with unfettered curiosity about and close attention to, the natural world. He had not left rural south Georgia, as I had, but had returned home after university to farm.

Now he had been in one place nearly all of his life at a time when country people in great numbers were migrating from family farms to burgeoning cities in hopes of finding easier and better lives.

So Milton Hopkins is an anomaly, a man going in one direction while most of us go in another. He is a man of character in the truest sense of that word, a man carved by seasons and weather and hard work. And by his love of beauty. He is one of a vanishing breed of country gentlemen naturalists, an unusual and a very special and a little understood calling.

That day when I drove into his yard, where loblolly bay was blooming, Milton came out to greet me, grinning from ear to ear, as was I, and those first minutes together designed our friendship, which has been a great gift to me. Milton is a delightful, generous, loyal man who loves life in all its manifestations and lives it to the hilt. From that first meeting our friendship could do nothing but grow.

I was living in Tallahassee at the time, pining for home, and so Milton and I began to correspond. He would send me essays—tales he called them—that he wrote on winter evenings to entertain himself and to record events of his life. The tales were about days on the farm and in the woods, and they were fascinating, engaging and colorful. What made them even more compelling was Milton's unique perspective—a well-educated man, a university trained scientist, who returned to his homeland and stayed in that place for fifty years.

Milton's tales documented a changing rural South from the time farming depended on mules, and turpentining and growing cotton formed a large part of work on the farm, to the present when his son and grandson work the Osierfield land with mammoth tractors, combines and irrigation systems. The stories told of folk-ways and traditions of rural Southerners from the 1930s to the 1960s. Not only were they entertaining, but they were a trove of knowledge about ways almost lost to our generation.

So I began to type them and, with Milton's permission, to gather them together. And now they form a book. Section One, "Boyhood in Fitzgerald," is about growing up on the outskirts of that small town. Section Two, "Osierfield Farm," is set on the farm where Milton has spent his adult life. Section Three, "Field Notes," is a collection of commentaries about the natural history of Milton's world.

This book stands as testimony to the greatness of a life-long love for one place.

— JR

TABLE OF CONTENTS

Preface

Part I.: Boyhood in Fitzgerald

Grandpaw Walker	3
Postscript: How to Prepare a Possum,	
Paw Walker Style	8
Cousin Contests	9
Growing Penders on Halves	11
Swapping Lunches	13
Rattlesnake	15
The Value of a Dollar	17
The Woodyard	20
Lucy, Our Contented Cow	22
My Neighbor, Mrs. Fohle	25
Greasing the Rails	27
The Railroad Trussel	29
Knot Hole and Other Near-Misses	33
Kite Flying	37
Corks	41
Postscript: Patent Medicine	43
Uncle Will Walker and the Bear	44
Boys Will Be Boys	45
A Stolen Boat	46
Vandiver's Five & Ten Cent Store	48
Allen's Supermarket	51
Wade Cleary, Fire Chief	54
George Eaton and the Greased Cable Line	57
Postscript: Making a Flip	59
Snipe Hunt	60
Trips in the Model A	62
Chain Gang	65
The Ocean	67

Postscript: Undertow	72
First Flight	73
Misgivings, At Least the Admitted Ones	75
Catastrophe	79

PART II:. OSIERFIELD FARM

Courtship and Marriage	83
Dr. McElroy and His Brother Pat	88
You Killed My Vote	93
Shoot-Out in Osierfield	95
Dr. McElroy and His Jay Bird Springs Water	98
Cotton Picking	100
Postscript: Picking Cotton When I was a Boy	104
Crow Foster, Plow Hand	106
Mister Fred and the Black Preacher	109
Henry Beavers and Mule Farming	111
Postscript: The Beavers Prepare a Sow	112
Turpentining	114
Postscript: The Turpentining Mules	118
Joe King and His Family	119
One Unique Individual	122
Postscript: Picking Up Pecans	125
Joseph Robinson and the High Sheriff of Irwin County	127
Drinking Likker	129
Tobacco	133
Postscript: Foot-racing for "Dopes" or Cokes	140
The Wisdom and Folly of Ear Marking Livestock	141
Screw Worms	144
Growing Sweet Potatoes	147
Root Doctor	150
Meeks Harper's Bear	152

Postscript: Gathering Honey	153
Dynamite	154
The Greek Stands	157
Postscript: Preparing Salt Fish	160
A High Class and Expensive Train Wreck	161
Riding the Rails	162
Postscript: Laying Rail	163
Sam Davis, Official Wasp Nest Remover	165
Dog Days	167
Wells	169
Postscript: Anthony Hines, Master Mason	172
Guano	174
Going Fishing in Lay-By Time	176
Making Sausage	178
Postscript: Making Mash for Hog Slop	182
Settlin' Up	183
Deep Sea Fishing	184
Flying	187
Funeralizing	195
"Dad" Dixon	198
Glory Be, All The Cows Are Gone	200
More Ways To Skin A Cat	205
Red-Neck Show	208

PART III: FIELD NOTES

Ode to Swamps	209
Hunting Pearls in Freshwater Clams of House Creek	212
Postscript: Bowen's Mill	213
Bird Watching	215
Early Naturalists	217
Dr. Francis Harper, Old-Time Naturalist	221
The Red-Headed Scorpion	224
Tektite	226

Herbert L. Stoddard, 1889-1970	228
Buzzards	231
Encounter With a Giant Snake	233
The Speed of Soft-Shelled Turtles	238
Smelling Fish Beds	239
Postscript: How To Cook Bream, Southern Style	241
Robins	242
Canines in the Wild	244
The Limey Bird Ringer	246
The Golden Mouse	249
Asafetida	251
Catawba Worms	252
Postscript: Catalpa Tree Pods	253
Seventeen-Year Locusts	254
Sandhill Cranes	256
Hunting Quail	259
Postscript: Cooking Quail Eggs	263
Thoughts Late of an Evening	264

ILUSTRATIONS PROVIDED BY THE AUTHOR

PREFACE

Sometimes late of an evening on the farm, I sit in reverie and write tales of years ago, for I have been here over fifty years now. These musings are fanciful products of the mind, simply notions, strange or impractical at best. But maybe it's somehow practical to record some things on paper before the remembrances are fugitives from one's mind; after all, a wise person once told me that the dullest ink is better than the best memory.

In the early 1950s, after leaving the University of Georgia in Athens, I went to Osierfield to be employed by father-in-law Dr. J.W. McElroy, who had been ailing for some years and wished me to look after the Osierfield farm. I was twenty-five then, had an M.S. degree in ecology and zoology under my belt and really wanted to go into wildlife management. I especially had in mind getting a position as caretaker of some Georgia barrier island, like Blackbeard. My wife, Mary, talked me out of this, wishing to get back near home, persuading me to go try to help Daddy.

Was this a revelation! Dr. McElroy proposed that I work for him and his interests at two hundred dollars a month and a Chevrolet pickup—brand-new but stripped to a bare frame and cab, no heater, no AC, no radio, almost no nothing. Mary and I had been living in poor accommodations for years, subsisting on a ninety dollars-a-month GI bill, one of the most productive pieces of legislation to ever leave the halls of the U.S. Congress.

Dr. McElroy commenced my farm and turpentine apprenticeship by putting me in the peanut field in the fall of 1951 with about fifty black hands, acting as straw boss and timekeeper. Husbands and wives were putting peanuts, recently plowed up and side-delivered with a John Deere rake, in neat rows. The men could not read or write, but by God they could count. We were working in the South Walker Cut (south of John Walker's house) in Tifton upland soil that was resplendent with red pebbles. The hands gathered up overhaul pockets of these and on the completion of a stack of peanuts transferred one of these pebbles to the right pocket. The contents of the right pocket at sundown indicated how many stacks they had put up.

Oft'times the women would not work as a team with their husbands, preferring to answer their own payroll call, since many of them were doing more work than their spouses. This was always the case in the cotton patch. The men just did not have their hearts and minds in this job, which they figured was women's work. The women were more dexterous, and a good many in the cotton-picking crew could top four hundred and nigh on to five hundred pounds in the run of the day, from sunrise, when the dew was still on the cotton and perhaps added a bit of extra weight, until just before sunset. The long day was called "caint to caint;" caint hardly see before the sun came up to caint hardly see as the sun went down. They always wanted to weigh up about a half-hour before sundown for it was hard to see how to cook by lamplight.

I once had the chance to work beside the best picker in the field. At the time we were growing near six hundred acres of the plant and gathering it all by hand. Except for the peanut acreage and about twenty acres of mule corn, cotton was king, hilltop to branch. My "opponent" was taking two rows at a time and I was steadily losing ground on one row, trying to keep up. The day ended and I weighed in a hundred and twenty-five pounds, while she had over four hundred. This was the last time I seriously tried to pick cotton.

PART I

Boyhood in Fitzgerald

GRANDPAW WALKER

Scott Walton Walker, my maternal grandpa who lived to about ninety-seven, was an obstinate old cuss, stubborn as a mule. All us grandchillun highly respected him for he was a strict disciplinarian, and by God, if he promised you a thrashing you had better hang around in his arm's reach to get your sentence. Woe to those unwise siblings or cousins who made the choice to run. He tenaciously stuck to his opinions and when it came to make a pronouncement, he did so in no uncertain terms and language.

Paw was also tight—amounts to being stingy. He'd come up hardscrabble and guarded his pennies until they numbered a hundred, whereupon he'd swap them to the bank for one cartwheel or silver dollar, then a major piece of money. He carried his change in a small, leather, snap-lock purse; I can still see him digging into it with his forefinger, looking for the smallest coin he could find—an Indian head penny—to reward some grandchild for a task performed. My mother and her siblings, when in their fifties and sixties, were proud to get a shiny half-dollar or later a silver cartwheel for Christmas from Paw, perhaps remembering the times when they got nothing besides some fruit and a Merry Christmas.

Paw Walker married his first cousin, "Charlie" Tyus. He said this was his choice—he didn't want to walk his mule team further than Charlie Tyus's home for his courting. He'd also been apprised of her abilities as a housekeeper and a doggone good cook. She later proved this and could be depended on to fix Paw his favorite breakfast, "the same," each morning. "The same" consisted of two one-minute eggs, cornbread, buttermilk and a piece of fatback, or if he was eating high on the hog, a slab of country cured ham smothered in red-eye gravy. Another favorite of Paw's was hog brains and scrambled eggs for breakfast, along with buttermilk and grits. I savor this too, but now it comes from the can. Strangely I get few takers—none, actually—when I offer this breakfast to guests. Paw would have told them, "Don't knock it if'n you haven't tried it." Paw always liked to end his meal with a little sweetening, cane syrup over a couple of biscuits or the cornbread. When he rose from the table, no matter the meal, Paw would say, "That was good. I feel just as well as if'n I'd eaten aplenty."

Paw worked on the railroads for nigh on sixty years. He reckoned it all started when, on a late July afternoon, he drove into Albany with a two-hoss wagon loaded with watermelons. It had been a hot twenty-five or thirty mile trip on two-rut wagon trails, plus a night spent sleeping under the wagon. This was in the 1890s when the watermelon broker was located at the railroad station near the Flint River. Paw offered up his wagon load of melons to the broker who was trying to fill a carbox for shipment north. The broker told Paw he'd give him a half-cent a pound, take it or leave it, for the load.

Paw thought this over for some time and had about decided to sell when he happened to walk quietly (he was barefoot) by an open window of the depot and overheard the broker say to the station agent, "Just watch that pore son of a bitch; when that sun starts to set over the river he'll sell out for half that price."

Paw went back in and asked once again of the broker what he'd give for the load. On getting the same answer, he swore to the broker that he'd back his team up to the bluff and dump the whole load into the river, rather than sell for that ridiculous price. He proceeded to do just that but not before splitting one of the finest with his pocketknife and eating the heart.

He told me that he then headed south with the team and after traveling all night he got to the homestead, loaded up the wife and three chillun and all their belongings, and headed back north. He hired on to the railroad section gang in Americus, where he shoveled Stone Mountain gravel as ballast, placed ties and drove spikes. Paw stayed with railroads until the late 1940s.

Paw Walker had a free pass on the railroads, and by golly, he intended to use that privilege. He usually traveled alone, probably not wanting to buy a second ticket. It was exciting to be around when he told Granny to get down his grip and pack him enough clothes for three days, just like in the ballad, "Hand me down my grip and cane, for I'm leaving on the midnight train." He'd pack a shoebox with fried chicken and homemade biscuits to get him through the first day, supplemented by cups of coffee bought for a nickel a cup with free refills. One time he rode his pass to Miami, boarded a train ferry, and went clean to Havana, Cuba.

Although he wasn't a heavy drinker, Paw liked his toddy—about a half tea glass full of good shine or store bought bourbon, one teaspoon of sugar and filled to the top with creek water. Granny didn't allow any liquor in the house so Paw Walker kept his supply in the mule barn. Paw like to tell a drinking story about the wildest Sunday school picnic he ever attended. It took place under the iron bridge over the Flint River, which separated Baker and Mitchell counties. Seems the good religious folks of Baker and Mitchell had organized this Sunday meeting with dinner on the grounds to celebrate something, maybe a revival. Paw said they came in mule and wagon from ten or fifteen miles around. Some fellows saw fit to bring in several charred kegs of homemade stump liquor in case the food ran out.

The event started on a high plane—some preaching, some baptisings in the Flint River, a lot of eating and singing and then the liquor surfaced. Within an hour hellation came forth and the gathering turned into a wild melee of cracked skulls, bloodied noses, river dunkings and some of the worst fisticuffs Paw had ever witnessed. Paw never got to crawling drunk, and abhorred those who did, so, for the sake of his wife and chillun, he hitched up early and cleared out. This event made a lasting impression on his mind for he vividly recounted it to me several times many, many years later.

At home he kept his personal toolboxes filled with all the tools a good carpenter might ever need. They were oiled, sharp and in good working order, and had no rust on them. He kept a strong lock on this box and wouldn't allow any of his children or "cowshed" carpenters who knew how to hammer, nail and saw, though when it came to cutting a rafter at the "bird's beak" angle to fit neatly on the ridge pole, they were lost.

Paw checked things out each evening and the work proceeded according to his plan. He insisted on having wide, four-foot overhangs over the rafter tails to protect the windows and screens from the weather. It only cost a few dollars extra and simply made a farce out of modern-day carpenters' practice of stopping the roof overhang about six inches from the end of the rafter tail, thereby requiring gutters and drainpipes to prevent rot. The original window screens, made of galvanized webbing, lasted almost fifty years.

Adjoining the kitchen there was a cupboard for Granny. It was a really big closet, lined from floor to ceiling with shelves. The upper shelves were crowded with Mason jars, all a pretty light green, but filled with home-canned vegetables that gave them a variety of pretty colors. Nowadays the empty Mason jars with their zinc lids, bottomed by white glass, sell empty for five or ten dollars apiece.

Paw put in three fireplaces, a big one in the living room, over which was placed an oil painting of the Mayflower in stormy seas. The other two were in the bedrooms. He liked coal fires, in particular bituminous coal, probably filched from the railroad supply at Westwood, brought into action with a few lightered knots as starter. I can picture him now, sitting in his cane bottom or rawhide rocker in front of the bedroom fireplace, smoking a pipe loaded with Prince Albert or enjoying a chew of Brown's Mule chewing tobacco. He didn't allow us grandchillun to poke the fire—said we'd scatter ashes and make a mess for Granny to clean up.

Granny Walker died in 1937. It was a sad day for me for we were really good, loving, faithful friends, but Paw Walker was completely disoriented without her. He lived alone for a spell until Mama Hattie Lee talked him into moving in with us. He brought only the clothes on his back and his beloved tool chest. Unwisely, Paw had sold his home to Dr. John Edward Smith but after a short stay with our family of five noisy children, he went to Dr. Smith almost on bent knees and begged him to sell the house back. Kind-hearted and compassionate, Dr. John Ed did exactly this and Paw spent thirty more happy years in his home.

Paw Walker had broken both his legs when he was in his eighties. He was supervising the doping of his car, greasing the steering joints and doping the transmission and differential. The car left the rack in neutral and pinned him between the front bumper and a brick wall. Nowadays it would have been grounds for lawsuit but Paw looked at it otherwise. "I shouldn't have been standing where I was," he said.

We owned a mare Tennessee Walker name of Lady, a second- or third-handed horse of a kind disposition. I'd ride her to town on a Friday afternoon when my children were small and keep her there in a small shed during the weekend for daughter Carol to ride. When Paw Walker was ninety-two years old he said, "I've ridden all kinds of horses in my younger days and would like to ride Lady." We were apprehensive, but when he turned up and said it was his time to ride we couldn't refuse him. Several of us offered to help him into the saddle, whereupon he said, "Shaw, a man don't need any help to mount a horse."

He and Lady set off down the dirt road at the smooth, rocking canter at which Lady was most proficient—that is, she could cover a long distance at a good rate of speed with the least discomfort to her rider. Paw passed from our view about a mile away and we were worried until we saw him returning a few moments later. He dismounted with no assistance and proclaimed how much this ride brought back old times. He did admit the day after, privately, how sore his muscles were, but said, "Then again at my age it takes a lot of groaning to just get out of bed."

POSTSCRIPT
How to Prepare a Possum, Paw Walker Style

Paw always ate well and liked to add a little zest to the usual fare by keeping several possums on hand in wire chicken coops. He was seldom without at least one possum. I caught a lot of them after he demonstrated how to chase one down in the woods, catch him by the tip of his prehensile tail and lift him up. The possums would sull and show their teeth but couldn't reach up to get my hand.

Possums are omnivorous scavengers—they will eat anything. Paw would "clean them out," converting them from eating anything to eating table scraps of the same things Paw was eating. When he deemed they were "cleaned out" and fit for the table, he'd grab one by its tail from the cage, hold it up and club it in the head, quickly skin and gut it and cut the tail off. The whole carcass was placed in a cast iron pan after salting and peppering—no herbs or spices. By the time he killed them they were extremely fat and cooked in their own juices. It was a traditional meal to bake six or seven sweet potatoes in the woodstove oven at the same time the possum was baking, then peel them when they were done and line them around the edges of the serving tray. I was twenty-one years old before I heard a modern version of a seven-course meal—I'd always thought it meant a baked possum and six sweet potatoes.

COUSIN CONTESTS

Granny Walker doted on her grandchillun and often went along with their fantasies and desires. We grandsons bragged so highly on her good homemade biscuits that she sometimes offered to go into the cupboard, mix up another batch for us, bake them and serve them with country-made butter and a jug of cane syrup. My cousins and I once decided to take advantage of the situation and had a biscuit-eating contest; I ate twelve of her creations. That was overdoing it and I had to go into the backyard and relieve myself of the overload.

My cousins and I liked these competitions. I well remember walking to Knot Hole, as the country boys called a wash hole on the Willacoochee River, on a hot July day, taking a washing, swimming a little, and later walking the five-mile dirt road back home. Most farmers and farmers wives welcomed us to draw a bucket of water from their surface well but others sicked their dogs on us and hollered, "Stay out of my yard." When that happened, we made the return trip with dry throats.

Thus evolved another contest. Paw and Granny were connected to a deep city well by black-iron pipe and there were faucets all over the yard. We went in and asked Granny Walker for a pint Mason jar, which she promptly produced. We took turns drinking from the jar filled with deliciously cool water. I can't remember how many times I filled it to the brim, but I won the contest. My overextended gut couldn't accommodate all I drank, but I had sworn I'd outdrink the whole passel of cousins. This was called "catching up."

A hurtling contest took place between us in my Uncle Warren's potato field. I recall that all us first cousins, his nephews and nieces, had answered his call to help gather the Irish potato crop. He had already gone down the middle of each row with his middle buster attached to the shank of the push plow and most of the taters were lying on top of the ground. We cousins were supposed to pick up the taters, place them in washtubs or baskets for delivery to his house, and spread them out on dry dirt for storage. We gathered everything down to half-inch and one-inch size taters.

All went well for a while. Then we male cousins got into a tater-throwing war, throwing them at each other. This was forbidden because it bruised the taters and they wouldn't keep well. Putting food by for his family was very serious business with Uncle Warren because he didn't intend to head to the store for many purchases.

The soil had many red pebbles in it, some up to the size of baseballs and larger. Cuz Billy Walker, thinking to improve on the taters as a missile, picked up a baseball-sized stone, made a quick pitch towards me and it connected midway on my forehead. Blood began to flow all over my face and eyes, and down my chin to my neck. The spectacle scared the shit out of Billy and he left the tater patch, fast-trotted two blocks home and hid under the front porch for nigh on two hours, thinking he had killed or maimed me.

T'warnt that serious. We cousins all dutifully lined up for a collective thrashing with a gallberry limb, administered by Uncle Warren for the crime of willfully bruising the taters. I can't recollect whether cuz Billy got his later or not but he suffered enough.

GROWING PENDERS ON HALVES

Grandpaw Walker suggested we break up the vacant lot twixt his house and ours. That meant getting a hand with his dilapidated mule and a one-hoss Oliver turning plow to turn the soil and streak off furrows, into which we hand-dropped penders, as he called them. He never called them peanuts, though he sometimes referred to them as ground peas. The best tasting variety, on account of their high oil content, was the Spanish peanut, a small-fruited plant that spread only eight to eleven inches and produced a good knot of taproot peanuts. After arranging for the plowing and seed dropping, Paw backed off and said, "I've showed you how, now take over and I'll tell you when to dig. We'll do it all on halves."

I anxiously watched the growth and when he said dig, I hand-wrassled the peanut vines from the soil and picked the nuts off by hand. Then Mama took over. We set up a cast-iron pot in the backyard, filled it half full of well water, tossed in the peanuts, added ice-cream salt (this was cheapest), brought the pot to a rolling boil over a lightered knot fire and boiled the penders for fifteen or twenty minutes, tasting all the while. Green boiled peanuts are an epicure's delight in the Southeast. They must be dug just before maturity when they are sweet and succulent. We popped them open to get to the kernels, munching shells and all and sucking the juice from them.

When they were boiled and sacked, a quarter-pound to the brown paper sack, I toted them to town in the bicycle basket and stood in front of the Grand Theater, the only picture show in town. This was a heavy selling spot, for patrons liked to buy a sack of boiled peanuts along with a soda water and go through them while watching the show.

I stood barefoot in my striped blue overalls, without shirt or other clothes. There was a good bit of competition, for I was far from the first to take advantage of this enterprise. I'd usually sell out before sundown, but if the sun got too low I'd begin hawking them, "two fer a nickel, four fer a dime," to get rid of my stock. Then I'd head home with two overall pockets bulging with buffalo nickels, look up Paw and make the final settlement on the kitchen table. Paw would take the pile of nickels and begin counting two piles, one for you and one for me. This was high finance and it intrigued me.

Growing penders on halves lasted only one season. Later on, we bought from a farmer about three miles west of Fitzgerald who would sell us all the green peanuts we wanted for ten cents a pound. We had to pedal out there, go to his pender patch, pull up the vines, take them all to a shade tree in O.M. Outlaw's front yard, where we picked them off by hand, then have them weighed by Mr. Outlaw, and finally, boil and sell the finished product.

Nowadays you'll see signs all over the South advertising fresh-boiled peanuts. They are fresh boiled all right, but not green boiled. The salesmen buy last year's crop of dried peanuts, boil them in a big pot over a propane fire after having soaked them in brine the night before. They are a travesty against the real product but some folks just don't know any better.

SWAPPING LUNCHES

At Third Ward School in Fitzgerald it was a customary habit to tote our dinner (I still can't call it lunch) to school in a used brown paper sack. At that time everyone saved paper sacks, string, tin foil, used hog grease and the likes. Some fetched their dinner in a syrup bucket, a one-gallon tin pail with tight-fitting lid, because it was reusable and the sometimes-wet sandwiches wouldn't fall through the bottom, as in a brown sack.

This brings to mind how good vine-ripened, homegrown tomato sandwiches are after sitting in the bottom of your desk for three or four hours. They had been made between seven and seven-thirty that morning with a generous amount of home-whipped mayonnaise spread on two slices of store-bought bread, interposed with two or three slices of the delicious berry, plus plenty of salt and black pepper. The juice of the ripe tomato completely soaked the bread into a soggy mess that took two hands to get to the mouth.

The rest of dinner consisted of one hard-boiled egg, alongside salt and pepper twisted inside of two small packages, which Mama had made from the new-fangled wax paper. Barnyard eggs that had been sitting in the cupboard for several days at room temperature after boiling were the easiest to crack and peel. (I didn't know until the late 1940s that they made eggs in the back of supermarkets.) We held the cracked egg by the big end and alternately dipped it in the salt and pepper. The last element of a shore-nuff good school dinner was the dessert, a peanut butter and jelly sandwich.

Another favorite for school lunches was fried rabbit, a delicacy provided with the help of a rabbit trap. I had been instructed on how to make a rabbit trap by Grandpa Walker when I was eight or ten years old. He made the first few with secondhand lumber and then turned them over to me, expecting surplus rabbits. The boxes were five to six inches wide, twelve to sixteen inches long, and six inches high. A hole was bored in the back end with a brace-and-bit, and a string attached to a fulcrum connected across the top with a notched lever. At the end of the string hung an inviting half apple or carrot. When a cottontail rabbit wandered by this contraption, he smelled, or saw, the delectable morsel, and entered the box. In the process of nibbling on food, he would pull too hard and trip the release mechanism, causing the front door to fall shut. When you found a shut box you slowly raised the sliding door and waited with a stick to bash the occupant as it backed out.

One day, on joyfully seeing another shut box, I quickly pulled up the sliding door and under my raised hand and stunning stick, out backed a polecat. This was my first encounter with this creature (also called a skunk or civet cat), but something told me to hold off. He quietly ran away and either was good-natured enough or too shocked to shoot his evil-smelling juice.

Another delight that went into school lunches was fried squirrel. These, like rabbits, I trapped until I was allowed to tote a gun. Grandpa Walker loaned me a brace-and-bit to bore one-inch holes into a freshly fallen log, or one we had cut down. Then I pounded six to eight finishing nails in toward the hole at angles so they rayed toward a central point. I baited the hole with pecan halves or peanuts, which would entice the cat squirrel to reach in with a foreleg. The squirrel got impaled on the nails and was easy prey, though the catch results weren't nearly as good as with rabbit trapping. Mama always said she would cook me anything I brought in, but she requested I first cut off squirrel's tails at the base—she said they looked too much like tree rats.

The city boys were gung-ho on wanting to swap their store bought meat sandwiches, cookies and cakes for a squirrel or rabbit hind leg and I was quick to oblige, happy for variation in my menu.

RATTLESNAKE

We hired an old itinerant black fellow, locally known as One-eyed Willy, who was full of old wives tales about snakes. I sat wild-eyed numerous times listening to his highly embellished stories. He never bothered about murdering the King's English because he'd never heard of it, and if there was a problem with expressing himself or a lack of vocabulary, that also never bothered him. He could string a line of snake stories that would stand your hair on end—about the time his cousin was whupped by a coachwhip or his uncle was hypnotized by a belltail.

One-eyed Willy could back some of this up by producing a well-worn set of diamondback rattles, complete with end button, from one of his numerous side pockets. All this time he was spouting a dire warning, "I'll let you hear the rattle in your ears but beware the dust from the rattles—it's shore death or a case of blind in both eyes if that dust gits in yore eyes."

He often suggested we go into the woods close by to let him demonstrate his accumulated knowledge of all snakes. Apparently Paw or Grandpaw overheard some of this, for I was forbidden to go into those woods with him. Years later Paw told me Willy was one of those "guys little boys shouldn't be alone with." Time went on as it naturally does and I saw less and less of Willy, but the snake tales have stayed with me.

My first encounter with a diamondback was about a hundred yards south of the homestead. It must've been 1935. We boys discovered a monster of a belltail in the mouth of a gopher hole. He was one of those adamant ones, full of fight, and highly vocal on the tail end.

Our operation to send him from this world required fetching a six-foot stepladder from Grandpa's well-stocked toolshed. This presented no small problem, for Grandpa highly regarded his tools and equipment. Nevertheless, this stepladder was necessary for us to carry out our plan, which was to climb to the top of the stepladder and from there somehow administer the *coup de grace* to this terrible foe of mankind without endangering ourselves. We first prodded him with the proverbial ten-foot pole, which only made him madder. We chunked sand and gravel in his face. He got madder and madder but stood his ground at the mouth of the gopher hole.

Then some smart member of the local gang—a group of us first cousins who in those days seemed to be a dime a dozen—decided more drastic methods of eliciting action from the adversary were necessary. "Fire will conquer anything," he said. He volunteered to swipe a gallon of kerosene oil from his Mama's cook stove, and was back in a jiffy with the big glass reservoir, not even bothering to pour it in a bucket.

From the top of the ladder, on which about four cousins were clinging, we sloshed the k-oil toward the gopher hole and someone produced a match. It ended up taking about half a box of cordwood matches to get the fire going and in the ensuing melee we set the broomstraw and pinewoods on fire. Luckily that big rattler found another hole in the ground to rush into, for if he'd come out under the ladder there wouldn't have been anybody but us and the washwoman to know our fear.

After jumping off the ladder, barefoot, one by one and sprinting to the house, we were all scared to go back down there. But Grandpa missed his ladder and Grandma her k-oil, and the truth came out. Naturally we got a thrashing but the rattlesnake tale told to admiring friends at school was worth it.

THE VALUE OF A DOLLAR

In the 1930s, a dollar in exchange value was worth one hundred American cents. We heard unbelievable tales of Henry Ford paying five of these dollars for one day's work on the assembly lines of his car factory in Detroit. He was smarter than us farm folks in south Georgia, for we were accustomed to figuring a cartwheel or silver dollar was a fair price for an honest, hard, cain't-to-cain't day's work on the farm. This, mind you, was for about twelve hours work by a grown, able-bodied man. Those lower in the workforce started at fifty cents a day, then a ninety percent silver half-dollar coin.

At the store, of course, one could swap silver coins for full value in merchandise. Delivery of the goods cross-town was included since delivery boys who didn't mind pumping their bicycle a mile or two were a dime a dozen. If a delivery boy was lucky he might get tipped with a full glass of fresh, unpasteurized cow's milk from a luxurious icebox or perhaps a fresh, pristine slice of the Madam's newly baked cake.

In pursuit of some dollars for ourselves we answered the call of a friend who farmed on the outskirts of town. He needed young, stout-hearted and strong-backed boys to shake his peanuts by hand. I should add *weak-minded* for it was all mule work, hand work, a lot of dirt and sweat.

It went like this. The farmer would lead his mule into the field of peanuts and begin turning them up on top of the ground with a one-hoss Oliver turning plow or a steel beam of some other make. We boys would follow very shortly behind, snatching up all the peanuts we could handle, shaking them vigorously and piling them in a row. The farmer turned at the end of the row and came back in the opposite direction, plowing up another row adjacent to the one already upturned. We'd shake this row, too, and pile them in the same row. It didn't matter that many of the peanut vines were half-plowed from the ground or that pusley (Florida purslane) had taken the field. The farmer expected to see bare ground behind him and all peanuts and associated weeds were thrown in the windrow to dry in the sun. Many times, after several weeks of this kind of labor, the skin peeled back from the base of all fingernails and about all that was left on our phalanges was bloody nubs.

Now this particular farmer, who was a half-cropper and didn't own the farm or much more than his bare ass and a change of overalls, stopped at the end of each long row to roll himself a Prince Albert. Even at age fourteen it was a relief to find the farmer had the tobacco habit, for it saved some in the crew from being "caught by the bear," or overcome by the sun and heat. Even at that young age it was a serious matter, for if one got "overhet" during peanut-shaking it was well-nigh a sunstroke or heat exhaustion. The older blacks on the farm always wore hats or turbaned red bandannas, and all had long-sleeved shirts buttoned at the collar. They would say, "Boy, you better put on a hat 'fore you catch the brain fever." We were grateful for the chance to rest and catch our second winds. If he hadn't smoked, we would soon have been put on the dirt road home with a third or half day's pay, not redeemable until Saturday evening at Haile's Drug Store in Fitzgerald. "Dr." Haile owned the farm.

Somebody had figured out a peanut had to be ten to fifteen percent moisture to store without damage, so we were paid well to stack them for drying—ten cents a stack. Sometimes we were paid a Mercury dime (ninety per cent silver) on the completion of a stack, otherwise receiving our pay at the end of the day's work at sundown. The young crew was invited, urged or begged back for this operation. We stacked the peanut vines and nuts onto cleats nailed in a pole that had been set in the ground at least two feet, ensuring that it wouldn't blow over in a fall hurricane. We used three-pronged pitchforks to stack the vines as high as we could pitch them. The smart farmers wanted the stacks short and stumpy, the bases broad and wide, thereby getting more vines on the stack. In reality, maybe they out-figured themselves, for a narrow, tall stack tapering like a Christmas tree to a reasonable three-feet-wide base probably dried quicker and was ready to pick sooner.

I could easily out do most of my friends and many times I exceeded the going day's labor of fifty to seventy-five cents a day. This meant putting up, to the farmer's satisfaction, a grand total of twenty to twenty-five stacks. One week during this time I was paid sixteen dollars, a tremendous fortune. My parents insisted I put this amount on my Fall-term school clothes. This dumbfounded me—I figured the whole amount was mine to spend as I wished.

I never did get to see a peanut crop all the way through, for by the time the peanuts were dried and ready to be picked off the stacks, pitchfork by pitchfork, it was up into Thanksgiving and I was back in school.

Back then we children perused the Sears Roebuck catalogue as if it were the gospel. I had spied a pair of eighteen-inch lace-up hunting boots that my heart desired. My parents told me I could have the boots if I'd earn the money—all six dollars of it, plus postage. The summer's peanut pay had already been banked and I was not allowed to touch it. I inquired around, for now only afternoons, after school, were free. Grandpaw Walker told me I could shake pecans off the trees and then pick them up and put them, clean, into croaker sacks for a penny a pound. He would sell them for cash at four or five cents a pound.

I proceeded to shake the trees by hand, squirrel-like, and then picked up and bagged six hundred pounds of pecans. I soon had the money I needed. In time, I was the proud owner of one pair of genuine leather boots. They served their intended purpose for a couple of years, with frequent oilings and polishings. I split the sides with my pocketknife as long as I could, and cut the toes out, until finally I outgrew them. I was, and still am, proud of those boots, for it took a lot of toil and trouble to be able to say that I'd earned them on my own, they were my own alone, and nobody could lay claim to any part of them.

THE WOODYARD

Somewhere long about the middle 1930s when the buffalo nickel was a big piece of money and he blinked his eyes when withdrawn from a deep, dark, secret overall pocket after long seclusion—when it was at long last decided that he should be placed in circulation once again to help improve economic conditions in our great country—I gathered up a few of the coins.

I had decided it would behoove my financial standing to spend this money for a good sharp ax, about seventy-five cents at that time, and brand new at that. The purpose of this decision was to go into the woodyard business, that is, to cut wood, which was free for the taking and toting, and sell it to nearby neighbors who almost always had a use for it, as either cookstove or fireplace fuel. I reasoned that wood was an essential item that one had to have, like it or not. I had heard of the cord of wood and what it was worth to city folks.

For about a month during one autumn I cut and toted to the house, piece by piece, some up to a quarter of a mile, enough wood to make up the magical cord. That was enough wood to reach between two stakes about eight feet long, four feet high and four feet wide. There ain't no way to tell how proud I was of that rick of wood and for several days, I took special pride in circling it, eyeing it, and thinking of just how pretty it was and how much hard labor had gone into its existence. At one point I just about decided to keep the cord of wood and forget the money.

Well, experience and reality are a wonderful, albeit sometimes heart-breaking, teacher. I quickly, to my chagrin, learned some facts of life. Ladies and cooks wanted their firewood cut into correct lengths for the Southern Comfort woodstove—maybe even a little shy of the firebox's length to give good circulation and even burning. My four-foot-long bolts wouldn't do.

I also learned the terms "hardwood" and "softwood." It appears hardwoods, mostly oak, had a higher specific gravity and would give off more BTU's per size piece. My cord was mostly dead pine, blown down by winds or chopped down by me. This was a terrible let-down that burst my visions of financial independence, kind of like a sure-fire prediction of the state of the economy. My pocketbook was to remain empty. The wood got burned in our fireplace mixed with oak, after halving again for size. Paw Walker later told me he knew folks didn't want dead pine to burn if they had anything else.

My Pa later told me he could have a full measured cord of red oak delivered to the house for seventy-five cents and cut into any length he wanted for another twenty-five cents. I should have thought of this for I remember the seller jacking up one rear wheel of his Model T or Model A Ford, attaching a belt around the tire and his cut-off saw shaft pulley and sawing it, then piling it neatly for the full price of a dollar.

Why didn't these loved ones tell me? Maybe they figured it would stick with me longer to find out for myself. It has. A moral from this tale? Don't go into new ventures plumb blind; ask some folks who ought to know.

LUCY, OUR CONTENTED COW

In the early 1940s Paw Walker urged Hattie Lee, his daughter and my mother, to purchase a milk cow. He convinced her that five younguns needed a dependable and cheap source of milk. "That big strapping son of yours (me) can take care of the milking morn and night—it will probably keep him out of trouble."

Paw Walker helped secure a fine-looking cow, half Jersey and half Guernsey, already broke to milk and named Lucy. We led Lucy home one afternoon and tied her to a tree with a well chain. Paw started showing me how to milk a cow. First, I had to get her attention and make her stand still, by way of mixing about a quart of cottonseed meal and a peck of cotton seed hulls, and dumping it in her trough. Milking came easy for me, for Lucy had big four or five-inch tits and my hands were a bit large for my age. Paw said to get a tit in each hand, wrap all your fingers, except the thumb, around it, bring your fingertips in about midway on the tit and squeeze hard. I milked into a ten-quart bucket and shortly became adept at the procedure, rhythmically squirting the left tit and then right, swish swish, plop plop. It was about a fifteen-minute job, sunrise and sunset, but I walked away with a ten-quart bucket each time.

Paw thought it shameful that Lucy had to stand outside in the weather, so he got us for free a condemned carbox. Back then they were all made of heart pine, two by six inch tongue-and-grooved. It was a big improvement during inclement weather to sit on the three-legged stool in the carbox and do the milking.

I became very accurate at aiming streams of milk, and by a slight twist of the wrist could shoot it into the face of any younger sibling who might be looking round the door of the barn, making smartass remarks. Paw's tomcat, Tom, would turn up like clockwork, and after I'd direct a stream towards him and he had it licked off his face, he learned to open wide his mouth and have a few ounces shot into it. Another visitor was Aunt Jean Walker who liked a glass of fresh, warm, unpasteurized milk.

Brother Jack and Charlie Lee had to take Lucy out in the mornings, stake her down for free grazing, bring her a half-filled washtub of fresh water at noon—cows can drink many gallons at a time—and then drive her in before sundown. When Lucy was brought in of an evening, Mama said to wash her udder down with warm soapy water before the milking job, which I did. I never did tell her though that Lucy occasionally stepped into the milking pails, and since Mama always strained the fresh milk through a cotton flour sack a couple of time it probably didn't matter.

We always had a surplus of fresh milk, which we peddled up and down Lee Street just north of the house. We sold buttermilk for a nickel a quart and sweet milk for a dime—both had our personalized cardboard cap. Mama also made pressed butter, indented with our logo, which we also sold, though I don't recall the price. Neighbors kept a big flock of Dominicker and Rhode Island Red hens, so we swapped milk and butter to them on a penny-an-egg basis. Another of the joys of surplus milk came from a six-quart, hand-cranked ice cream churn. We usually made plain vanilla ice cream, but when peaches were in season we took advantage of them.

To keep a good milk cow "coming in fresh" she must be bred once a year. It was easy to recognize when a cow was in heat for she'd walk around with her tail heisted. I recall a time when Paw and Daddy and I were going to lead Lucy out to Diemel's Milk Dairy for Lucy to meet their prized Jersey bull. All went well until we reached a wooden bridge south of town. When Lucy thumped her forelegs onto the planks and heard the reverberating noise, she sulled and refused to go further. Paw Walker says, "Cut me a stout gallberry limb and I'll coax her across by heating up her flanks." This didn't work, so Daddy fetched the Model A Ford and commenced pushing her from behind, whereupon Paw yells, "Stop, you're gonna break her legs and maim her!"

Paw figured a minute then said, "Boy, jump the ditch and fetch me some pine straw and one of those turpentine cups." He proceeded to build a lively fire behind Lucy in an attempt to make her cross the bridge. As the hair on her hind legs and tail began to singe she reared up, turned around and faced home, still standing still. There was a hasty conference and the consensus of opinion was that we'd better lead Lucy the long way around to the bull.

A cow's gestation period is about the same as a human's and Lucy's calf arrived shortly after nine months, a healthy one hundred-pound bull. We didn't cut it, so within six months he was a robust yearling tied out to graze with his mama. Paw told me to leave one tit for the calf when milking. At first the milk was a bit bloody and we discarded it but in about two weeks she had "come in fresh" and was giving more milk than ever.

Some of the cousins allowed it would be good sport to lead the young bull under a pecan limb and for me to drop onto its back as it passed beneath. This was a wild ride as far as rides go. I got bucked off in the first hundred yards, fell to the ground, got a leg tangled in the chain and then was dragged on the ground for the last few hundred yards to the cow lot. This was the end of calf riding, as I could not get any riders for further attempts.

MY NEIGHBOR, MRS. FOHLE

Over on the south side where the houses stopped and the pine woods began, our neighbor Mrs. Fohle had a five-acre pecan orchard. She constantly patrolled her acreage from the time the pecans began to swell in the husks until they fell from the trees, in order to keep the cat squirrels from harvesting part of the nut crop. On one of her shoulders she toted a double-barrel 12-gauge shotgun, a really old-model, rabbit-eared hammer gun. She knew how to handle the gun and often knocked two squirrels from the high limbs with one blast.

I was scared shitless of Mrs. Fohle, as were all the boys on the south side. We heard she was an Indian and she looked the part. She was short, dark-complexioned and wore her long hair in braids. An old gnome with very stooped shoulders. Once she caught me in the woods beside her orchard with my new .410 shotgun. She was toting her own gun, and when she hailed me, I was afraid to run. Instead, I walked up to her and underwent a lengthy interrogation, all the while imagining terrible things about to happen.

"What is your name? How old are you? (Nine). Where do you live? What are you doing on my land?" I answered all her questions. Thank goodness she knew my grandpa, who lived nearby. I fessed up as how I was looking for a squirrel to shoot. She said it was all right if I'd bring her half the squirrels I shot. As the conversation warmed up, she invited me to come see her sometime.

In a few days, I got up the nerve to carry a squirrel to her back door. She asked if I knew how to clean the game and I admitted I'd only watched the process. She went inside, got a sharp paring knife, a pair of scissors, one 20D (penny) nail and a hammer. Next, she took the squirrel, walked to a nearby tree and nailed it to the tree through its head. Then, she quickly cut a circle around its neck and a short way down its belly and adroitly had him skinned and gutted within minutes. The last operation was to clip the tail off next to the body.

Mrs. Fohle and I became fast, trusted friends, for many things about her fascinated a young boy, among them her pigeon loft where she kept pigeons and sold the squabs. Many folks in Fitzgerald ate squabs, which were tender and juicy, having been fed on pigeon milk, a secretion formed in the parent-birds' throats.

Mrs Fohle must have been in her seventies or early eighties, but she easily climbed the ladder and gave me a tour of her many boxes of pigeon eggs and squabs, instructing me to pick up some to determine whether or not they were fat enough to kill. She cautioned me to listen and look carefully, for she was going to turn the gathering job over to me.

Regular visits continued, interlaced with a glass of cold milk and a delicious slice of home-baked cake—she could outbake my own Mama and Grandma! When the winter was about over, Mrs. Fohle asked me to clean her homemade fish pool. She had previously called me one bitter winter day and told me to come and look. I stood by the fish pool and watched the goldfish swimming under the ice; I thought this fantastic and vowed one day to have a fish pool of my own.

Mrs. Fohle grew a large banana tree in a half oak whiskey barrel sitting in a wooden wheelbarrow. She kept her banana tree from about late October until middle March in a root cellar, something I'd never heard of or seen, but when I did I thought it dark and exciting. I was amazed to see bananas growing on her tree in south Georgia. Putting the tree in and taking it out when she deemed it safe turned into another of my chores.

All of this was almost sixty-five years ago but I look back on Mrs. Fohle with kind remembrances of a wonderful world she showed to me. I finally built my fish pool in 1990 but haven't yet produced bananas like hers.

GREASING THE RAILS

All's quiet in Osierfield as I reminisce. In the middle and late 1930s the Atlanta, Birmingham and Coast rail line had a spur line running from Fitzgerald and terminating in Thomasville, with stops at Mystic, Tifton, Moultrie and Coolidge. Besides hauling turpentine, bales of cotton and such, in July the biggest manifest consisted of watermelons supplied by farmers meeting the train at one of its stops with their loaded wagons. The melons were shipped in boxcars on beds of oat straw, stacked about three or four feet deep with two by six inch holding boards in place of standard sliding doors. Back then the horticulturist hadn't developed a watermelon with shipping characteristics, such as cannonballs and ice-cream melons—the yellow-meated one. So the melons would vibrate and jelly up into unrecognizable mush as they bumped along.

The older boys saw the steep upgrade on the south side of our town, where the steam engine huffed and puffed and slowed to a walking speed, as a cherry needing picking. I was invited to participate in the stealing of watermelons, a privilege gained by furnishing several gallons of Mama's and Grandmama's hog lard or oil, already used several times for cooking, and intended for making lye soap when it became too rancid.

To reach the top, level portion of the hill the train had to gain traction on the grade. We greased both rails with an ample supply of hog lard and cooking grease. When the watermelon train, probably only fifteen to twenty boxcars, reached the greased portion, the driver wheels began to slip and start spinning; that was our signal to climb into the boxcars and begin passing out fine watermelons as the train came to a stop. The engineer and fireman were at the front of the train, the conductor was in his passenger car or caboose. None of them wanted to leave their posts and come backward or forward while the train stood still, waiting for an additional engine or double-header to back out from the local Westwood shops and couple onto the engine in distress. This was our opportunity to get a week's supply of melons.

It took a lot of river sand liberally spewed on both rails to get the train moving again, and by that time we had helped ourselves and friends to all the watermelons we could handle (just the hearts for starters.) It didn't seem a crime, just a way of garnering a supply of watermelons using our wits and backs.

THE RAILROAD TRUSSEL

The railroad trussel, more correctly called trestle, spanned Town Creek, later called the "old ditch" and even later "Shit Creek"—all towns back in the 1930s had one—since it carried off the liquid effluent of Fitzgerald's septic tanks, mainly by gravity flow. The trussel was one of our favorite hangouts and readily accessible, so near home and Town Creek about twenty-five or thirty feet below.

We used the trussel for various and sundry adventures, including the challenge that likely always surfaces among boys playing together—who can piss the farthest. We could try to outdistance our companions on level ground, but why not do it in a spectacular way? It was pretty well agreed, with a vote among ourselves, who had pissed the farthest.

The span had a line of eight by nine inch timbers on the north and south sides. We often dared one another to ride his bicycle across on the nine-inch surface. This was real crazy, in retrospect, for if you made a one-inch mistake you could find yourself plunging twenty-five feet into the creek run. Most important, it'd probably bend up the bicycle. I did it once or twice on a dare—"I double dog dare you to try it."

Probably the most "death defying" challenge was to dangle from the beams supporting the cross ties and rails and let the steam train from Pavo to Thomasville pass over the trussel while you hung from the cross-arm. The steam train approached from the southwest on a downhill grade and began gathering up speed to climb the incline to level ground and thence to the local station.

For an eight- or ten-year-old it took a lot of guts but I mustered enough to hang on to the crossbeam, hearing the whistle of the approaching steam train, listening to its warning. The engineer had seen us scrambling off the upper part of the trussel, to disappear below and hang on for dear life. The first time around it was terrifying—the many-ton train (probably forty or fifty thousand pounds of steel and cast iron engine, plus twenty or thirty freight cars) passing overhead, with a showering of cinders and live steam, plus the accompanying vibration of the bridge timbers. I could only hug the beam and hold on tight. After my initiation, having survived the debacle, losing only a shirt to cinder burns, I figured I was a veteran. I could tell the younger guys, "No sweat, just hold on tight and it won't hurt you."

Around the same place we used to tote a six to eight foot piece of roofing tin to "snowslide" down the embankment. We'd bend back the first two feet of the tin for a shield, pile one or two on and slide downward to the bottom, crossing into a thicket of briers and bramble. It was an exhilarating slide downwards but hell to pull the tin back up the sandy steep incline if one wanted another slide, like climbing in loose dune sand. It would have been nice to have a ski lift.

When we'd worn ourselves out dragging the tin uphill, we'd catch a second wind and begin climbing pine saplings to sway them over for a graceful and exhilarating ride to *terra firma*. We always went barefooted, but still it was a hard feat to shinny up a loose-bark pine to a height that would make it bend or sway. When we got up fifteen to eighteen feet above ground, we'd grip the bole of the sapling tightly with both hands, push hard against the tree and jump into space. The top of the tree would bend or sway with your weight and usually gently bend for a ride down. We'd try to pick a slash or longleaf pine for swaying, for they were more resilient than knotty loblolly pines and not apt to snap off.

Other days we'd decide to wade Town Creek clean to Lake Beatrice five or six miles south of home, barefooted with short pants on, for a moccasin killing foray. We'd all carry long stout sticks and clobber any snake that showed itself. We thought, wrongly of course, that we were benefiting our fellow man. At every bend in the creek we'd flush a great blue heron, called big blue crane or pond scoggin by our elders, and a few wood ducks, called summer ducks, because they were the only breeding ducks in the area. The heron would launch itself into the air amidst awful guttural squawks and fly out of sight around the next bend of the creek. The summer ducks would leap from the creek and utter a squeal, hence their occasional name of "squealer."

A common inhabitant of the creek-run was the "shitepoke" or "shit-up-the-creek," a small green heron. Both sexes careened themselves into space, gave a squawk and defecated, hence shit up the creek. This is not a habit specific to green herons and occurs, apparently spontaneously, in many species of birds. Maybe they are frightened, maybe they want to lighten their guts.

These wilderness encounters set me on fire. Truly, they were wilderness experiences, for remnants of virgin forests lined the creek's banks, outside of town, and few, if any, folks trod the path. I don't remember any encounters with *Homo sapiens*, except once I came upon a couple stretched out on the creek bank blissfully screwing away. I distinctly remember the guy saying "Step over us and get out of here," all the while never missing a stroke.

At times we found numerous nests of the golden swamp warbler (the prothonotary), along with those of the downy woodpecker, in hollow, rotten willow stumps. The warbler nests sometimes contained several light-colored eggs with brown splotches. Once, looking into a large hollow stump, standing in water, I found several tiny coons. They were the cutest of the cute, but I realized they were suckling babes and resisted the impulse to carry some home. The sow coon definitely had to swim to the stump for the nesting or birthing.

The highlight of our meanderings was to follow close behind a steam shovel, run by a man who'd been hired to clean up and deepen the creek. The machine did the work of the modern backhoe but actually had a steam engine stoked by the operator. He'd fire up the steam engine early, get up a head of steam by shoveling stoker coal into the fire box and then begin digging operations, amid a cloud of black coal smoke, the clanking of gears and the swish of steel cables attached to the bucket. The monster traveled on steel tracks and when the operator had cleaned out several yards of the creek, he clank-clanked downstream for a new digging angle. Quite often the operator had to stop to hastily shovel more stoker coal into the firebox.

The steam shovel operator led a solitary existence, not so quiet but lonely, for only one man was needed to run the machine. The operator seemed to welcome us curious boys as long as we stayed at a safe distance. I remember countless snakes, turtles, small alligators, and other denizens of the muck fleeing for safety. They were our prey and our *raison de etre* for being there.

It was all good, healthy, invigorating activity and didn't cost a cent. My fellow participants and I were probably ridiculed by the usual "drugstore cowboys" who held forth on the downtown street corners and never ventured outside town limits. Methinks those guys missed the best part of growing up, an appreciation of what wonders were to be had just outside of town.

KNOT HOLE AND OTHER NEAR-MISSES

Knot Hole was known far and wide as a good, deep swimming hole. It was on Coochee Creek also called Willacoochee River, which passed under a wooden bridge on the old dirt Ocilla-Fitzgerald road. It was only a few miles from town, an easy pedal except for the times when George Eaton conned me into pulling him astride the back fender of the bicycle. Downhill was easy but George didn't do his part on the uphill grades. (George, by the way, had a good-looking, blond-headed, blue-eyed sister I admired. When his Mama once directed to me, "Don't look so close at Mary, you little bastard," I thought she had made me a complimentary remark.)

One small area of the route passed A.B.C.D. Dorminy's home, which we were a bit afraid of, since Mr. Dorminy kept two big, ugly pit bulldogs to help gather his cows. Fortunately his place was on a downhill grade, easy going on hard-packed clay. We'd pump up all the speed we could attain, put our bare feet up on the handlebars and coast by faster than the dogs could run. We knew we could not outdistance the bulldogs pedaling uphill, so circumvented them on the return trip by traveling the Seaboard Air Line railroad tracks back home. Have you ever pedaled a bicycle over the crossties and between the rails? It's a bone-rattling ordeal.

Around the end of May, when school stopped for summer, we boys on the south side of Fitzgerald had our minds on Knot Hole and a chance to swim. After several spring freshets, Coochee Creek had swift currents and the flow of water had washed out really deep holes. Plenty of tupelo trees lined the banks, with high limbs to try a spectacular dive from. The swimming trips were *au natural*, butt naked, so no girls were allowed. One of the common practices, known as the "moon rise," was to show your bare ass on a surface dive.

Sometimes we attached a cotton plowline to one of the high limbs, using enough line so that it dangled about six feet above the water's surface. The dangling end was tied to a holding bar, about two inches in diameter and two feet long, which we cut from a small tree on the bank. Taking turns, we would bring the bar over to the high bank with a long stick, grab hold with both hands and back up as far as the line would reach, then taking a high-spirited run and sail out over the creek for a release at the apogee of the swing. Entry into the water was via a "cannonball." The object was to see who could make the biggest splash. Others tried diving from the bar, but they weren't too graceful for it was difficult to arrange yourself in a diving position while holding onto the bar.

We once had a contest as to who would jump from the highest limb into the creek. I won it with a jump from forty-two feet up, the record verified later by carrying a ball of kite-flying string out to Knot Hole, pulling it from the limb to the ground, and carrying it home to measure with a yardstick. Maybe we stretched that string a bit, for nowadays the only way I'd jump from forty-two feet was if the ship was going down or I got pushed from behind.

One early spring day I volunteered to be the first one in on the plowline swing. I hit the water after loosening my grip on the bar and became entangled in a rusting Model T Ford car body that had been pushed into the creek, lying submerged just beneath the surface of the water. Maybe the landowner had pushed this car frame into the creek to discourage the crowd of town boys from using the place. The accident resulted in rather severe cuts on my feet and calves.

Children are highly resilient, and I came out sputtering, bleeding profusely but with no broken bones. The problem came later when we got home, for blow flies had attacked the fresh cuts and laid eggs, as they'd been taught to do eons ago. My parents recognized that flies had "blowed" the wounds, so promptly and thoroughly washed their egg casings out and applied spirits of turpentine and rubbing alcohol to make them antiseptic. When the spirits hit raw flesh, talk about Indian yelps and a dance!

This wasn't the first home doctoring I'd endured. If you were sick enough to visit a real doctor (there were a lot of root doctors around) and pay his three-dollar fee, or worse, if you had to "turn in" to the Ben Hill County Hospital, you were really in bad shape. Most folks figured the next they'd hear your name would be in an obituary with subsequent burial in Evergreen Cemetery.

Once while hanging upside down, reaching for succulent grapes on the grape arbor, I fell headfirst into the woodpile and got a three-inch scalp wound. Grandpaw Walker had me lay down face-up on the kitchen table, lathered my scalp with his shaving brush, took his straight razor which he'd stropped on the leather strop, and shaved the top of my head. He treated the cut with methiolate, let it dry, then pulled the two sides together and taped them tightly.

On another occasion I jumped off the cow barn with an umbrella and landed on a scantling that had a twenty-penny nail sticking straight up. The nail pierced my foot about midway and came clear through, protruding about two inches out on the topside. This sight terrified me as I hopped to the house on one good foot. Grandpaw, the patriarch of the family, was called in for consultation and he said, "Boy, sit in this chair and let me look at your foot," whereupon he knelt down and snatched the nail and board downward so fast I didn't know what had happened. That solved getting the nail out, for I already had visions of going to the hospital, having it cut out and maybe suffering for a long time on a lame foot.

The folks consulted among themselves and decided since the nail was rusty and in a cow lot, I'd better see Dr. Coffee for a tetanus shot. Lockjaw was incurable. The tetanus shot was administered. My parents bought me a big ice-cream cone, and I was escorted home and given a good thrashing for my imprudence, for I'd been told many times to quit jumping off the cow barn with the umbrella.

The cry of "mad dog" was as bad. Few people in the 1930s went to the care and expense of having their yard dogs innoculated against rabies. It was agreed among us boys that if one of us saw a dog running toward us, foaming at the mouth, we'd holler "mad dog" as loud as we could and take to the nearest tree to shinny up out of its reach. We also agreed there wouldn't be any crying wolf, for this was serious business. We'd heard that a bitten person would be subject to multiple shots in the stomach, maybe up to twenty, with a six-inch needle, if the head of the suspected dog, cut off, packed in dry ice and sent to Atlanta, showed evidence of rabies.

After each accident I wasn't allowed to swim for a few weeks, not until the wound healed. And sometimes Knot Hole would be dry by then. Nowadays, any of the incidents would not only eliminate some swimming, but would also require a trip to the emergency room.

Upstream from Knot Hole, Coochee Creek flowed across a flat arch, spreading out. In the spring it was grassy and the swift-moving water was about two feet deep. This place was known locally as Martindale and the fishing was excellent and exciting—the catch was red-finned pike, one of the best-tasting fish in the country. Coochee Creek was an intermittent stream, as are many south Georgia creeks and rivers, meaning they don't flow continually as do most mountain streams, but rage fast and furious in the spring rains and dry to a trickle in mid-summer, except for deep holes that contain all the fish. The water was always dark-brown due to the cypress swamps it flowed through, where it picked up tannic acid. Sadly, this boys-growing-up paradise, all for free and a little walking, has been channelized, dug out in straight lines with huge backhoes to take the curves out and hasten the stream's rush to sea, forever destroying, in my mind, what adventure a boy could find around the next bend of a meandering creek

KITE FLYING

I can't remember at what early age I was introduced to kite flying, when a good, hard-pulling kite sailing in a stiff breeze was more than I could handle alone.

Good-looking, brightly colored kites were displayed in merchants' February and March offerings, but they cost from a dime to a quarter, the likes of which we often didn't have, not when grown men and women were being paid fifty cents or a dollar a day for hard labor. The next best thing, probably the best, to a store-bought kite was to make your own on the kitchen table. We made at least three types, the box, the triangular shield and the butterfly kite.

The box kite took two thirty six inch sticks and one twenty four inch stick. We used bamboo or reeds cut in the woods and let dry, or sometimes Grandpaw Walker would run a thin board through the table saw and cut a great number of sticks about a quarter-inch wide and less than that in thickness. We crossed the sticks as illustrated, tied them securely at points A, B and E, then cut notches or channels in the ends of all the sticks and stretched a good cord around the whole frame. Now the frame was ready to lay on the floor or table and the paper put on. Ordinary newspaper tore too easily so we used paper from dry cleaning bags, which had one slick side, or meat wrapping paper, which had one waxy side.

We laid the frame on top of the paper and snipped around it, allowing about four inches on all sides. We then got Mama or Granny to cook up a batch of flour glue made of flour and water, spread it liberally around the four-inch overhang with a brush or our fingers, then folded this overhang back over the string frame and patted it down. The flour paste made a good, homemade glue and dried in a few minutes.

To further increase the strength at stress points—A and B where a string bridle was attached and C and D, where another went—we doubled the paper and glued it on top of the points over the other paper. Bridles were tied from A to B and from C to D; it was wise to use strong string for the bridles. The control string was attached to the bridle between A and B and the tail was attached between C and D.

We always begged for the brightest colored scraps to form the tail. They were in good supply, for Mama and Granny kept all cloth scraps for making patchwork quilts. We snipped them about two inches wide and as long as the scrap, knotting them at each joint with a couple of half hitches. It took a good long, heavy tail to keep the box kite steady in the sky and prevent it from doing the loop-ta-loop. Sometimes we'd fetch the kite in and add more tail to stabilize it; for a stiff breeze we'd make them twenty feet long.

As to kite string, all families kept all the twine that came their way rolled into a big ball. Oftentimes on visits from neighbors and kinfolk the different balls would be brought forth, commented on and bragged about, to compare and see who'd saved the most.

In spring and late winter the old folks gave us boys the twine to fly our kites with. They had carefully tied various lengths together to make the balls, always with a square knot—granny knots would slip and come untied. Of course, kite flying string was available for about a nickel a roll, but it was wound on a cardboard spool to make it look larger and never contained over two or three hundred feet. We wanted our kites to ascend to at least one or two thousand feet into the heavens.

When the wind was from the south, a couple thousand feet of string would put the kites from the fields on the south side of Fitzgerald to past the center of town. When, after flying them several hours, the string would break at some weak point and the kite would go into a lazy dive, we'd jump onto our bikes and pedal furiously, following our string over trees and rooftops to the fallen kite. We'd try to go in pretty good numbers, for guys on the northside tried to claim anything that fell on their turf, like manna from the skies. There were a few fisticuffs and some wrassling, mostly bluff and nothing serious ever came of it.

Often we were the cause of the string breaking for we southsiders were continually sending up "messages" to our kites. This was done by cutting out a round piece of paper, making a sharp cut to the center with Mama's scissors or our pocketknife, and slipping the paper over the control string. Since the route up the kite string had to be blown by the prevailing south, southwest or southeast wind up the string, it was exhilirating to note its speed. We even tried sending up handkerchief-sized parachutes on a crook of coathanger wire and at any point on their ascent we could release them with a violent jerk on the cord. We sent up so much stuff, it would get too heavy for the kite, and the weight would bring it down.

When the string didn't break, which was seldom, we'd reel in our kites for another day and another flight. The wind usually diminished or quit blowing late in the evening, and it took some fast and furious winding the string around a stick to bring the kite in. C.M. Copeland continued flying kites into his adulthood and had an ingenious method of letting out and taking in string. It consisted of a large saltwater fishing reel, which he mounted on a stand with the crank handle at a comfortable height.

Another type of kite we often fashioned was the triangular shield type. It only took two sticks as illustrated and the paper was applied as on the other kite. These weren't nearly as stable as the box kite, being a little more prone to looping, especially with a short tail, but were probably more exciting to fly. This type was the most common store-bought kite.

The last type of kite was the simplest, and required very little material. We called it the butterfly kite. We took a common eight by eleven inch sheet of good bond paper, and went to the field and broke off at ground level two of the longest stalks of broomsedge to be found. With an ice pick we punched a round hole at the four corners of the sheet about one inch inside each corner, inserted the butt ends of the broomsedge stalks in the shape of a cross and there we had it. The control string was tied where the two stalks of grass crossed.

It was flown without a tail and usually with No.8 sewing thread. It was a lightweight, delicate kite flown in light breezes that wouldn't hold up the larger kites. This was like fishing for big fish on light tackle and really took tender loving care to fly it without crashing.

Boy, what a durable kite I could make nowadays with heavy poly, instant glue, polyurethane clear acrylic sprays and monofilament fishing line up to almost any test strength. But I'm not going to do it, for it would ruin the fond memories of creating something unique with my own hands, then test-flying it, with all the accompanying anxieties and uncertainties, successes and failures.

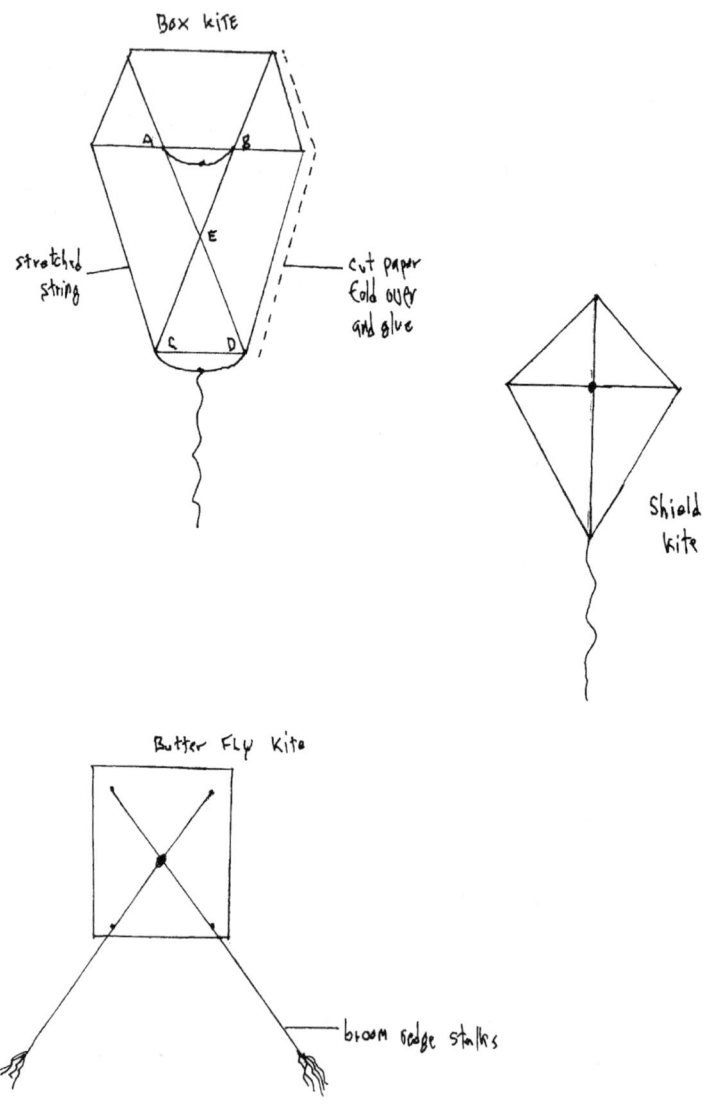

CORKS

Many products were once sealed in bottles with real corks, which came in all lengths and diameters. They were tapered from the upper end down to where they fit into the bottle. A slight upward twist took them out, and a slight twist and bump of the hand put them back in. These corks, the genuine ones, came from the outer bark of the cork oak, an evergreen oak native to the Mediterranean. The only country producing them, as I recall from a picture in a grammar school geography text, was Portugal. It showed two men stripping the thick bark from the cork tree.

Corks were a real necessity and easy to use—none of these child-proof, difficult-to-open plastic tops. But the main purpose of corks for a growing boy was as fishing floats. Granny and Mama saved all their corks when bottles were empty. The little slim ones that stoppered the thin bottles of spirits of turpentine were too small for fishing. You needed a stout cork from a bottle of "Syrup of Black Draught" or "666" to fill the bill.

To make the bobbers, we took the corks from a Mason jar, full to the top with all sizes, picked out the best ones, split them halfway with a pocketknife and inserted the fishing line in the cut. Then we'd cut a wild reed or bamboo stalk for a pole, tie the line on the end and attach the cork an inch and a half or two inches from the hook, depending on the depth of the water.

My first attempt at fishing was probably at nine or ten years of age. I'd watched the older boys fishing. They got some No.8 sewing thread from their mamas, plus a straight pin, which they'd bend in a crook on the sharp end. The bait was red wigglers. They'd never use the whole worm but pinch off half-inch portions to bait their hooks. Usually the redeyes, a sunfish, would first attack the worm. Since they could get off easily, there being no barb on the pin, one had to quickly snatch back on the pole with a quick backhand movement. I'd catch a nice string of redeyes to carry home and after I'd scaled them in the backyard, Mama would fry them for my supper. This proceeded until I found one could buy real fishing hooks, several for a penny from the hardware and thereby land bigger fish such as stumpknockers or redfin pike along with an occasional catfish.

About the only other use I know for corks, besides those tied on a three-foot string and shot from a popgun, is for capping homemade wine. When the bottles are laid on their sides, the wine permeates the cork during the aging process. When the wine is nine-tenths worked off, you put in a pinch more sugar and cap it; the build-up of CO_2 gives it the pop-fizz-fizz bubbling effect. Just a little too much sugar makes things dangerous. I once had several bottles explode in the wine closet while the wife was hostessing a church circle. She told the group of ladies that neighborhood younguns were shooting firecrackers outside. Some of the more pious ones bought this, but some knew better. There were glass shards buried a half inch deep in the closet when I inspected it in the cool of the evening. This stopped wine or champagne storage inside the house for the damn stuff was almost as finicky as nitroglycerin.

POSTSCRIPT
Patent Medicine

One of the most common uses for corks in the past was for stopping up patent medicine bottles. Some patent medicine men put bitters in their concoctions; I know not of what bitters consisted but the effect was to make the patient think that if he or she was ailing, something that tasted so bad had to be good for combating the ailment. Maybe they thought that the dose was a bigger devil than the one inhabiting them and would prevail. A dose of castor oil could fall in that realm, but thank goodness, Mama didn't believe in castor oil. Instead, she followed her mama's prescription of a tablet of calomel, epicat and soda on Friday evening, followed by a cup of Granny's home-brewed sassafras tea the following morning. This was a powerful cathartic used to clean us younguns out in case we took in any strange foods. It did, all right, and we ended up with asses red as a fox's in pokeberry time.

It's now pretty common knowledge that most of these "cure all that ails you" potions were laced with up to sixty percent grain alcohol or shine liquor. The liquor served its purpose in giving the patient an almost immediate euphoric high and feeling of goodness, about like sidling up to the bar and ordering a double bourbon on the rocks or with creek water, letting it trickle down your throat, hit bottom and almost instantly send messages to the brain saying, "This is good, my pains are gone, when should I or can I take the next dose?"

UNCLE WILL WALKER AND THE BEAR

Uncle Will turned up at our home late one evening and told of being in Coffee County the day previous and losing his new Model A Ford somewhere east of there. From his description, it sounded like it was near the sand ridge east of Douglas on Seventeen Mile Creek. He was down there on the hog, sipping a little. Coffee County back then was noted for its rye whiskey, made from rye or wheat shorts instead of cracked corn. Drunk, he had wandered off over the sand ridge to take a leak and forgot where his roadster was parked. He spent the night nearby.

He told Daddy that a black bear had approached him walking on his hind legs in a menacing fashion. There were then hog bears wandering all over Georgia. The year before one had dragged a hundred-pound shoat from Pa Walker's fattening pen about two hundred yards south of our homes. Anyway, Uncle Will said he ran from the bear and lost his bearings, then couldn't find his car.

Daddy was overly sympathetic to Uncle Will's dilemma and offered to take him back to Coffee County in his own Model A Ford. Paw Walker, who was Will's daddy, pronounced he'd not take part in the search. I begged and pleaded to accompany the two, for I wanted to see a live black bear walking on his hindquarters, preferably charging. I was sure I could outrun him, barefooted, climb a tree and watch the action.

Uncle Will finally admitted that he didn't know what part of Coffee County he lost his car in, nor whether it had been a bear, a painter or even an elephant that had charged him. We returned home late in the evening after looking all day and stopping to ask for leads—no bear, no nothing. The car never did turn up.

BOYS WILL BE BOYS

There was, south of Fitzgerald on the old dirt road to Ocilla, a Mr. Stokes who grew some of the finest, sweetest watermelons in creation. The word got around our neighborhood that he'd let you pick out the biggest one in his field for a buffalo nickel. We got up two nickels, tied a red wagon behind the bicycle and made an expedition out there one Saturday morning. It was only about three miles out, and downhill nearly half the way. We inquired at his farmhouse after drinking about half a well bucket full of his cool water. When he appeared, he said sure, he'd sell us two melons. The field was over a hill about half a mile away. He told us to go ahead and look the melons over. "I'll walk on that way and meet you." We'd already picked out two big melons that weighed over forty pounds apiece but waited for him to cut the stems before we loaded up. We thought we were experts in picking a ripe melon, having heard that if the little curlicue near the stem attachment was dried out and brownish in color, the melon was ripe.

When Mr. Stokes arrived we asked about this, he said, "Maybe yes, maybe no. Let me thump them and I'll tell you." He thumped them with his middle finger and pronounced them ripe, then cut the stems. To this day I thump watermelons before buying one, but they all sound about alike to me. We took a bit of time loading up and retying the string holding the wagon tongue as he bade us good-bye. Just as soon as he disappeared over the crest of the hill we hurriedly loaded another big one, all the wagon would hold. We justified this by rationalizing that one of them might be green and we wanted our money's worth. Besides, he had hundreds of them. We proceeded back to town by a different route and at the first wooden bridge over a creek, took one out of the wagon and opened it with our pocketknives, consuming almost three quarters of it and throwing the rinds into the creek.

We were steady customers of his for the next couple of weeks, after which he said, "These are the last ones I'll charge you for. They're going bad and I'm going to turn my hogs into the field." I have a good idea he knew what we'd been doing all along. The old saying hereabouts is that a stolen watermelon always tastes better than a storebought one.

A STOLEN BOAT

Having a burning desire to know all the birds and their habits, I thought it would be a good idea to steal one of Mr. Eli Vickers' bateaus, or wooden boats, which he kept chained to cypress trees ringing his Lake Beatrice frog pond. He'd rent them to fishermen or ladies for fifty cents a day, but I didn't have fifty cents so I slipped a pair of side cutters from Grandpaw Walker's tool chest and clipped the lightweight well chain while no one was around. Or so I thought.

I still don't know how Mr. Vickers got on my trail, unless it was because a couple of men fishing that day spoke to me as I paddled off. They must have given him a good description. I hurriedly paddled as far north of the millpond as I could, near where the main creek entered. Here I secreted the boat for several weeks before Mr. Vickers tracked me down.

Late one afternoon I arrived home from school to find a strange pickup truck in the side yard. Daddy says, "Mr. Vickers thinks you are the boy who stole one of his boats." I had to 'fess up as being guilty, for I'd been lovingly and strongly taught not to steal anything. A multitude of horrifying thoughts raced through my young mind. "Is he going to call the sheriff and arrest me? Am I going to the dreaded chain gang or to that great fear of young boys, reform school?" Just a few months ago, a partner in my cave digging was pronounced incorrigible by the local judge and taken from his widowed mother to be sent to a reform school. We boys heard they treated you like an animal, fed you little and whipped on you morn and night.

I, in short, was scared shitless, though I was not permitted to use the word, and was shaking in my boots except I was barefoot. Daddy dressed me up and down. Kind Mr. Vickers says, "If you'll have the boat back at dawn tomorrow I'll not press charges. Just bring the boat and paddle back and replace the well chain and we'll forget it happened."

Daddy stepped in about then, saying, "Thank you, Mr. Vickers, for your consideration. It won't be tomorrow. It'll be before sundown today." He put me on the Seaboard Rail line right-of-way to Ocilla and said, "Run all the way and get that boat back to where you stole it by sundown." I happily did this very thing and thanked some unseen power bigger than I was that I'd gotten off so lightly. But I really learned a lesson that I already knew: don't take anything that doesn't belong to you, never, never. If you can't buy it or trade for it or offer labor for its value, forget it and tell your friends the same thing.

I got the boat back and replaced the chain. It took way into the night hours to walk back to town and get a good thrashing to refresh my memory of the episode. I was too embarrassed to face Mr. Vickers for several weeks, although Daddy encouraged me to do so. When I did, Mr. Vickers was very friendly and understanding and said, "I hear you are one of the best paddlers around. How about turning up a couple times a week this summer to paddle me for trout fishing?" He was using the local idiom for largemouth black bass.

I guess nowadays this would be called probation. I turned up and paddled him quietly into the back recesses of his pond, Mr. Vickers all the while sitting on the front seat with a four-inch rod and reel with a Heddon River Runt Plug, a big, long wooden plug with fish-like parts painted on it. His method was to throw the plug overhand really hard, bounce it off a cypress buttress and let it fall into the dark-brown, tannic-acid-stained water. More often than not, a big trout struck the plug, got impaled on the treble hooks hanging from it, and was brought into the boat to be placed in the live box. Rarely did Mr. Vickers get skunked. Eli had regular customers for the bream and trout, keeping them all alive until called for. I don't know any modern day bass anglers who use his technique but it sure worked for him.

He bragged on my expertise at paddling, never once mentioning a stolen boat. In later years we often recalled the boat-stealing incident and had a good laugh. He died in 1994 when he was in his eighties and probably had more friends in Fitzgerald and Ocilla than any other person. He had given me a second chance and made another friend for life.

VANDIVER'S FIVE AND TEN CENT STORE

One Saturday afternoon, Brother Jack and I entered Vandiver's Ten Cent Store on East Pine Street, Fitzgerald. We were both attired in the uniform of the day, short pants, no shirt, bare-footed, and sun-tanned from the summer sun.

Mama and Daddy were parked diagonally on Pine in their polished Model A Ford. Daddy took great pride in the ownership of a nice-looking car. One of their favorite pastimes on a Saturday afternoon was people watching, which they did for entertainment since it didn't cost a penny and there was little else to do. At the time, Ben Hill County was probably eighty percent agricultural and Saturday was the farmers' big day in town. There were then still quite a few ox carts and one- or two-hoss wagons on the streets. Seems everybody in the county was in town, having either rode or walked in. East Pine was where the action was. A steady stream of humanity passed by, all sexes, all sizes, all ages, and probably all temperaments. Few had any money to spend and were mostly window-shopping, visiting friends, and looking up at our tall buildings.

We had one huge building, five stories high above the street level. The owners tried to call it the Garbut-Donovan building, but it was then and is still called the "five-story building." It and the Lee-Grant Hotel are probably pictured more often on pre-1908 postcards than any other buildings in early Fitzgerald. The building even had a uniformed Negro elevator operator who announced the floors as would a train conductor calling out station stops. A small, hole-in-the-wall sandwich shop on the main floor, a forerunner of fast-food joints, specialized in hand-patted hamburgers. Most of the occupants were medical doctors, tooth doctors and lawyers. Dr. William Peter Coffee had his office there, the same doctor that delivered all five of us younguns in the middle bedroom of our home on Roanoke Drive.

Further on down East Pine Street there were vacant lots occupied by at least two medicine shows on Saturday. These attracted huge audiences, for the little soft-shoe dance accompanied by banjo music was free. Most were hawking patent medicines and guaranteeing their concoctions would cure anything that ailed you. Sales were few and far between.

Mama and Daddy were parked in front of Haile's Drug Store. Dr. Haile's title was of dubious and uncertain origin. One of his signs, which I still own, read, "Dr. Haile's Old Injun System Tonic for the Kidneys, Liver and Stomach for Sale Here." The other said, "Dr. Haile's Fly Skeeter Knocker. It kills 'em dead. Get the genuine blue label, T.J. Haile & Co., Mfg. Chemists, Fitzgerald, Georgia."

Vandiver's Store was across the alley and facing Pine. Mama and Daddy allowed us younguns the pleasurable privilege of wandering up and down Pine Street, going in and out of the various stores. Vandiver's was especially intriguing because the store had an inventory of hundreds of items—all under or up to a Mercury dime. (The Mercury dime had on the obverse a female figure with wings on her cap, intended to symbolize liberty of thought, and on the reverse a fasces, a bundle of rods with an ax in them, supposedly borne before Roman magistrates as a badge of authority.)

All this money business mattered little to Brother Jack and me because we didn't have even an Indian penny to spend. We were just looking over the merchandise, fantasizing about what we would purchase if we had the means. Mr. Vandiver sidled up and says, "If you guys, street urchins or whatever, don't have any money to spend, keep your hands off the merchandise and, furthermore, if you don't get out of my store and onto the street, I'll call the law."

Naturally we beat a hasty retreat but this talk upset us mightily since we were only looking and wishing, and for certain didn't dare steal anything—in fact, didn't even harbor such a thought. We returned to the Ford downtrodden, with gloomy faces.

"What's the matter?" Daddy says. "Y'all ought to be enjoying yourselves and having a good time."

We had to relate what Mr. Vandiver had said to us. It didn't sit right at all with Daddy. He was awful proud of his younguns, their honesty and integrity. Daddy says, "I need to have a few words with Mr. Vandiver," whereupon he left the car and proceeded toward the dime store with us two in tow.

Mama calls out, "Keep your cool and don't do anything you'll regret." This wasn't necessary, for the worse cussing Daddy ever said was, "I'll be doggoned." It now seems almost impossible, him being a bona fide U.S. Navy sailor, that he didn't learn any better cuss words. I honestly believe he respected and adored Mama so much that he would not offend or even think of offending her by ungentlemanly conduct. Pray that I could have such control.

Daddy gave Mr. Vandiver a real dressing-down and told him he ought to be ashamed of himself. Vandiver sputtered a forced apology and hung his head. He lost several potential customers that day and I learned a lesson. If a person enters your store, give him or her a royal welcome—you can never tell when a customer might come back with money jingling in his pockets.

ALLEN'S SUPERMARKET

My very first grocery store job had been up Pine Street at a small grocery store called The Swannee Grocery. It seems that on my first day a lady shopper told me they were selling cabbage across the street for a penny a pound less than "we" advertised them for. I politely told the lady that's where she should buy her cabbage, whereupon she says, "But they're out over there." Like a smart aleck, I told her we sold them at half that price when we were out. Unfortunately the manager overheard this conversation and as a result dismissed me at the end of the day, handed me fifty cents and told me he didn't need me anymore.

In spite of my record I was hired by Owen Seagraves who was the first man in town to realize the attractiveness and convenience to the customer of a modern supermarket with a full produce department and meat counter. The store was on East Pine Street and was about seventy-five feet across the front and at least a hundred feet deep. The restocking warehouse behind made it larger by three or four times any other grocery in town. He had rows upon rows of plain and fancy groceries, even down to rattlesnake meat. I remember watching this particular item, packed in a small container about like a tuna fish can. The item never needed restocking as long as I was employed there.

There were two checkout lines, one manned by Mr. Lightsey, and his sacker, and the other by Emma Lee Liles, with me as her sacker. Customers could pick up a wheeled cart at the front, wander up and down the aisles, and fill it with various and sundry items. The meat department had a couple of long refrigerated display cases with ordinary cuts of ham, chops, hamburger meat and the like, but the meat cutters specialized in custom-cut portions. The floor was covered with planner mill chips and sawdust, as were most meat markets back then.

Owen bought his biscuit-making flour by the railroad carbox, which held fifty or sixty tons. Almost every housewife made biscuits at least two times a day and some again for supper. He got a good price on the flour by the carload, way below other grocers in town, and passed it on to his customers, thereby cornering the market. Hog lard in fifty-pound cans was another big seller, for it took lard and flour to make biscuits.

This brings to mind the time Owen hired John Oliver Warren and me to unload a full boxcar, offering us an unheard of five dollars apiece for the job. We started by emptying the carbox, piling two to three hundred pounds of flour onto a hand-pushed dolly, then unloaded this into a motor truck. In the process we picked up the flour three times before it was in the store. We started at about sun up and were still unloading the car late that night. We'd had no time off for dinner or supper, so Owen told us boys to pick up a loaf of bread and a pint of mayonnaise, come back to the meat counter and eat all the sliced meat sandwiches we wanted, plus a free nickel soda water to wash them down. Of course he stayed in sight to be sure we didn't eat over two sandwiches apiece.

Five dollars for the day was a windfall, since our regular wages were a dollar per day less two cents Social Security withheld. This dollar workday consisted of turning up at sixty-thirty or seven in the morning and going till around midnight, when Owen would go to the front door and look up and down Pine Street to be certain no one else was coming in to shop. Even then a knock on the door would gain admittance for a late shopper. This midnight closing time ran into one or two a.m. Sunday morning, as we were expected to cart groceries from the warehouse to restock the shelves for the coming week.

I remember one terrifying incident in the warehouse when I was the first to unlock the door and switch on the lights. Wharf rats as big as house cats went screeching and running over the tie beams and along the walls. I knocked on a post to frighten them and a huge rat jumped, landed on my back, tore my shirt, and left bloody streaks where he had clawed me. I am to this day afraid of wharf rats.

One day in 1941 when pennies became scarce due to World War II beginning, Mr. Lightsey handed me a five-dollar bill and said to go to the bank for more. At the bank, some cashier went to the safe and brought out ten rolls of pennies. Lo and behold, when they began opening them, it turned out they were all brilliant Indian head pennies, uncirculated, just as bright as the day they left the presses. Mr. Lightsey refused to let me buy even five, for he said he needed every last one to make change for customers.

All shoppers were encouraged to fill up their carts before coming to the checkout. When the groceries were rung up—yes, the cash registers had a bell—some customers didn't have enough to pay the bill, whereupon Owen would begin removing items till the remainder equaled all the money a customer was carrying. Most black women carried their cash tied up tight in a handkerchief or bandanna usually secured by several knots.

Owen was the tightest man I ever knew, unless it was Esbon Faulkner later on at Osierfield. Owen on a good Saturday, his best day, took in six to eight thousand dollars and that was big money in the early 1940s. He invested a lot of his money in worn-out farmland in North Ben Hill and Wilcox counties and subsequently planted them in pine trees. This proved to be a far-sighted move for he made a bundle from this venture.

Owen mellowed in his old age and made many generous gifts of cash and land to Fitzgerald and Ben Hill-Irwin Tech School and his beloved Methodist Church.

WADE CLEARY, FIRE CHIEF

Wade Cleary was Chief of the Fitzgerald Fire Department for near on forty years. He was an Irishman who took his responsible position in stride and lived up to the townspeople's expectations. I can't relate precisely where he got his expertise or *modus operandi* but the little town of Fitzgerald for many years had one of the lowest fire losses, business and residential, in the nation, and as a result one of the lowest fire insurance rates.

Chief Cleary didn't put up with any bullshit. He drilled his crew continually to instill in them the know-how and wherewithal of approaching a fire, putting it out, and leaving the scene knowing they had preserved for rebuilding the largest part of the structure, whether commercial or private. The firemen drove or rode on one of Fitzgerald's two fire trucks, one chain-driven and probably 1920s vintage, the other a big handsome American LaFrance, really impressive at the time, especially to a young fellow.

On top of the fire station and city hall building sat a very loud siren that could be heard all over the square mile the city covered. There was no radio contact with the station, only a three-digit telephone number to call. The manual operator always politely asked, "Number, please." I distinctly remember that no number was really needed; if you yelled "Fire!" in the mouthpiece the lady would immediately put you in touch with Chief Cleary who had a separate number for fire calls. On the first ring of this phone the truck was cranked, and firemen scrambled aboard while the chief tried desperately to get a street address from the excited caller. It's quite difficult to remember your street address when your house is on fire!

We younguns loved to answer fire calls. On hearing the ominous scream of the fire siren, we'd hop on our bikes. Was the engine coming toward us or going away? The older guys said you could listen to how many times the siren wailed and know which ward of the town the fire was in. We didn't put much credence in this but rather trusted our ears. If we could see smoke or hear the fire engine coming our way, we sometimes beat the truck to the fire.

Our Aunt Nita Walker was a fire chaser too, and kept an old Model T Ford truck parked on a slope. If we were anywhere near her house, we'd race to the truck, give it a push—there were always a lot of first cousins around—and hop aboard as Aunt Nita let out the clutch. Uncle Will wouldn't go to the extravagance of buying a battery, saying that taking off the brakes or getting a little push forward would get all four cylinders a'poppin'. Aunt Nita got very adept at these sudden starts downhill. If a cousin wasn't quick-like-a-rabbit, he'd get left behind. She had three daughters, but they weren't allowed on these trips.

On one occasion we were witnesses to a shanty fire in our own fourth ward and watched Chief Cleary's crew promptly extinguish it. Probably a frying pan of chitlins got too hot and spilled over the top of the wood or kerosene stove and set the wood floor on fire. Just as the shanty fire was put out some well-meaning citizen, one of the few in town who had a phone, came a'running, waving his arms and hollering to Chief Cleary that there was another fire on the north side of town.

The chief yelled to his crew to load up then called to us, "You boys want to go?"

Immediately five or six of us boys eagerly hopped on and held on for dear life. We scratched off from the dirt and gravel street and went roaring away to the next fire, amidst the screaming of the hand-cranked siren and the clanging of the hand-pulled bell clapper. We boys felt mighty important, like we were part of the crew, as the truck slid to the next stop. Things were a bit more informal back then, except the seriousness of fighting the fire. All citizens respected Chief Cleary highly and cleared the streets when they saw or heard the fire truck coming.

Sometime in the early 1950s, I took the farm crew to town to tear down a two-story wooden house that had seven bathtubs and probably eighteen to twenty rooms, built by Lon Dickey, a local lumberman and entrepreneur. We began by taking off the roof of wood shingle overlaid with two or more asphalt shingles. None of this was salvageable so we stacked it up in a huge pile in the back yard, set it on fire and shortly had a raging, black-smoke blaze going. Some good citizen turned in the fire alarm, and in minutes Chief Cleary and his crew were on the scene, laying out hoses and directing streams of water onto the pile of shingles.

Chief Cleary yelled in a loud voice, "Who in the hell started this fire?"

I knew I had to face the music so stepped forward and fessed up, allowing as how we were standing by with a garden hose for protection.

Chief said in another loud voice, "Boy, I don't give a damn about all that. I'm good mind to arrest you on the spot for setting an open fire in the fire zone," a four-block downtown area which the wise city fathers had set aside years ago after some disastrous fires were set near wooden buildings. Some prominent citizen pleaded my ignorance of the fire ban in this zone, but I still thought for a minute that Chief Cleary was going to carry out his threat. He cooled down a bit—Irishmen never cool down all the way—and directed his crew to put a lot more water on the fire than was necessary. This episode put the house-wrecking back a full week for we had to load the soggy mess on farm wagons, one shovel or seed-fork at a time, haul it ten miles to Osierfield, then unload it.

My son-in-law, Darrel Weeks, worked for the city of Fitzgerald for a short period and one of his duties was to accompany Chief Cleary to Atlanta for some sort of "fire meetings." The chief was in his late sixties or early seventies, but insisted on driving his red chief's car. It so happened the chief got on a one-way street and sideswiped several cars. Darrell said, "Chief, you done sideswiped a car back there."

"To hell you say," the chief replied and barreled on down the street.

GEORGE EATON AND THE GREASED CABLE LINE

Some of the older guys put up a line of abandoned steel loggers' cable in trees near home. They attached the upper end of the cable to a tree about forty feet above ground and anchored the lower end some hundred or hundred and fifty feet away, about six feet off the ground. The length of cable was greased to cut down on friction. They made a handle by heating a half-inch diameter steel rod in a lightered knot fire, bending it into a hoop, and then flaring out the two ends for hand holds. It looked kind of like a Sherman's necktie, a rail heated in an oak fire and twisted around a tree. A boy would then take the handle and climb up the tree, hook the hoop over the cable and jump into space to take a quick, death-defying slide down the cable. He got a fast, exhilarating ride to the ground, gracefully trip-ta-a-lu, and walked away unscathed, to the admiring yells of the audience. The greased cable line was quiet most of the week during school term, but from Friday afternoon until dark Saturday it was used constantly.

The guys who built this contraption didn't like to let us snotty-nosed younguns use it although some of the older guys let us ride if we paid an Indianhead penny. One day some smart son of a bitch told George Eaton and me that if we'd climb the tree (at least forty feet), each of us grab one side of the hoop and jump off into space together, they'd let us slide for free. This sounded like a fair proposition to me, and George thought so, too, so we readily agreed to take part in the episode. George and I climbed the tree and reached the top of the cable anchorage. We stood on a flat plank that the older guys had stolen from somewhere and tacked onto the limb. I thought I could trust George. We stood on the plank at the upper end of the cable's anchorage and prepared to jump into space. He held onto the right fork of the steel hoop and I onto the left side. We only needed the blare of trumpets and rattle of drums. Instead of the simple "one-two-three" we called loudly, "one for the money, two for the show, three to make ready and four to GO." At the last word we were to jump.

I did and George didn't. Naturally the hoop spun left off the cable and I plunged over forty feet toward Mother Earth. I remember crashing through several lower limbs and landing with a loud thump and that was the finale for me. This took place a few hundred yards from home, where I remember waking up about an hour later. The older guys had dragged or toted me home and placed me in a high sidebed. I'd been knocked out cold but had no broken bones.

George Eaton may be alive today: I heard he got a belly full of shrapnel at Battle of the Bulge, the last big Nazi offensive. Several of the other boys went off to service in 1941, never to return. My favorite was Tater Morgan, killed on Guadalcanal.

POSTSCRIPT
Making A Flip

  Tater Morgan's pa furnished him with a steady supply of small steel ball bearings from the A B&C railroad shops. Tater could put one of these bearings in the leather cup of a slingshot and knock a robin out of a tree. He rarely missed.

  We got our slingshot frames from the woods, carefully picking the desired natural fork in a tree. After cutting the forked branch from the tree we took it home and scraped it with a pocketknife to make it smooth. Then we cut a shallow circle about half an inch from the end of each fork to give a good grip on the string that bound foot-long rubber innertube strips to the forks. On the ends of the rubber bands we used more string to attach the leather cup—seems the best leather came from the tongues of well-worn shoes because it was soft and pliable. We called the weapon a "flip." The city guys who used band-sawed forks called them slingshots.

SNIPE HUNT

A few of the older boys regaled us youngsters with the excitement of snipe hunting, its trials and tribulations and the final reward of catching a couple of succulent snipe for the family table. They'd advise us to try it, saying how proud our mama and daddy would be.

I'd been apprised of the intricacies of snipe hunting by an older guy who had an eye for my older sister Ann, a tall, good looking, raven-haired girl coming into her own. To win the privilege of participating in a snipe hunt, all I had to do was speak kindly of this guy and to introduce the two. This sounded like a win-win proposition so I went along with the deal, since I had the secret of what snipe hunting really was. We had many takers—mostly younger boys in our scout troop, the tenderfoots. I entered into the game with relish, but slipped off before the innocent guys who, after crouching in a desolate place for hours holding the open bag, might take out their wrath on me.

There are many versions of the snipe hunt, here is ours. We'd take the young boys, one at a time, to some God-forsaken tract of wild timber or marshy area around a stream or pond edge; snipe were reported to be fond of wet areas. Then we told the boy to squat and hold open a hemp croaker sack, which he had to furnish, and wait for the snipe to come while he called, "snipe, snipe!" When the snipe entered, close the bag quickly and head home with your prize. The best time to catch snipe was late in the evening.

A few boys, determined to catch a snipe or fearful of coming back to the ridicule of not having caught even one, spent most of the night in a swamp, then trudged home empty handed feeling they'd been taken. On a few occasions we'd get a bit apprehensive about the welfare of some of the youngest ones and would go looking for them. This wasn't always a simple matter for often they had wandered off and got lost. A few weak minds insisted on being carried out for a second night's snipe hunt.

The snipe was a mythical bird, and the method of hunting it had passed down from untold generations of older boys trying, for their entertainment, to put one over on the younger boys. Snipe hunting was indoctrination into growing up—what to believe and not believe, and who to listen to. I can't even remember what a snipe was supposed to look like—bird, amphibian, reptile, or mammal?

A few years later I discovered, or Robert Norris taught me, that a Wilson's Snipe was a real bird of the shorebird family. The bird was long-billed, with over four inches of beak for probing in soft mud. It was a legal game bird, although one of the most difficult to bring down with a shotgun. We located an open grassy bog south of town, which caught the effluent from a nearby abattoir, turning it into snipe heaven. We first took shots of the flushed, erratic-flying birds, which took off crying a rasping call, without much success. Then we noticed their oft-repeated habit of circling in a half-mile arc and diving right back where they had started. Our success rate immediately increased, and we found snipe meat delicious.

TRIPS IN THE MODEL A

One year, Daddy and Mama took us to northern Georgia in their Model A Ford in search of Daddy's roots. Mama encouraged this, since from time immemorial she had heard of his sibling brothers, Jack and Hubert, who just vanished into space and anonymity around World War I and were never heard from again. I was intrigued by the strangeness of this tale, as was Hattie Lee. Folks just don't disappear. We questioned Daddy concerning this and he always came up with blanks.

So the trip was planned although it didn't take much planning, taking just the clothes on our backs and a huge lunch prepared from what was already in the home. In hard times a couple with a passel of younguns just doesn't pull up to a restaurant, go in, and order from the menu. Fact is, there were few cafes or tourist courts back then.

We went north to Harris County and neared Daddy's birthplace, Chipley, Georgia. It was a real adventure for us younguns from flat south Georgia, seeing all the high mountains, which in retrospect I know were only the foothills of the Piedmont. At one point Daddy's Model A Ford slid off of a slick clay road, ended sideways in a deep ditch, and Daddy trudged for a country mile to get to a local farmer to pull us out with his pair of mules. My remembrances are of successive red clay roads, slick from recent rains, leading in every and all directions, no road signs, and blank stares from almost everyone we questioned. Were they typical of the local folks? I didn't know then and I don't know now. Our entourage must have spent the night somewhere up there for it was too far from Fitzgerald to have made the round trip in one day driving a Model A Ford and traveling dirt roads.

We traveled a lot within a fifty-mile radius of Fitzgerald. One trip we especially liked was bending north out of Fitzgerald on a blacktopped road towards Bowens Mill. This ten-mile stretch of paving was an oddity back then, there being few paved roads in Georgia outside the metropolitan areas. We'd leave the paving at Bowens Mill, then hit the dirt roads to Abbeville, crossing a mile-long wooden bridge over the Ocmulgee River and its flood plain. Then by a circuitous route we went through Rhine, reportedly one of the meanest places in the state, China Hill, and on into Jacksonville, one of the earliest settlements in the interior of Georgia, where there was a two-car ferry over the Ocmulgee River. This ferry ride was the high point of the trip for us. The ferry was pulled along a tight cable strung across the river and anchored on each bank to a stout tree. The motive power was supplied by two men pulling on a system of pulleys, using also the downward flow of the river to get us across. The fare was twenty-five cents one way until the state began operating it years later. The trip would end with about a twenty-mile trip back to Fitzgerald on dirt roads.

On one of our drives south into Berrien County, we came around a curve and saw five or six tough-looking men holding hands and blocking the two-rut road. Daddy first slowed down, then made up his mind not to stop with Mama and us younguns in danger. He shoved the Ford into second gear, accelerated rapidly, all the while blowing the uga-uga horn, and rushed towards the guys. They held hands, playing chicken, until the car was a scant ten or fifteen feet from mowing them down. Then they broke up and dived for the ditches, their bluff having been called.

Daddy had his own adventure another time when a local doctor told him that he needed to have his tonsils taken out. For some reason Daddy headed south alone to Valdosta, where he'd heard there was a doctor who'd cut out tonsils while the patient sat in a dentist's chair. After the operation, the patient could immediately return home. Well, he nearly bled to death and was in pretty bad shape for days following. To top it off, a turkey buzzard flew up from a road-killed hog and went through the passenger side of the windshield. It broke out the rear window too, they were only plate glass back then, and Daddy returned home with turkey buzzard blood and broken glass all over the car.

Our family once took a fine weekend trip to a new-fangled tourist court on U.S. 41 between Sycamore and Ashburn, Georgia. Daddy had found out about this brand new place on one of our previous trips to Ashburn, when he'd put us younguns on the fast Southern Railroad passenger train, with its green and gold engine and tender, and instructed the conductor to put us off in

Tifton. The highway paralleled the railroad tracks nearly the whole trip so we younguns could sit at the open windows of the passenger coach and wave wildly at Mama and Daddy as they raced along the highway trying to keep abreast of the train. Of course, we opted for this excitement several times in spite of no air conditioning, open windows and a lot of coal-smoked cinders.

The tourist cabins were a circle of white-painted, two-room shanties with a hip shelter on the rear for a small kitchen. There were only two beds in the cabins, but there was running water and an inside toilet. The local entrepreneur had scraped out a huge lake, using mule scrape pans, for a place to swim. It probably covered less than an acre in area but the use of this lake came with the five-dollar cabin rental fee, which paid for the whole family for the weekend. This weekend was a memorable one, camping out, but camping out in style.

CHAIN GANG

I always had a bit of a problem about correctly hearing what was spoken. I took the Wednesday night prayer meeting at the First Baptist Church to be 'pram' meeting. It took two sittings of the Saturday cowboy movies or of Tarzan of the Apes series to pick up the dialogue and understand what the actors were saying. This is why I always thought the old folks were saying 'chang' gang instead of chain gang.

The Georgia chain gang, like those in Alabama and Mississippi, were foremost in cruel punishment. Incarcerated men wore chains on their ankles, put on by a competent blacksmith. The incorrigibles had an iron ball attached with just enough slack in the chain to permit a short step. They wore these all day, and then at night, when they lay on their straw-filled mattresses, an iron rod was passed through their chains to keep them in one position.

Their food was spartan and the same every day—in fact, in some of the worst camps it was poured into a common trough and the convicts went at it like slopping hogs. Convicts were roused way before daybreak, fed and counted, then carried to jobs on mule wagons or 1920s trucks, sitting on benches exposed to the weather. They put in close to a twelve-hour day doing mostly pick-and-shovel work, usually on county dirt roads. Far back, it had been legal to hire them out for so much per diem to work in private sawmills and turpentine camps. To compound their misery, the contractors could sublease them to others for almost unmentionable labors.

In Ben Hill County, at least, the prisoners were treated almost as humans if they toed the line. One of the free entertainments of the mid-1930s was a visit to the convict camp north of town on Sundays, the only day when the chain gang was not working on roads. Most were kept in crude barracks, but the really tough guys, especially murderers, were kept in iron cages and still had their chains on. Their cages had a small hole through which food and water was passed, very much like the feeding of wild animals in a zoo. We were led past the cages, hands held by our parents, looking upon the poor wretches in their misery. I well remember some of the guys in the cages putting on an act, rushing to the side walls, dragging their chains and balls, and growling and spitting at us gawkers. I distinctly remember one incident at the Starke, Florida prison. An old woman rushed at me, "You've finally come to see me, my baby boy," she said. "Come here and let me love you." She embraced me with an iron-tight hug, and kissed and hugged me almost to strangulation. It took my parents and several attendants to drag her away from my neck. I was terrified and swore I'd never go there again.

We were also carried to Milledgeville, site of the State of Georgia asylum for the insane. Most of the patients were behind bars, a far cry from the modern treatment of the mentally disturbed. The reader may think my parents were sadistic or macabre in their attempts to instill in us younguns a resolve to tread the straight and narrow path. This is far from the truth. We had a very, very happy childhood, knew we were loved and adequately provided for, and figured these bizarre trips were part of our education.

THE OCEAN

My first sight of the Atlantic Ocean was from the beach of St. Simons Island, Georgia when I was four or five years old. St. Simons is one of a string of barrier islands separated from Georgia's mainland by an estuarine system of vast marshes, tidal creeks and waterways like the deeper intercoastal waterway.

I was amazed and dumbfounded at the sight of the ocean and immediately fell in love with it—the sight, sounds, smells and the whole euphoria of stepping onto an ocean beach and looking seaward at the vast expanse of water. Daddy pointed east and said, "France is over there, more than three thousand miles away." He knew because he'd been there in the battleship *Ohio* in World War I.

Most of my earliest remembrances of the beach and ocean center on St. Simons Island, for Daddy and Grandpaw Scott Walker had bought some cheap lots on the interior of the island, paying probably less than two hundred dollars for the two or three. These lots were more than a mile from the beaches over two-rut oyster shell roads, shaded by magnificent live oaks festooned with large streamers of Spanish moss. The Model A would get us to the open beach in a few minutes, sister Ann and I riding on the front fenders and hanging on to the head lights.

We did have to suffer the restriction, in the form of a huge wooden fence, of going onto the private Sea Island Cloister beach from the public beach, but of course those beachfront owners had paid an arm and a leg for their view. Sometime in the 1950-60s, a few wise legislators in Atlanta declared all beaches on the coast to be public as long as one stayed on the beach itself and didn't trespass behind the dune lines. Nowadays, what few are left of these beach front lots sell for $500,000.00 and upwards. And they are in continual jeopardy from erosion and threats of hurricanes each fall.

Daddy and Paw Walker had a small cabin on their lots and a free-flowing artesian well of sulfur water. We began going to the island in the early 1930s, carrying mattresses, linens, food, and bare necessities on a two-wheeled flatbed trailer Paw had built at the local railroad shops in Westwood. On one of these early trips, Daddy, Paw and I sat together in the front seat of our Model A. Daddy pointed to the circular, liquid filled speedometer and told Paw that the car, which was doing almost fifty mph, would probably do sixty if we didn't have the trailer behind us.

Just then a wheel ran off the axle spindle of the trailer and, as Daddy braked, the wheel and tire came rolling along the road and overtook us. The lost wheel was no big problem. Paw said, "jack up the trailer," as he came rolling the lost wheel back down the road. He got a can of dope from the trunk, put the wheel back on after locating the spindle tap, and looked around for something to replace the cotter key that had broken off. He spied an 8D nail in the trunk, inserted it in the hole, bent it over with a pair of pliers, and then found a Vienna sausage can in the ditch to serve as a hubcap. We were on our merry way again, with thanks to Paw and to Henry Ford, who always furnished the bare-essential repair tools in a little folding kit under the front seat. It was barely enough to get you out of trouble: a pair of pliers, an eight-inch monkey wrench and one screwdriver.

The hundred and forty-mile trip, pulling the trailer, took only five or six hours over mostly, if not all, dirt roads. Thank goodness we had not had any blowouts on the whole trip though we had passed several cars on the shoulder of the road, jacked up, and with the male occupants patching an inner tube. Tires and tubes back then were notoriously fragile, and every driver carried a spare or two, plus a do-it-yourself patching kit.

The cabin had kerosene lamps for illumination, really roughing it, for we'd had electricity in Fitzgerald for a good number of years. This enthralled us younguns. Granny Walker and Mama built a fire in the wood stove and commenced cooking supper. The two had brought along most of what we were to eat in the ensuing week, primarily "iron rations" including grits, corn meal, side bacon, syrup, flour and what bare seasonings they thought necessary. There was no refrigeration, so Mama carried many cans of Carnation evaporated milk for us younguns. She mixed it half and half with sulfur well water for drinking, cereal, coffee, and cooking. Somehow I drank this strange-tasting mixture and learned to like it.

The meager diet was supposed to be supplemented with the catch of the day from local bridges and boat docks where Paw and Daddy used their piscatorial skills to "bring home the bacon." Their fishing rigs consisted of the very basics: thirty to forty feet of heavy cotton twine, No. 3 hooks and a few ounces of lead sinkers which Paw had molded at the Westwood shops. That was it. They would coil the twine in one-foot loops on their left hand, put some bacon rind or, more rarely, storebought shrimp on the hook, rapidly swing the hook and sinker around and around then release it and let it sail out a good distance where it landed in the salt water with a loud ker-plunk. No bobber corks—this was bottom fishing. After they threw out the line they would reel in the slack, then hold the line in a taunt position, feeling for a nibble. Saltwater fish of any size didn't just nibble though, they snatched the bait and tore off with it. When there was a steady pull, they'd begin reeling in, hand over hand. It was not uncommon to catch two-pound drum, sheepshead, sea trout, whiting and other saltwater fish on a regular basis. Blue crabs were bad about stealing bait and we gingerly pulled in a few but didn't know they were delicious when boiled.

On one memorable occasion I was standing too close to Paw Walker when he wound up and made a mighty heave towards the water. The big hook caught me in my right ear and the force of the throw pulled about a quarter inch gap in my ear. There was plenty of room for backing out the barb. I distinctly remember not crying, although it hurt like hell and a lot of blood flowed. I was afraid to complain for they might have put me on the road home. It was just another lesson learned the hard way. Don't stand too close to a hand line fisherman.

Close by our lots was a small Mom-and-Pop grocery run by a local couple. The husband began every sentence with "Ok, ok" and was known locally as M.F., which stood for "Mighty Fine." His sobriquet even reached the pages of *The Atlanta Journal Sunday Magazine*. M.F.'s grocery was one of the few on the island, if not the only one so he did a thriving grocery business and also pumped gas. One of the most intriguing items he had was sea turtle eggs for sale by the dozen (fifty cents) or by the bushel for around five dollars. During the warm months of the year, immense numbers of loggerhead sea turtles and a few green sea turtles came ashore on St. Simons Island to lay their eggs. They'd usually come out of the ocean after dark and crawl up past the high tide line near the first dunes before excavating a hole to lay their eggs in. They'd lay a hundred or more eggs, cover them with sand and head back to the ocean. Their crawls left tracks easily discernible because on the smooth beach it looked as if a small bulldozer, or nowadays four-wheel-drive vehicle, had come ashore.

The sow turtles had a trick for protecting their nests. They dug several false holes in random fashion before digging the real one where the eggs were to be deposited, probably an attempt to mislead coons who loved their eggs. The locals knew this and had figured out a way to save digging in every false nest. They'd get to the beaches very early and carry a long metal rod to punch into all the holes that had been dug the night before. When the rod came up with egg yolk on it, they knew they'd hit pay dirt and, with a few shovels full of sand removed, would be at the eggs.

M.F. had another attraction that brought many potential customers to his store. He had hired a steam shovel to dig a deep circular pond behind his store and kept it full of clear artesian well water. In fact, he kept it flowing over, since artesian water was free, not having to be pumped. He built a dock out some ways over his pond and stocked it with catfish, bream and bass. He always encouraged customers to go see his fish, dropping the hint that they loved light bread and crackers. Naturally, he sold huge quantities of bread so that children could piece-feed his fish, making a good profit on the bread and getting his fish fattened too—he had many catfish that weighed in at four to eight pounds. He also caught some for sale. He'd get an order for so many pounds of fish, then go out to the pond and bring up a few with his cast net, throwing back what the customer didn't want.

Sometimes Sister Ann and I just played around our cabin and one day learned a useful lesson there. We were under some huge live oaks near the cabin, pulling down garlands of Spanish moss to put on our heads and wrap around our bodies. We had never heard of chiggers or red bugs, but soon learned they loved the stuff too, especially that fallen on the ground. In a few hours we were scratching all over and had red welts on most body parts. Mama got sulfur-impregnated washcloths from M.F.'s store and scrubbed us down, but really there isn't an instant cure. The chiggers dig in, lay their eggs and reproduce, and it takes nearly a week for the cycle to go around.

One evening Daddy and Paw Walker were invited to go mullet jumping. A local carried them out in a rowboat with a couple of bright lanterns placed mid-ship. From hearing them tell the tale, all one had to do was pull into a school of mullet after dark and the fish would begin to jump in the boat, attracted by the bright light. Hard as this is to believe, I found out later it's the truth and explains why this way of fishing is called mullet jumping.

Before we left the beach on my first trip to the ocean, Daddy told me to pick up one of those big whelk shells and carry it back home with me. I did as told and, back home, I'd often put it to my ear and hear the booming surf.

POSTSCRIPT
Undertow

Undertows or rip tides are, in part, caused by the backward flow of ocean waters receding from waves thundering on a beach. They are very strong currents that flow in the opposite direction of surface waters and on the Atlantic shores the initial rapid flow goes eastward to the sea but then usually turns south or north and runs parallel to the shore line. They are a real threat to swimmers who get caught in them and knocked from their feet; they are almost impossible to swim against.

While we stayed at St. Simons, the beach was our destination for a few hours each morning and each afternoon. On one occasion I swam out beyond the breakers, only a few yards beyond my Daddy who was standing in water about four or five feet deep. I yelled to him. "I can't get back to you!" I had been knocked off my feet by an undertow. Immediately he made a few strong strokes and was beside me, but did not make body contact. We both began to tread water and dog paddle and he cautioned me not to fight the undertow, but to go with it and said, "I'll stay close to you, don't panic."

I understood him, but following his instruction was agony. He talked to me constantly, always in a low, calm voice. "Just keep paddling, this thing will play out shortly, then we'll be in calm water and you'll be able to feel the bottom and walk out." We drifted several hundred yards, perhaps a quarter mile down the beach and eventually he was proven right. Where did he get his expertise? Several swimmers had drowned on this beach, which had no lifeguards. Perhaps they had tried to fight the pull of an undertow and expended their last energy trying to reach the beach.

FIRST FLIGHT

The first aeroplane I ever saw was the "flying Jenny" type of World War I vintage. It roared over the homesite at about three hundred feet with two helmeted occupants sitting in open cockpits. They were barnstorming out of some local pasture. I longed to go there and ride if possible, or at least watch, but money was short and my dreams were not then to be fulfilled.

Later in the mid-1930s a local boy, Hubert Dowling, purchased a fine-looking radial engine biplane. He and his partner often flew low over the city. One Sunday afternoon, Hubert decided to jump from a parachute. Sitting on the front fender of Daddy's Model A Ford, I was witness to his fatal fall. It was awful to see but did not discourage my interest in flying.

I was in the eighth grade when a fellow student and young entrepreneur named Billy Kent turned up at school mid-week selling tickets good for a circle over the city in a Ford Trimotor aeroplane. I scratched up the fifty cents and excitedly told Mama and Daddy I was going to go up in an aeroplane come Sunday. Mama didn't cotton to the idea, but Daddy said, "That's fine. I've never been up and I envy you."

I was on Cloud Nine the rest of the week. I'd told Brother Jack to come along, baiting him with the promise that I'd be bold and ask the pilot if Jack could ride on my lap for the one ticket price. We pumped our bicycles across town and then about a mile north, to a field owned by two local farmers who had agreed to take down their landline pasture fences in return for a free ride.

There was a huge crowd, mostly gawkers and non-ticket holders. This plane, designed by Ford engineers, was the largest plane ever to visit Fitzgerald. The sides were built of aluminum that looked like barn roofing and had its large engine in the nose or nacelle. Brother Jack and I approached and produced the one ticket. I asked the pilot, who was also the ticket taker, if my brother could come on and sit on my lap. Fortunately he said yes. "This plane will pick up twice the load it's supposed to."

Man, was this excitement. The huge silver bird was sitting there idling on one of the smaller engines. It was a taildragger and sat on the ground pointed up at a sharp angle. There were at least fourteen wicker seats in it; I can't remember seeing any seat belts. The pilot gunned all three engines, roared down the pasture and in a few hundred feet left Mother Earth. This was exhilarating to the 'nth degree. We craned our necks to pick out prominent landmarks, our home and various and sundry sights. The flight seemed to last thirty minutes or longer but in retrospect it probably was only ten minutes. I relived this first flight in many fantasies and vowed someday to pilot my own plane.

Years later, Mary and I attended an air show in Albany. Lo and behold, there sat a Ford Trimotor offering rides over the city for ten dollars. I left Mary immediately and proceeded to the waiting line to board her. This was nostalgia at its outer limits. At that time there were only three Ford Trimotors still flying in the world; the one I flew on that day had been on a Mexican airline for twenty-five years. There it sat, just like the one in the farmers' pasture so many years before, pointing up, one engine idling, wicker seats and all. Unless the nose was down, the Ford Trimotor probably cruised at only about ninety-five miles per hour but it was an excellent platform from which to observe the local terrain and those poor earthbound inhabitants below who didn't know what a thrill they were missing.

MISGIVINGS, AT LEAST THE ADMITTED ONES

In case the reader thinks I might be setting myself up on a pedestal and trying to be the knight in shining armor or the cowboy with the white hat, let me set you straight with a few adventures from my boyhood.

George Boney, a local mule dealer, and Bennie Anderson, local Ford dealer and peanut buyer, owned about a hundred and fifty acres just southeast of Fitzgerald. Boney kept a huge flock of free ranging turkeys on this place. These weren't wild turkeys but did often wander off into nearby woods. Neither my friend Jack Farmer nor I had ever shot a turkey so we decided here was an unpicked plum. Since Thanksgiving was coming up, we thought bringing home a big gobbler would raise our status in the eyes of the parents.

We carried out the hunt not knowing that our presence and the sound of shooting had been noted and a call put in to George. This snitch met us on the wooden bridge spanning the creek and started up a conversation, almost insisting we stop and rest. It sounded like a good idea, for the two big gobblers were getting heavier with each step homeward. They probably weighed twenty pounds each but after the first mile they felt like a hundred pounds. While we were visiting, up drove George Boney who accosted us saying, "I hear you boys have been shooting my turkeys." We couldn't deny we'd shot some turkeys for we had the evidence, but tried to plead to him we thought they were wild turkeys.

George said in a loud and authoritative voice, "Unload those guns, put them in the front seat and you two boys get in the back, I'm carrying you straight to the jailhouse and have you locked up." Naturally we were scared shitless as he pulled up in front of the big county jail. He sat there for a while, wondering out loud about whether to put us in jail there or carry us to the city jail. He asked us our names and ages and gave us a choice of which jail we'd be put in. We offered to somehow pay him for the gobblers but he wouldn't listen. He just wanted to teach us a lesson about trespassing.

Finally Jack got up the nerve to tell Mr. Boney that his bu mammy (big mama) Nellie Paulk was Captain Jack Dorminy's sister. Jack lived with her on South Grant Street just two blocks away. George, on hearing this information, let up on us a bit for he and Captain Jack regularly traded mules. He then said he'd let us go if we promised not to come within a mile of his place in the future. I don't remember what happened to the two big gobblers but mine sure didn't reach home.

Speaking of Jack Farmer, we were good buddies and got into a passel of trouble together. We both owned fighting cocks and would tie them in our bicycle baskets and ride around town looking for challengers. One of our favorite pastimes was trying to shoot out the flame of a candle at fifty feet without hitting the candle itself. We aimed at the upper tip of the flame with a .22-caliber bullet and didn't have to actually hit the flame to snuff the candle but just come close enough for the wind of the bullet to do it. Mind you, this took place two blocks from downtown, but folks then were pretty calm and didn't bother about guns going off in the city limits, unless you hit someone or destroyed property.

In grammar school I got paddlings from about the third grade through the seventh grade, not just one or two but a multitude of them. All the teachers kept wooden paddles in the cloakroom and didn't hesitate to use them. Back then, they paddled you squarely on the butt and if you had any promise, you'd beforehand slip a writing tablet or something similar in your britches on the backside, hidden below the belt line. We boys always emitted mournful wails at each lick of the paddle and it sometimes shortened the punishment. One of those paddlings came about when I carefully lettered a "Please kick me" sign and clipped it on the back of Martha Stone just before recess. As she walked across the school yard both boys and girls began kicking her till I felt so sorry for her I ran up and removed the sign. This didn't lessen the severe paddling Miss Hildreath Castleberry gave to me.

My own Daddy did not hesitate to administer a whipping when he deemed it necessary. Once I found a washed-out grave at a black cemetery about two miles south of Fitzgerald, picked up a skull, cleaned and polished it after getting home and placed it on the middle of the mantel. On Daddy's arrival home I proudly pointed it out to him, but from start to finish he didn't take to the idea one iota. He thrashed me good then told me to get a flour sack, put the skull in carefully and take it back exactly where I'd picked it up. It was almost dark then but I followed his instructions to the T. I hoofed out the Seaboard Airline Railroad to the burial site, replaced the skull right where I'd found it, and hoofed it back home to another whipping.

Halloween was a night to howl when my friends and I were twelve years old. We shot out streetlights and tossed sand bags through glass windows along with turning over wooden outhouses—not considered a big crime if we first knocked on the door and asked if anyone was inside. A gang of us on the south side had just sand bagged a big picture window on South Main Street and the owners had called the cops. We heard the siren of what we called the Black Mariah, actually a black painted Ford panel truck with a wire cage separating the driving compartment from the prisoner hole.

The Black Mariah driver was my Uncle Dean Hopkins who was on the local police force. As they pulled up, I let fly a pound sandbag in the direction of the panel truck and it connected with the side of Uncle Dean's face with a loud smack. Unluckily he recognized me and called me by name, adding, "Boy, I'm gonna get you for that and whip your tail when I catch you." He popped open the door and ran for me and I taunted him by yelling, "You ain't gonna whip me cause you ain't gonna catch me."

Uncle Dean had been the high school football team captain for three years and starred on the track team but had added a lot of pounds over the years. Besides, he was on my turf and I was barefoot and swift on my feet. He chased me across several dark lawns, up and down a couple dark alleys until he gave up. I outdistanced Uncle Dean even though I had really not tried to run fast, just fast enough to play cat and mouse with him.

Shortly after this, I returned home to receive an unexpected inquisition from my Daddy. He'd gotten a call from his brother, Uncle Dean. Dean was really mad and told Daddy if he let me out of the house again that night he'd arrest me. I spent the rest of the Halloween night at home.

CATASTROPHE

    Today is December 28, 1993. For years I had thought of making a return trip to the surroundings where this story took place. I had planned to made the trip on the fifty-year anniversary but somehow put it off for fifty-one years. This morning I took up the abandoned right-of-way of the Seaboard Airline railroad tracks just south of Fitzgerald, Georgia, and walked three or four miles south to where Emory Wilcox and I went camping in December of 1942. We had walked to our campsite the day before and built our lean-to at a railroad trestle over Coochee Creek, really the Willacoochee River. We intended to camp without a tent, only a hastily-built lean-to and pine straw laid on the cold, wet ground to sleep on. This was to be a three-day, live off the land trip, approved by our parents and talked about many times, though by the time it finally happened both our fathers had died; Daddy in June and Emory's father three years before, in June, 1939, when he had been sucked into an undertow on St. Simons Island and drowned. We had packed one blanket each, some hog lard, salt and pepper and a few Irish potatoes, intending to drink creek water and probably go hungry. The only other equipment was two single-barrel 12-gauge shotguns and a couple of pockets of shells. We never could afford a whole box of twenty-five but bought them singularly at about three for a penny. We had already had one moment of excitement when the cordwood matches rubbed against the shells in my pocket and caught fire.

    We did fairly well the first evening, as well as breakfast the next day, December 28, 1942. We had one dove, one quail, one squirrel and one robin and put them all into a hunter's stew, seasoned by wild onions, salt and pepper, potatoes and a lop or two of hog lard. We complimented ourselves highly and ate heartily, drinking creek water and preparing for the day to come. The night was cold but uneventful except for courting barred owls, the eight-hooter, which kept us on edge for a couple of hours. Hindsight says it was probably two males announcing their whereabouts, seeking lady owls, and probably prepared for defending their territories.

We awoke to find thin ice on the edges of Coochee Creek but were determined to spend the day duck hunting on Lake Beatrice, a mill pond about one mile east of the campsite. It had formerly been called Minnie's Mill Pond and had an operable grist mill in the east end of the dam. A little south of the pond was a steam-train stop also called Minnie. My Daddy had told me of riding his Indian motorcycle out over the pond's bridge planks to a pavilion or dance hall sitting on pilings over the water. Over the years the millpond had sprouted pond cypress and made a most pleasing sight, the cypress being festooned with Spanish moss.

At this ephemeral mill pond or frog pond, Emory and I were to spend a few hours that day in pursuit of wild ducks, epicure's delight. At that time the waters of Lake Beatrice covered several hundred acres, nowhere over four to six feet deep, and produced wonderful habitat for wild ducks, mostly wood ducks. An extensive cattail marsh on the west side was highly attractive to migrating mallards, considered to be the chef's first choice and a delight to the palate when baked in a wood stove or roasted over oak coals.

We hiked in the dark to Lake Beatrice through some awfully big pine timber and arrived between four and five in the morning, prepared to paddle each other through the myriad trails of cypress to secure some ducks to enhance and change our menu. I paddled first in the stolen boat, which we had secluded in the north end of the pond after having clipped the chain where it was padlocked. Emory was in the bow and I sat in the back, paddling fervently ahead, quiet as an Indian, to give him good advantage as the first shooter. He knocked down two wood ducks and shot one diadapper, pied-billed grebe.

We were both armed with 36-inch barrel, 12-gauge shotguns loaded with high-brass No. 4 chilled shot, which we had bought for about five dollars apiece. Emory had used his try and now it was my turn. I left the stern, or back of the boat, and he proceeded to pass me and assume the paddling position on the rear seat. As he sat down he took his duck gun and shoved it, butt down, into the bottom of the boat. The hammer caught on a rib of the wooden boat and pressed the firing pin into the percussion cap.

I was sitting down, looking forward, when I heard a tremendous explosion; Emory hollered my name and shouted, "I'm shot," and as I turned to face him he was falling backwards out of the boat. The three words were the last thing he said as the boat capsized and immediately filled with water. I quickly stepped over the gunnel of the boat, picked Emory from the near-freezing water and placed his now-limp body on a nearby stump that was sticking just above the water's surface. I quickly rocked the boat from side to side to splash the water out, pulled him back into the boat, and did the only thing I'd been taught in Boy Scout first aid, placing a wet handkerchief over his protruding intestines. The load of duck shot from close range had entered his body just below the rib cage, tore through a leather belt and leather jacket and made a hole through which his intestines flowed.

I remember paddling Emory to the dam over half a mile away, shouting as I went. We were met by several people and someone called an ambulance. Today I can't remember any of those people, but someone called my mother and she sent my sister out close to our campsite to pick me up. It was a dazed trot back to that site and I cannot remember any of it

On arriving home Mama said, "You must clean up and go talk to Emory's mother." This struck me as almost as bad as the accident but Mrs. Wilcox was a kind, loving mother of three boys and we both tried to console each other. Someone in the crowd said there would be a coroner's inquest, whereupon Mrs. Wilcox said adamantly, "No, there will be no inquest. I take Milton's word for the truth!"

Emory was a gangling, freckle-faced redhead, full of good-natured mischief and able to hold his own. We were dear, compatible friends, always ready to back each other up in all conflicts. I've done a lot of soul-searching over the years wondering how the accident might have been prevented, but have always run into a void. It just happened that way—it was his time to paddle. It could just as well been me.

PART II

OSIERFIELD FARM

COURTSHIP AND MARRIAGE

Mary and I first met in the late spring of 1946, after I returned from the Pacific—a ten thousand mile voyage on the return trip alone. The occasion of the meeting was a fishing trip to Devils Den, a pond owned by Mary's maternal grandfather Captain Jack Dorminy. Sister Ann had intended to introduce me to Caroline McElroy, Mary's older sister, but she was still at Athens pursuing her degree in English, so Ann, Mary and I went together on the fishing trip.

After catching a few bream and catfish and even a two-foot alligator that I managed to hook and bring in, we three went into Captain Jack's hunting lodge. As we sat together on a davenport the subject of kissing came up. Ann, and I think Mary, could not believe that at over nineteen years of age, I had never kissed a girl.

In fact while in the Navy I'd carried a picture of a good-looking first cousin and claimed her as my girlfriend, embarrassed to tell my shipmates that I didn't have one.

Well, Ann suggested for Mary to put one on me. Mary obliging, slowly leaned over, parted her lips and gave me a moist and delicious kiss. As Victor Hugo said so well in *Les Misérables*, "Oddly enough the first symptom of true love in a young man is timidity, in a young woman, boldness." My God, why had I been so stupid; why hadn't this happened long before? With that first kiss long dormant passion exploded. There may have been fireworks and bells ringing, too.

Mary agreed that I could pick her up in a 1937 Ford car that evening and we would go to a drive-in movie. We did attend the movie but to this day I'm unaware of the picture or actors and actresses. We spent the whole movie lips to lips, tightly embraced. It was the most passionate evening I'd ever experienced. We were both oblivious to Disraeli's advice, "The magic of first love is our ignorance that it can ever end." I could think of nothing else, saying to myself that this was the girl I wanted to spend my life with. The next day she invited me home for dinner, prepared by Rosa Merritt, the family cook of over forty years. After I paid a generous dollar tip, Rosa confided to me that Miss Mary had already told her she had finally met the man she was going to marry.

I continued the chase, seeing Mary every night and driving off to our rendezvous on some secluded country road to park for hours on end. Mary taught me some delicious aspects of smooching and embracing like French kissing. These experiences raised passions I'd never imagined existed either in my mind or other parts. Mary had some experience in these matters. In high school she was the life of the party and always had around her a group of adoring young males. Her popularity with them earned her the nickname Mert, short for the moniker, Mert the Flirt. She was a year behind me, but I had admired her even then although I had been too embarrassed and timid to speak to her, in fact had never met or had any contact with her before our fishing trip.

Mrs. McElroy stayed up to see Mary come home from her dates with me whether it was eleven o'clock or even midnight. As I walked Mary from the old Ford to her front door, Mrs. McElroy would be patiently sitting on the living room sofa knitting an afghan under the only light showing in the house. I once told her I'd love to have one of her afghans, long enough to cover my legs and feet on short naps. She produced one within a week in my favorite green; it is still among my favorite possessions.

Mary had uncanny common sense and, pardon the hackneyed expression, it wasn't really so common. From whence it came I cannot say, perhaps from a hard scrabble upbringing during the Great Depression, intuitiveness, and her own observations of what worked and what didn't. I always asked her advice when making important decisions. She didn't hesitate but immediately came forth with a good and quick solution to most problems.

When I went to Athens in the fall of 1946 to attend the University of Georgia, I was miserable and homesick for Mary and south Georgia. I transferred to South Georgia College so that I could be closer to home, but after the first quarter we decided to become permanent mates, to get married and finish college together.

Finally we decided it was past time to tie the knot and on September 21, 1947, a beautiful fall day, we carried out our plans. We already had the license and rings and went to tell Dr. and Mrs. McElroy of our intentions. He reached into his pocket and handed me a hundred dollar bill and the keys to his Chrysler touring car. We took off on the run and when we just happened to see a congregation coming out of a church in Douglas, we pulled up and asked the parson if he would perform the ceremony right there under a big oak tree. He hesitated but a moment then said he would be glad to if his congregation could stand with us as witnesses. The vows were spoken and we were officially united as husband and wife.

Mary wasn't an outstanding beauty but to me, in 1947, she was the prettiest girl in the world and continued to be for thirty-four years of marriage. She had beautiful, shoulder length auburn hair, full of natural streaks and highlights from time spent in the sunlight—no modern spray-on stuff. Mostly at my insistence Mary kept her long seductive hair at least until the birth of our second child. She occasionally complained of the endless shampooing, curling and combing so I sometimes took over, sitting behind her and combing her hair. She liked this and so did I; she probably didn't realize how erotic the activity was for me but it was often a prelude to deeper and more profound encounters of love.

Following the natural course of events, a daughter, Mary Carol, arrived in 1950 followed by Milton N. in 1952. Mary Carol called him Bubba and soon so did everyone else. A decade later, in 1962, our third child, Donna Raiford, was born, to live only six years before dying from an inoperable brain tumor.

In the late sixties Mary and I used to spend quiet afternoons together at the pond house, formerly the old Cooty house. We had moved the house down from the top of the hill and set it up next to the pond we'd built in 1966 and 1967. Mary would come out to the farm at Osierfield and look me up while I was working on some project with Mister Fred Deese and Rob Dixon, then call me over to the car and say, "Let's go to the pond house." I would give the hands the rest of the day off and Mary and I would drive over to the pond house to spend the afternoon together.

It seems we were attracted to structures moved from somewhere else. In the fall of 1974 Mary and I began to make arrangements to move the old Osierfield railroad depot to a favorite spot in an area of piney woods on our property. The depot had already been moved once, in 1951, when paw-in-law Dr. McElroy bought it to use as a tobacco-curing house. The railroad company stipulated that it had to be relocated at least one hundred feet beyond their right of way so Doc contacted a local mover. He agreed to take on the job, promising to complete the work in six weeks.

The promise was an optimistic one for the move took place in the old fashioned way. The building was jacked up from its brick foundation and solid oak or blackgum rollers with iron axles laid evenly under the entire structure. Because the ground was soft, the mover had to lay planking along the path he intended to take. A cable ran between the depot and a drum that took up the cable as it revolved around, turned by mule power. By this method the several hundred tons of depot advanced a few feet at a time sometimes only reaching the end of the eight or ten foot length of planking by the end of the day.

Mary and I did not need to rely on such antiquated methods. The Green Brothers from near Ocilla moved the building a mile and a half, guaranteeing that a glassful of water placed on one of the windowsills wouldn't spill a drop in the transition. They did balk, though, at the prospect of including the thirty-five foot steeple that rose above the old ticket office and said it had to be removed. We thought the steeple gave the depot its distinctive style and Mary immediately told them that without it she didn't want the building. The Green Brothers finally agreed and proceeded to move the depot to our home site in two stages, one thirty by sixty foot wing at a time.

The depot looks now nearly as it did for the many long years it stood in Osierfield and visitors sometimes wonder how such a large and unusual building came to be where it is. The major change is in the roof, which was originally covered with beautiful Ludowici tile. Unfortunately, they were so badly cracked in the first move that they had to be torn off and replaced with a tin roof.

Now, in the year 2001, trees that had to be replaced after the move have grown to be forty feet tall. It is still my home, though no longer shared with Mary, who died in April 1981.

DOCTOR McELROY AND HIS BROTHER PAT

Dr. McElroy was a flamboyant individual, a ladies' man and a quick combatant who sported a temper with a very short fuse. He figured he could stand up to any man if he had enough fire power. It worked out that he stirred up so much trouble he needed a bodyguard to cover his rear. His brother, Pat, got the job and did virtually anything Doc told him to do.

Dr. McElroy had served in the British services as a medical officer and surgeon, after graduating from Atlanta Medical College (later Emory University Medical School). He entered the British army before the U.S. joined the war against the German Kaiser. While in England Doc attended lectures by world-renowned physician Sir William Osler and on returning to the States became a resident surgeon at Bellevue Hospital in New York City. After all this he returned to Osierfield and took up where he left off.

The doctor was a man to be reckoned with. He confided to me that he'd killed his first man (besides military killing) by cutting the jugular of a fellow worker with a surgical scalpel, the victim a jealous boyfriend of a woman he was consorting with. Dr. McElroy once shot Jimmy Lester Jinright in his right arm, intending only to injure and not kill him for Les was Doc's scratch foreman on the Osierfield farm. Afterward Doc said, "Jimmy Lester, I could have killed you but I'm saving you for later. If you ever again shoot at me with my baby girl Mary nearby, I'll kill you for certain." Another time he shot a neighbor, again in the arm. I know not the reason for this fracas but without a doubt Doc put his bullets where he wished them to go.

I once had the youthful impertinence of making a negative assessment of the "God's truth" as spoken by Dr. McElroy at a crowded Osierfield country store gathering. He'd been bragging about how many hands he had working and how many tractors he had plowing at that time. I made the asinine (in retrospect) statement that he had about half of that going on. The truth was half a dozen hands and one tractor. He pretended to joke this away and said no more except, "Let's get out of here and tend to some business."

We'd barely left the store and the enthralled cracker barrel audience when all hell broke loose. He turned on me and said, "You little wet behind the ears, smart-ass son of a bitch, who thinks he knows so much. Try to keep your Goddamned mouth shut when I'm telling a story. Them folks were enjoying my story, not really seeking the truth, and by God a good story with a passel of lies is always better than the truth."

I smarted a little from this rebuking but have had many years to think this over and must agree he was right, especially since he was one of the original first-rate raconteurs.

Pat McElroy, brother to Dr. McElroy, was named Andrew Greer McElroy by his loving mama. Pat walked the streets of Fitzgerald nigh on forty years or more, and all the while tales about his backwardness and his sorriness followed him. Doc was a bit evasive as to why Pat was the character that he was but alluded to the fact that Pat was probably a victim of early spinal meningitis. Dr. McElroy had made a deathbed promise to his mother, Caroline, that he'd look after his brother and so from the time Pat dropped out of school until his death he was a ward of his brother John and the state.

Pat was caught several times snitching merchandise from the Dorminy-McElroy turpentine commissary at Osierfield. Using a sixteen-foot cane fishing pole with a fishing hook wired to its tip, he would stick the pole through the iron bars that took the place of windows, direct it towards merchandise on the shelves, then snare the items and pull them out through the iron bars. He was sometimes selective and then again indiscriminate in his shopping. If the items didn't go for immediate personal use, he could always swap or sell them for cash.

Pat was addicted to toting a fully loaded .38 Special in the right hind pocket of his overalls. He carried the Special with the handgrip down and the barrel pointing upward, protruding about two inches above the top of his pocket. Pat made a point of letting everyone know he was toting a gun and most knew that he was not afraid to use it. Alvin "Bozo" Jordan once saw Pat walking towards town when a small feisty dog (any of the terrier tribe and highly combative) barked furiously and snapped at his heels. Pat hardly broke step as he pulled his .38 Special from his hip pocket, shot him dead, and walked on.

Pat often left the McElroy home on Merrimac Drive, walked to the intersection of West Central Avenue about a half block away, then stepped in front of any vehicular contrivance and demanded a ride downtown. The startled motorist always braked to a stop and picked him up. I don't think he ever brandished his pistol to commandeer a car; most folks just stopped for him. Once I thought I'd call Pat's hand as he stopped me on Merrimac Drive. He said he wanted a ride to town and I said, "Sure, hop in." He got in the pickup cab, slammed the door, and as he settled down I reached under the seat and pulled out my shotgun pistol. I inserted a shell, snapped it shut and informed Pat that I intended to rob a bank, saying, "Your brother Doc McElroy don't pay me enough to support my wife and children and I need some cash." Well, Pat looked a little apprehensive but rode on towards town, glancing at me, then the pistol, all the while holding onto the right door latch. I turned into the line at the drive-in bank, newly in vogue at the time, and drove up to the teller's window. As I reached for the pistol, Pat jumped from the right side with the truck still moving and raced off to his hangout on Sherman Street.

Dr. McElroy and Pat were continually arguing, but it was mostly bluff and tough talk. Once the three of us were in Doc's big red Chrysler (Doc always liked to travel in a big, good-looking automobile). With Doc and Pat in the front seats and me in the back, we had just pulled up to our "private" railroad crossing connecting the shelter field lands with those he owned north of the railroad tracks. Pat commenced bragging about how he'd stood down some really tough hombre and how he'd called him a lowdown son of a bitch and so on. Whereupon Doc says "I'll bet you told him all that trash when he was a quarter mile away across the creek." Pat took awful offense to this remark and reached for his pistol, and at the same time Doc drew his .38 from his right coat pocket. Both men pulled back the hammers and both said, "I'll kill you, you son of a bitch." Pat lowered his pistol, knowing for certain which side his bread was buttered on, and Doc grabbed it and ordered him out of the car. Pat meekly unlatched the right door and stepped out. The last we saw of him he was walking east on the railroad right of way.

Later, Doc and I were touring around the Osierfield farm, my only duty being to drag open gates for his egress or ingress, there never being a gate on the farm which swung on hinges. We turned up at Miss Julia Faulkner's store—she was a daughter of Mrs. Bradley, who operated an Osierfield store for eons. Pat was standing outside. Doc said, "Pat, you want a soda water and cigar?" Pat took him up on both. There was no mention of the fracas of an hour earlier, and I began to get the picture—their actions were part of a game and didn't amount to anything. A short time before I'd surely thought someone was fixing to shoot the other's brains out.

One evening, however, Pat, Doc and I were returning to Pat's North Merrimac Drive residence. The two had been arguing and threatening each other for several hours on the Osierfield farm. We got out of the car and Doc walked onto the back screened-porch with Pat following. Suddenly Pat picked up a six-ounce dope bottle from a wooden case on the screen porch (they drank a passel of Cokes) and hit Doc on the back of the head. I immediately grabbed Pat from the rear and pinned his arms behind him. I didn't anticipate Doc's reaction. He grabbed another coke bottle from the case and commenced beating Pat on his bare head, reducing it to a bloody mass. I felt guilty for my part, having held Pat with his arms pinned while Doc clobbered his head to a pulp.

Dr. McElroy was my boss, he paid my salary; I had mixed emotions. To show my allegiance I tossed Pat clean through the screened door and down onto the ground. Pat got up hollering something awful about Doc trying to kill him and hobbled off down the alley to Dr. John Ed Smith's home. Dr. Smith cleaned Pat's head, sutured the openings in his scalp and life went on.

I figured Pat would be looking for revenge and probably laying up to get me. It never happened; in fact the incident was never mentioned, either by him or Dr. McElroy. Pat was a meek coward and would only show his so-thought toughness when he was certain he had the upper hand or a backup from Dr. McElroy. We became friends on my terms. In the future I listened to all this bull and discounted it, but I was always ready to hit the floor, grab my pistol and take up Dr. McElroy's side of the argument.

Dr. McElroy mellowed a bit in his last years; he'd outlived most of his antagonists. He began to go to church, Miss Thelma's Methodist church, but he still carried a .38 caliber revolver in the right hand pocket of his business suit, just in case.

YOU KILLED MY VOTE

Dr. McElroy's feelings ran high when it came to politicians, a characteristic he may have inherited from his father. The two of them once went to visit Thomas E. Watson (1856-1922) whose fiery oratory had so impressed Dr. McElroy's father that he thought Watson a reincarnation of Jesus Christ himself. Tom Watson was truly a master of politics. Although he was often characterized as a hayseed rebel or a southern demagogue, he was one of Georgia's most famous trial lawyers and a fervent supporter of Georgia farmers. He was a power in state politics for many years and a potent force in the United States Congress during the one term he served there. While in Washington D.C. he managed to tack an amendment onto a Post Office Bill that brought Rural Free Delivery to farmers. Now they, like their city cousins, would have mail delivered on a daily basis regardless of muddy roads or high water.

Dr. McElroy and his father drove a horse and buggy to Macon to see Watson and entered into the inner sanctum of his office expecting to find the great man ensconced on a throne waiting for the visitors to kow-tow on their knees. Watson asked the elder McElroy the purpose of his call, whereupon he answered, "Mister Watson, I've listened to your oratory relating to Rural Free Delivery and think you speak for the forgotten man."

Watson quickly rejoined, "Old man, I thought you came here with something worthwhile on your mind and here you come up with this infantile prattle about speeches. Get out of here. I'm a very busy man. Why don't you get back to your farm and slop hogs!"

Dr. McElroy was flabbergasted and so was his father who swore that this was his last tribute to Tom Watson and as far as he was concerned the man could go to hell. He finished by saying, "I'll never vote for that son of a bitch again."

The matter of voting rose between Dr. McElroy and myself many years later when Eugene Talmadge, was running for governor of Georgia. I asked Dr. McElroy for permission to run into Fitzgerald to cast my vote. Permission granted, I took off and did my civic duty, marking my ballot for Ellis Arnall, a young progressive running against Talmadge.

On my return to the farm, Dr. McElroy asked if I had voted, and I responded that I had. He then asked for whom I had cast my vote for governor. I probably should have lied but that isn't my nature so I told him that I had voted for Ellis Arnall. Dr. McElroy exploded with expletives and said, "Why you little son of a bitch! You took off in my truck and on my time and killed my vote!"

I didn't exactly see the situation in the same light. I had nullified his vote but had voted my choice as he did his. His man won but died before taking office. The matter was put to the Georgia legislature which awarded the office to Talmadge's son, Herman Talmadge, who had received enough write-in votes to claim the position. So both our votes were killed.

SHOOT-OUT IN OSIERFIELD

One of the first questions Dr. McElroy asked me after I started to work at Osierfield in the late 1940s was, "Boy, do you have a pistol?"

Osierfield was known as a rough town. Floyd Glenn of north Georgia tells of his arrival in 1932. "When the train stopped rolling, I grabbed my grip and headed down the coach steps," he told me. "There were three fisticuffs going on beside the train. Two combatants rolled under the train, whereupon the conductor signaled the engineer to hold up the train until he could get the fighting parties from under the coach."

"I've never had any reason to tote a gun 'cept for hunting," I answered, but nevertheless Dr. McElroy handed me a loaded .32 long Smith and Wesson revolver and said it would be a good idea to carry it. He had recently gotten the pistol from Grady Jinright, via the Coffee County High Sheriff. Seems Grady was on the hog in Douglas and started walking toward Osierfield. After thumbing several cars and being passed up by all, he put four out of six slugs into the rear of one. For this he landed in the Coffee County lock-up and was bailed out by Dr. McElroy. Back then nothing usually came of gunplay unless someone complained or was killed. I learned of a shoot-out that occurred in these times from an eyewitness, Doris Glenn Colson of Osierfield. At the time, which was on June 1, 1933, she lived one half mile east of town on the AB&A railroad track and had accompanied her father, Floyd Glenn, down to Osierfield to ascertain what all the shooting was about.

The reason, I heard, was some heated disagreement over who in Osierfield was to disburse some W.P.A. funds allotted to the town. There was a lot of "make work" going on around the country, and the federal government was dispensing sums of money to the more distressed areas. Osierfield, sometimes called 'Oceanfield' for an area that was frequently under water in the late winter and early spring, received some of these funds for the digging of drainage ditches. Dug by pick and shovel into the Georgia clay, many of the straight-sided ditches are still evident in the 1990s where they pass through rises in the terrain. Dr. McElroy had posted a sign behind a plate glass window of Mrs. Bradley's store (Mrs. Bradley was Miss Julia Faulkner's mother) announcing that anyone interested in digging drainage ditches for the W.P.A. at one dollar per day should see Dr. McElroy at his office in the Dorminy-McElroy turpentine commissary just across the railroad tracks.

Dr. McElroy, his brother Pat and Mark Crawford turned up late in the evening, when the gaslights had already been lit and found that somebody had removed the sign from the store window and torn it up. Dr. McElroy saw Arch Tucker walking down the main street and asked, "Who took my sign out of the window?"

Arch doffed his black wool hat and answered, "I did. What are you going to do about it?"

Doc, Pat and Mark were armed with .38 Smith and Wesson revolvers and two Browning Automatics loaded with buckshot and Arch was carrying his pistol so they all commenced firing. Arch shot wild a couple of times and ricocheting bullets blew out the plate glass window making one store clerk jump into an open wall safe for cover. Dr. McElroy, Pat and Mark fired from behind gas pumps in front of the store. Tucker was fully exposed and had nothing to hide behind. He was shot down and then beaten up with a black jack made of a hunk of lead wrapped with copper wire and held by a leather wrist thong. Somebody got him to a doctor who sewed up Tucker's scalp, including grass, dirt, and gravel, trying to make him look presentable for burial display. The next morning he was still alive so the Doc undid the work, cleaned up Tucker's head and put him back together a second time.

Dr. John McMillan kept Doc hidden for several days following the shooting and no one was ever arrested or tried for attempted murder. They all claimed self-defense, and it might well have been, since every man in the community toted a pistol and had a shotgun or rifle in his vehicle.

To his credit, Dr. McElroy helped Arch Tucker with his needs for the rest of his life. In my possession I have a paper signed by A.L. Tucker on November 14, 1933, acknowledging the receipt of $1,500.00 "in full and complete settlement of any and all claim or claims for civil damages on account of an alleged assault with intent to murder committed on me..."

DOCTOR McELROY AND HIS JAY BIRD SPRINGS WATER

Dr. McElroy swore on his mother's honor that bottled water from Jay Bird Springs, Dodge County, was the best, the safest, and most healthful of any water to drink in this world. Doc drank Jay Bird Springs water with all the meals and was convinced he could tell it from any other water in the universe.

Each week a small dried-up man, steering a two-ton Ford truck with wooden racks on the flatbed, delivered ten gallons of Jay Bird Springs water to Dr. McElroy's back screened porch. The man unloaded the water there, all the while telling pitiful tales of his life in an orphanage and complaining about his pittance of a salary. To ease the pouring, the supplier furnished a rocking metal holder in which the demijohn sat. A linked chain around the neck secured it and forestalled the jug from falling from the cradle when it was tipped forward for pouring.

All the five-gallon demijohns sported an impressive white paper label listing the many (fifteen or twenty) minerals contained in the water. One could have sampled most any water in Georgia and found similar mineral content but somehow Jay Bird Springs had built up a reputation of being the best of the best. Probably the state chemist got his drinking supply free.

One hot July day Dr. McElroy asked me to refill his glass from the Jay Bird Springs water cradled on the back screen porch and please add a little ice from the ice box. I'd tried the water many times and couldn't tell it from Fitzgerald's deep well water so, feeling a bit devilish, carried his glass to the back porch, did nothing, then passed through the kitchen and filled it up with local tap water. He said thanks, tipped his glass, and made loud and vociferous braggadations about the wonderful taste of Jay Bird Springs water, whereupon I said, "Doctor, you're drinking Fitzgerald water straight out of the kitchen tap." He exploded with expletives and directed his comments to me loudly, "You dirty little wet behind the ears son of a bitch, you shouldn't have played this trick on me." I've played a lot of situations plumb dumb, even to my own detriment.

A few weeks later the driver of the water truck was pulled over by a perceptive Georgia state patrolman when the water truck braked for a quick stop at a railroad crossing in the middle of Fitzgerald. The officer had noticed that half of the demijohns of water had a distinct bead on the top, a sure sign of white lightning or strong liquor and called the driver's attention.

The driver told him one of his sad tales but it didn't stick. For years he had been hauling half a load of moonshine liquor and half a load of spring water and getting rich in the meantime. So things ain't always what they appear to be.

COTTON PICKING

When I married into the McElroy family, Dr. McElroy was growing upwards of five hundred acres of cotton, all tended with mules, picked by hand, loaded sheet by sheet, tromped down and carried to the gin.

This was the time of big families, because more hands, regardless of age, could pick more cotton. The parents took all their children's income and carefully dribbled it out to them at the end of the week—just enough change for soda waters or ice cream at the country store. I never heard children complain and most stuck with the grind, until they reached fifteen or so, at which time both boys and girls got a little wanderlust in their bones and started to say "shoes." The earnest pickers liked to be in the cotton patch at sun-up for they figured the dew on the lint would cause it to weigh more. They carried two rows at a time and only stopped for a half hour at dinner. They also wanted to pick until just a few minutes before sundown. I can remember how bad the gallinippers, a huge mosquito of the genus Psorophora, were late of any evening in the lower parts of cotton patches, near a branch or creek run. They were vicious biters.

Oft' times the women would not work as a team with their husbands, preferring to answer their own payroll call, since many of them were doing more work than their spouses. The men just did not have their hearts and minds in this job, which they figured was women's work. The women were more dexterous; a good many in the cotton-picking crew could top four hundred and nigh on to five hundred pounds in the run of the day, from sunrise when the dew was still on the cotton and perhaps added a bit of extra weight, until just before sunset. They always wanted to weigh up about a half-hour before sundown for it was hard to see to cook by lamplight.

Serious pickers bought their own tow sacks at about two and a half dollars from John Henry's Hardware. They were about six feet long with a rubberized plastic undercoating and a good, strong-sewn shoulder strap and could withstand a whole picking season of dragging across sand and red pebbles. Those who preferred to crawl on their knees also bought genuine leather kneepads. These cotton pickers might have been ignorant concerning current events, or events of any time, but by God they could pick cotton, weigh it and correctly multiply pounds times picking rate and out-figure you—or at least come to a common bottom line on what was due them at day's end.

Weighing-up time was a joyful time of day for the hands and with it came frequent explosions of laughter along with a clapping of hands and all sorts of banter. "There you go again, Bertha! Lawd, chile, you done hit yo' fo' hundred again, I knew you could do it." Or, "Uncle Joe, you just wasting this man's time. Why don't you jes' weigh up once a week?"

The hands always gathered around the scale begging not to have "up weights," where the distal end of the scale bar pointed upwards instead of level as it should have. I'd insist on giving them even weights using the eight-pound pea to pull the bar into a level position. At the last notch, the eight-pound pea weighed three hundred pounds of seed cotton and was usually all that was needed to do the job. If the sheet weighed over three hundred pounds, one would start moving a three-pound pea on the opposite side of the scale bar until it was level.

Sometimes a man who half-cropped with Dr. McElroy called me when he was busy elsewhere on the farm to weigh up his cotton-picking hands. He always told me to give them "up weights." Some farmers had even gone to the low-downness of melting extra lead, pouring it into the hollow on the bottom hole on the big end of the pea and daubing black paint over their mischief. I listened and said, "Yes sir, I understand," but then did it as fairly as I could, for I knew by experience what hot, monotonous, grueling work cotton picking was. I wanted to see them get a fair day's pay for a fair day's work. Besides, as I rode up one day I noticed them putting their own set of scales in the trunk of their Hoover buggy and surmised they'd already weighed the sheets. A good number of these people came by in later years and looked me up to tell me how much they had appreciated my honesty and good faith.

Many a night I've slept on a load of cotton in the long line waiting to be ginned. The farmers behind you would respect your place in line, asleep or awake, as long as you were with your wagon, but if you sidled uptown for a beer or two, or made a trip to a fancy cafe, they'd pull around you. Ginning a bale took fifteen or twenty minutes and we usually carried five bales. On the long nights I'd sometimes take a job in the ginhouse for free just to kill the time. I liked to run the powerful suction tube on the front of the gin. I ended up trying all the ginning jobs and eventually got to the pressroom where the cotton was pressed into bales. Pressers tried to come up with near as possible to a five hundred pound bale, although government classers would accept anywhere from three to seven hundred pounds. The warehouseman especially disliked the larger ones, for all handling was done with a two-wheeled, hand-push cart.

While one bale was being rolled out to the loading platform, a worker dressed down the press by placing a big webbed sheet of jute on the bottom. When the desired size was pressed, another sheet of jute webbing was placed on top of the bale. There were six slots on top and bottom of the pressed bale through which steel bands passed. When the hydraulic press was down, these bands would be cinched and then the pressure let up. The bands would groan and crackle as the bale expanded. It was very, very important to cinch the bands securely, for if one or two broke, the rest would follow. This occasionally happened, shutting down the whole works because a bale of cotton, when turned loose from the bands and jute, will almost fill an eight by ten foot room.

In 1958 we were still paying two and a half to three cents a pound for cotton. I see son Bubba's name on a September 20, 1958 picking payroll and he's now forty-nine. At six years old he spent the entire hot day picking alongside over twenty-five hands and weighed up twenty-three pounds for sixty-nine cents.

In the late 1940s and early 1950s Harris McMillan was going to school at Athens trying to learn to be a veterinarian. Back then they were called hoss doctors. His Pa, Dr. J.E. McMillan, owned a one-stand cotton gin at Osierfield through defaults on debts. It sat idle for some time but young Harris put it back in working order and then opened for ginning. The old gin was run by a hand-cranked International Harvester tractor engine and took one hour to gin a bale of cotton, but the staple length was over an inch long and very bright. Most of his bales graded strict middling, one and a sixteenth inch fiber length and brought the highest prices on the market, twenty-five to thirty cents per pound. Modern gins turn out a bale every six to eight minutes but the machine-picked cotton is lower in grade, mostly low middling to strict low middling. It is light-spotted and the staple length is hardly ever over one inch.

The cotton graders, or classers as they were later known, graded the cotton entirely by hand, working under a strong light. A grader would send a hand into the cotton warehouse with a sharp butcher knife, a face-brick to sharpen it, and a bunch of numbers to identify the bales. The hand slashed open the jute wrapping on the designated bales and brought back a sample stuffed into a brown wrapping paper cone. The cotton grader would take the sample, pull it between his thumbs and forefingers, and immediately call out a grade. Graders were all old men who had been at it for two or three generations. They wore green-shaded bills on their caps and were as proud of their jobs and expertise as a first-class bank teller counting greenbacks.

When the boll weevil overtook south Georgia, cotton farmers were in desperate straits trying to control it. Some resorted to paying their younguns a few pennies to walk the rows, collect weevils in a glass jar, and bring them home for counting and smashing between two bricks. Others had their younguns mop the cotton squares (immature bolls) with lead arsenate or had them walk the rows and whip the stalks with gallberry limbs, "pruning" the plants so that they would put on more squares. Now, we have the boll weevil pretty well under control, mostly through traps, baited with artificial sex pheromones, set around the fields. For the time being, cotton is king again. A gin in neighboring Ocilla ginned over seventy-five thousand bales last year.

POSTSCRIPT
Picking Cotton When I was a Boy

   I tried my hand at picking cotton in the mid-1930s on Mr. Spell's farm southwest of Fitzgerald where he cultivated a small acreage. Mr. Spell hired blacks to do the major part of the picking, for a good hand could pick three to four hundred pounds a day, but Mr. Spell appreciated any additional help he could get because it took from twelve to fifteen hundred pounds of seed cotton to make a standard five hundred-pound bale. The Spell boys, John Elie and Billy, were classmates of mine at old Third Ward School in East Fitzgerald and when the cotton was ready to pick, Billy invited me to come to the farm after school and on Saturdays to pick. Mr. Spell was paying the going rate of a half-cent per pound. This sounded like a good deal for a lad needing spending change, so I turned up there on my bicycle several days in a row.

   I was consternated to find out just how much, or should I say, how little, cotton weighed. It was almost weightless. Nevertheless, I continued to turn up for the picking. I soon realized, though, that I was no good at it. After several afternoons plus a half-day on Saturday I barely made picture-show-and-soda-water money. The best I could do was to get about fifty pounds in my tow sack on long afternoons and seventy-five or eighty pounds on Saturday.

   In spite of this, I later on bicycled out Old Ten Mile Trail, a well-known Indian route, to pick cotton in Mr. O.M. Outlaw's cotton patch. I went along with a bunch of city dudes (I should have known better) and we put in a full day except for dinner, which came from our syrup buckets, washed down with all the free well water we cared to draw. Outlaw, a typical south Georgia farmer, wore overalls, a long-sleeved shirt buttoned at the collar and the ubiquitous black wool hat. This last would make you sweat profusely early in the day but later you had your personal air conditioner right on your head.

   One of the city dudes put a twenty-pound citron under the cotton in his sheet, but Mr. Outlaw had seen this trick many times. Sometimes it was several handfuls of red pebbles or a few pounds of sand but the effect was the same—to add weight to the sheet of cotton. Mr. Outlaw knew, though, that the small sheet of cotton couldn't weigh as much as the scales said it did, so he told the young fellow to untie his sheet and spread out the lint cotton. The big green citron stood out like a sore thumb.

At this discovery, Mr. Outlaw said a few well-chosen words, then told us to get on our bicycles and get off his place. He didn't even finish weighing up the rest of our sheets. I thought this grossly unfair since we other five boys were playing by the rules and had no foreign material in our sheets. But sometimes life rains on both the just and the unjust

Years later, after coming back to Osierfield I had the chance to work beside the best picker in the field. My "opponent" was taking two rows at a time and I was steadily losing ground. The day ended, and I weighed in at one hundred and twenty-five pounds while she had over four hundred. That was the last time I seriously tried to pick cotton.

CROW FOSTER, PLOW HAND

Crow was a real maverick; a happy-go-lucky sort of fellow and a good time Joe. He would put in six hard days and sometimes work till Saturday noon in the field, but then the rest of the weekend was his to frolic, and did he know how! His name was Clyde Foster but everybody called him Crow. Dr. McElroy thought the sun rose and set on Crow and was continually bragging on him to others. Once Doc took a visitor on a tour of the farm and I rode along, listening to their talk from the back seat of the Chrysler touring car. The conversation got around to plowhands, whereupon Doc told the visitor, "I'm about to show you the best one in the country."

We pulled up to the North Walker Cut where Crow was planting cotton in east to west rows astride a brand new Super C Farmall tractor. He was making good time on the turn as he stomped one of the rear wheel brakes causing the tractor to spin around on one rear tire and head in the reverse direction down the next two rows. Doc says, "Just watch him, no wasted motion and doing good work too; you could set your watch by the rounds he makes and it wouldn't be off two seconds."

We sat down to watch the demonstration and after a while, long enough for Crow to make three or four rounds, we had not seen him return. The visitor asked, "Wonder what happened to your plow hand on the west end?" There was a good crown in the middle of the cut that blocked our vision of the other end. Doc says, "Mind you, Crow's had some minor trouble but he's a good mechanic and will appear in a minute or so." Well, we must have sat there for at least fifteen minutes with no show of Crow so Doc cranked up and drove to the far end of the field. We found Crow stretched out on the ground fast asleep with the tractor still idling. This was a blue Monday, about ten a.m., and it seems Crow had a terrible hangover and needed a short nap. I expected Doc to blow the horn and rouse him but he only said, "I'll be damned," and we drove off to see the rest of the farm.

Crow didn't think anything about occasionally getting sticky hands and appropriating other people's property for his own use or to swap for shine likker. We used to keep hundred pound bags of shelled corn for hog feeding in the old railroad depot under lock and key. Crow somehow got inside, heisted a bag on his shoulder and headed home about one-half mile away through the pine woods. He hadn't noticed a small hole in the bag that trickled a steady stream of corn grains all the way from the depot packhouse to his back door step. He was confronted with the evidence and the trail he had left. He didn't deny the theft, only commenting that he'd really worked hard for that sack of corn, and had wondered why it seemed to get lighter and lighter as he neared home.

Another time Dr. McElroy and I were riding past the Hiram Mobley Cut when we both saw someone out in the cornfield with a croaker sock over his shoulder, gathering corn ears. Doc said, "Did you seen a man out yonder in the field?" and I answered "No," not having been on the farm long and not wanting to see a man shot for stealing a little corn. He told me to walk out there and see if his eyes were fooling him. I proceeded out into the field a couple of hundred yards and came on Clyde stretched flat on the ground with his corn sack beside him. I looked away and told Clyde to stay put until we drove out of sight. I had to lie the second time and tell Dr. McElroy there was no one out there.

Once we followed Crow as he drove a tractor to the shelter field, staying about twenty feet behind, when the extended rear axle struck a solid black gum tree too near the road. The tractor completely broke in half, Crow falling backwards with the rear end and transmission and the engine end falling forwards. It was a terrible-looking mess, what with all the black transmission and rear end fluid splattered on the ground and Crow sitting there holding the steering wheel that he'd somehow managed to pull loose from the front end. He didn't get a scratch from the accident, but the tractor was ruined and had to be lifted on the tractor company truck with two lifts of their hoist. We carried Crow home and Doc immediately got two of his best axe men from the quarters and by sundown the black gum tree was cut off even with the ground.

Crow had several tricks up his sleeve to impress people. We had an 8N Ford two-plow tractor that he would back up to, then grab the front bumper with both hands, bend his knees and lift the two front wheels about twenty inches clear of the ground. I tried this several times while no one was watching and couldn't budge it even one inch. When I asked him what the secret was, he grinned and said, "First put the tractor in gear so it wouldn't roll, brace your back on the radiator and snatch it up all at once," thereby shifting the center of gravity to help the front end clear the ground. That didn't help me much—I don't believe he told me all there was to the story.

He was full of tricks but one that unnerved me was seeing him stall a four-cylinder tractor engine by pulling the spark plug wires loose from the plug with his bare hands. I could see his hand and arm tremble as he pulled the first one. He admitted this was the toughest. As the tractor began to skip and pop, he'd quickly pull the other three wires to completely stall the engine.

Crow died in Philadelphia about ten years ago. One of his sisters said somebody poisoned his liquor with wood alcohol.

MISTER FRED AND THE BLACK PREACHER

Fred Deese told me this true tale forty-five years ago.

Along then most all roads leading to and from Osierfield were dirt and only the major roads had culverts under them to take care of the flow-off from big spring rains, the frog stranglers and gully washers. On smaller roads a sho'nuff big rain, the lightered-knot floaters, flowed over the roadbed, creating a lake of shallow water sometimes a hundred yards across. Most of the watery roads had sand bottoms and local folk knew if they slowed down and crept through them, they could "ford the creek" without drowning out. They also knew if they hit the water too hard and stalled, they could usually wait a spell and the engine heat would dry the plugs and distributor.

It wasn't a Sunday so one of the local black preachers figured it was a good time to do some serious drinking and contemplating. Mister Fred himself loved a drink of shine and bootlegged a fair amount on the side. I don't know whether you could say he really bootlegged or not, for if he'd had the whole operation to himself he would've drunk all the profit. He just toted five-gallon demijohns from his hiding place to his house and poured up pints and fruit-jar quarts and often just a fifty-cent swallow, one-half teaglass full. His wife, Anniebell, handled the money angle from the security of the house.

The preacher stopped at Fred's house, purchased a gallon jug and asked Fred if he'd like to ride around a bit in the preacher's automobile. Fred thought that a good idea so they went by the store and put in a dollar's worth of gas so they could cruise the countryside sipping and talking trash.

About a mile west of Osierfield on the Prospect Church Road they came to water-covered roadbed forcing them to "ford the creek." The preacher hit too hard and drowned out the engine. He said to Fred: "Never mind, hit'll dry out terreckly."

The preacher took another sip then picked up his Bible from between them on the front seat and began to read scripture.

About then the water began to rise on the floorboard and well nigh came up to their knees. Preacher said to Fred, "Ain't you got no sense atall? Open your door and let this creek water out of here." Mr. Fred obliged but the creek began flowing into the automobile, running upstream. The preacher says, "Excuse me, Mr. Fred, I'll open my door and let it flow downstream."

He did and they sat there for a spell. The preacher put down his Bible and tried to crank the car, to no avail. "Mr. Fred, it's going to take some more drying," he said. "Open the glove compartment and hand me my straight razor and shaving cup."

The preacher sat there knee-deep in creek water, dipped his brush in the water, lathered up his face and took a shave, looking in the rearview mirror. He got finished and told Mr. Fred he would try cranking again, and if that didn't work he was prepared to do some serious praying.

The car cranked that time and the preacher thanked the Lord and eased on out.

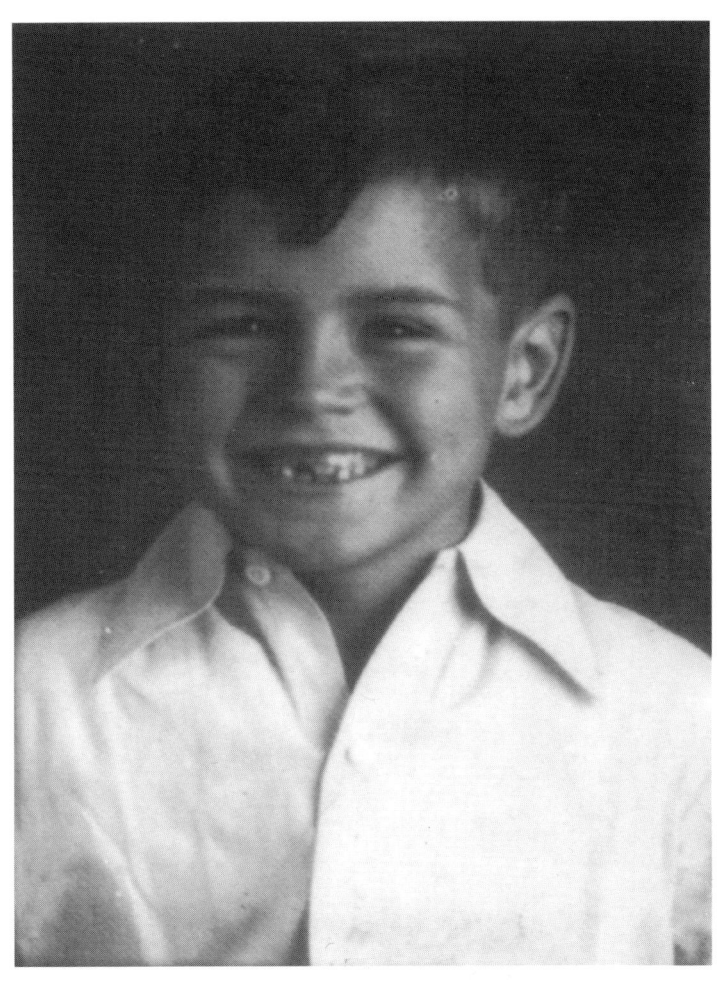

A Young Milton Hopkins, Jr.

Milton Hopkins, Sr.; Milton Hopkins, Jr.

Hattie Walker Hopkins and Milton Hopkins, Jr. 1944

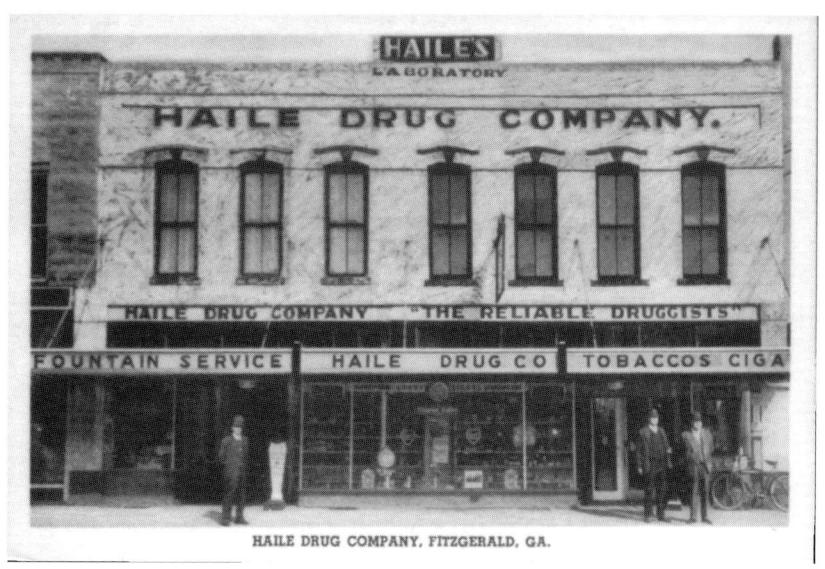

Haile's Drug Store, Fitzgerald, Ga.

The "Five Story Building", Fitzgerald, Ga.

Center: Dr. McElroy; Left: Pat McElroy; Unidentified

Left to right: Milton, Carol, Mary, Bubba, Donna Hopkins, 1968

The Osierfield depot on the Hopkins' Farm

Rob Dixon and Sam

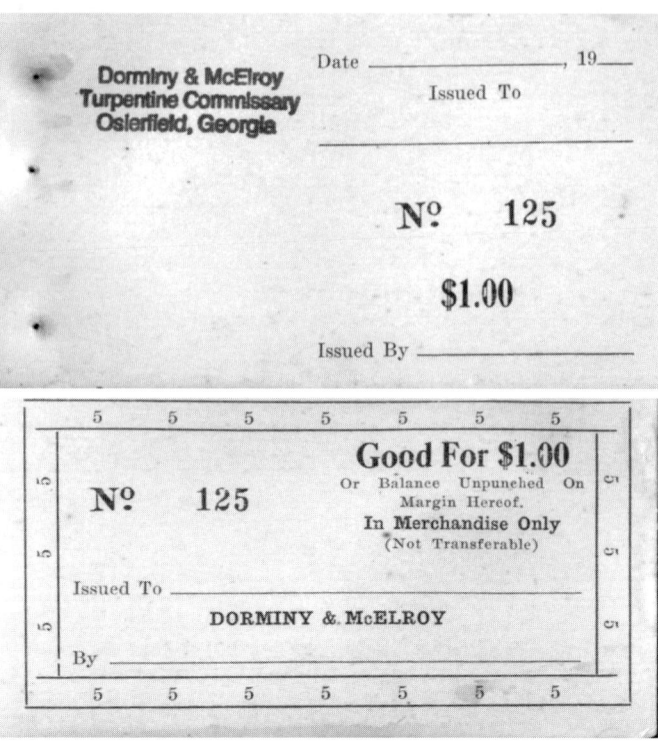

Commisary Coupons

Talley Sheet for Turpentining

A "crop" of turpentine boxes

Hattie White and Martha Dixon: 1966

Thrashing Peanuts: 1951

Picking cotton: 1950's

Weighing cotton
Left to Right: Fred Deese, Sam Davis, Bipp Deese, Clay Porter

Donna and Bubba

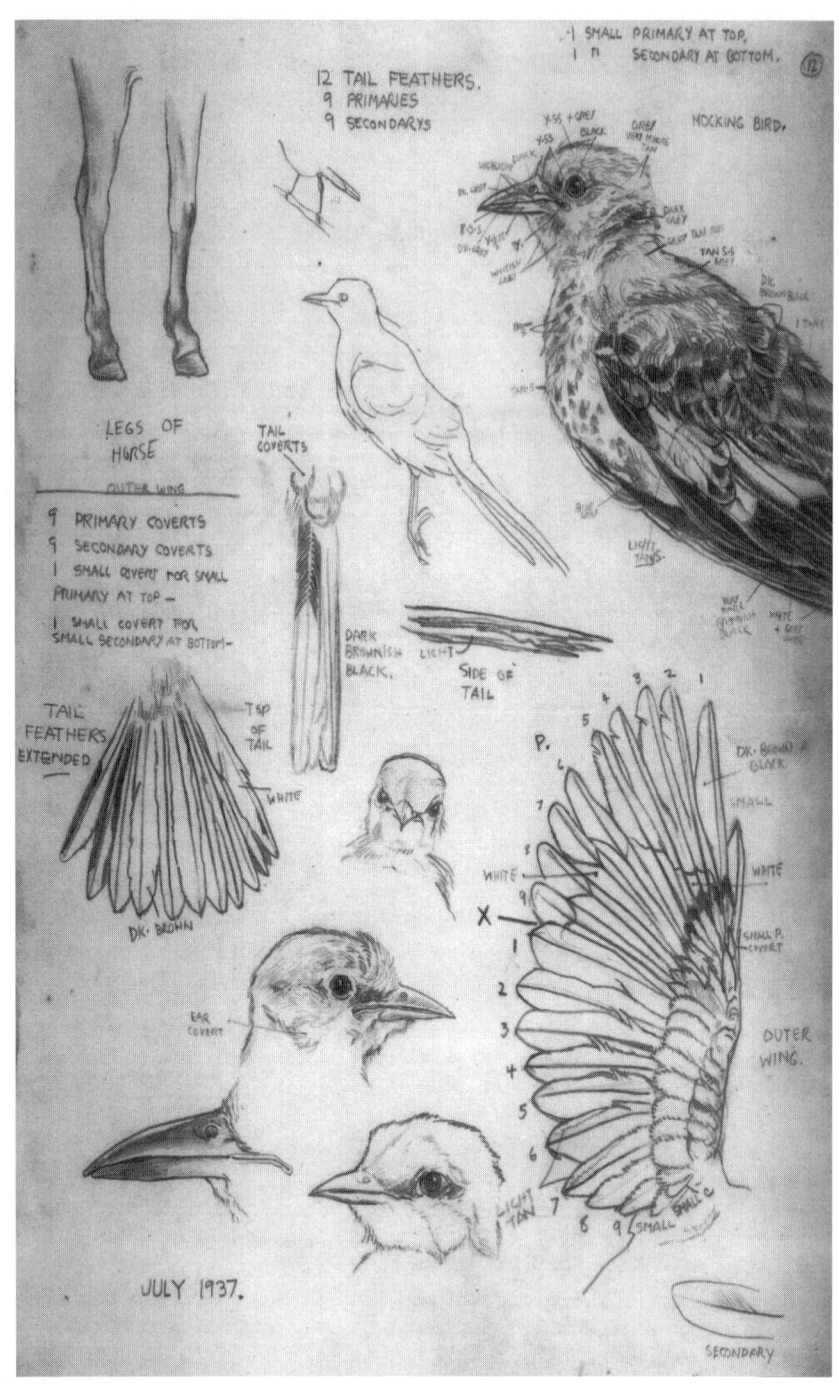

Field Notes by Bob Norris. 1939 Fitzgerald, Ga.

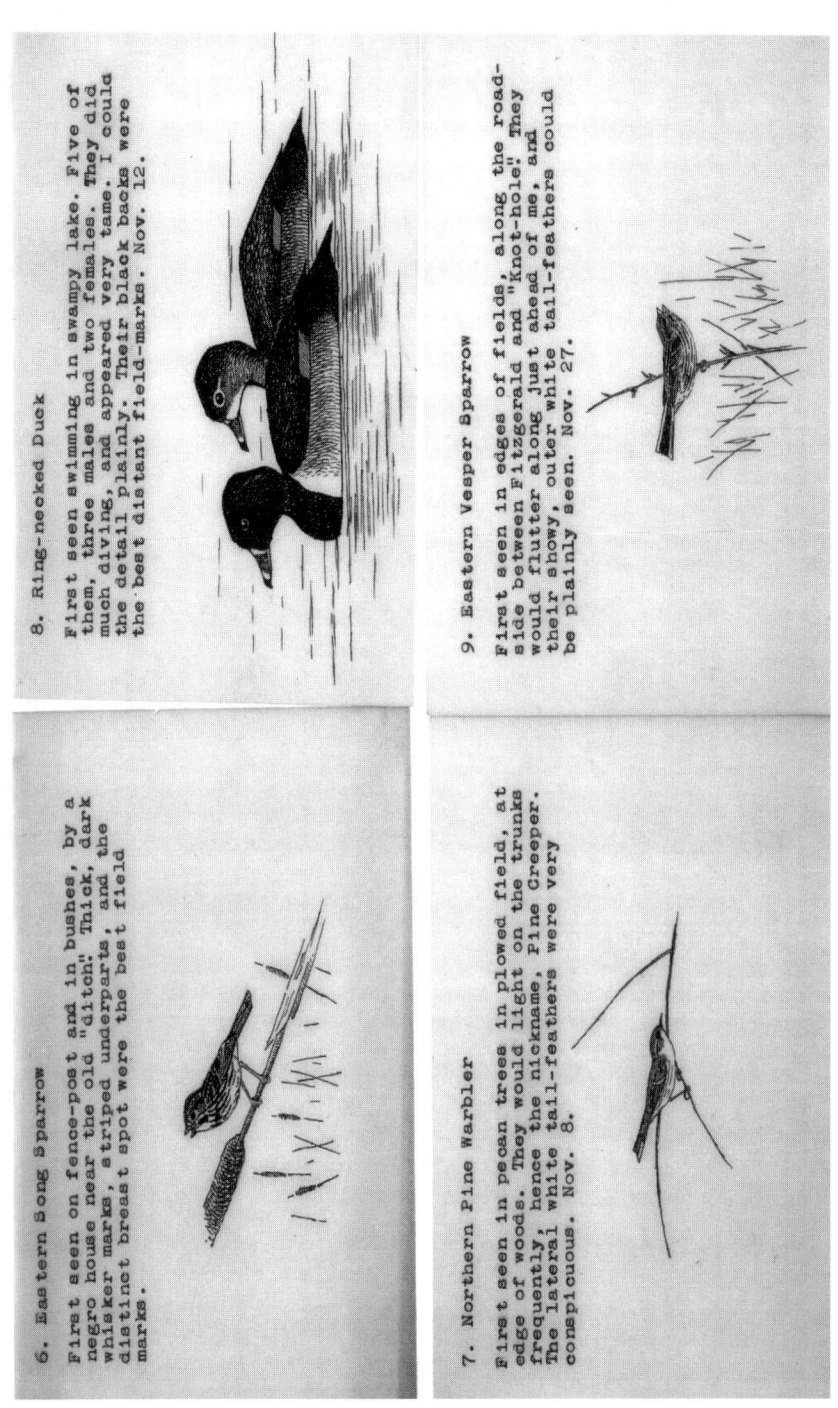

6. Eastern Song Sparrow

First seen on fence-post and in bushes, by a negro house near the old "ditch". Thick, dark whisker marks, striped underparts, and the distinct breast spot were the best field marks.

7. Northern Pine Warbler

First seen in pecan trees in plowed field, at edge of woods. They would light on the trunks frequently, hence the nickname, Pine Creeper. The lateral white tail-feathers were very conspicuous. Nov. 8.

8. Ring-necked Duck

First seen swimming in swampy lake. Five of them, three males and two females. They did much diving, and appeared very tame. I could see the detail plainly. Their black backs were the best distant field-marks. Nov. 12.

9. Eastern Vesper Sparrow

First seen in edges of fields, along the roadside between Fitzgerald and "Knot-hole". They would flutter along just ahead of me, and their showy, outer white tail-feathers could be plainly seen. Nov. 27.

Field Notes by Bob Norris. 1939 Fitzgerald, Ga.

HENRY BEAVERS AND MULE FARMING

In the early 1950s a man name of Henry Beavers, with a wife and a passel of hungry younguns, turned up at Osierfield straight from Sand Mountain, Alabama, wanting to rent or work on halves at least a two-hoss farm. A one-hoss-farm of thirty acres could be handled by one man and one mule who together could harrow the land, break it open with an Oliver turning plow, plow the furrows in three-foot rows, hand-drop the seed, then pass by with a Hammon stock on both sides of the row and cover the seed with a four or five inch shovel. Henry assured Doc McElroy that with the help of all his younguns and wife he could easily do all that for sixty acres and make both of them richer. Dr. McElroy liked the sound of this and stood for Henry's mules, plows, seed, guano, one-hoss wagon and a tad of running money each first of the month.

Henry Beavers was a mean son of a bitch. Although on first meetings he was a prince of a fellow, when the shit hit the fan his real character emerged. He was obstinate, tyrannical, overbearing, dictatorial, macho and opinionated, and most generally a hard man to deal with. Once the family had been given a yearling beef to raise for meat. We noticed one day that the yearling had a swollen eye and large knot on its head, and got the vet to check it out. The vet said to Henry, "Looks as if someone clobbered this animal with a stick," whereupon Henry replied, "I'll go get my gun—ain't nobody accusing me of beating an animal." I used to carry the family to town on a Saturday afternoon, Henry and I in the cab of the pickup and his wife and chillun on the open back. Once they had a little altercation about the distribution of their meager funds. Henry told his wife "Youances have your love stories and weunces want our beer."

The Beavers had arrived in the late fall. To tide them over the winter, Dr. McElroy furnished them with a house in the pecan orchard and a four hundred-pound sow. The farming got off to a slow start in January and February when Henry and the boys began breaking land with a two-hoss Oliver turning plow. Turned out Henry intended to boss the operation, do little, if any, of the work, and to make a crop with his chillun and wife. It was just too much for the young ones, and Henry wouldn't put his mind to it except for short demonstrations on how to do it.

I happened to turn up near noon one day where they were breaking land in the Hiram Mobley Cut. Henry had parked the one-hoss wagon with the front wheels in a shallow ditch, making it closer to the ground and thereby easier to step off the seat. He had already perched himself in the middle of the seat and was telling the boys to unhitch the mules from the turning plow, back one of them between the shafts, attach the trace chains to a singletree and hand him the plow lines. About that time, as the boys scrambled aboard, Henry shouted "gitup mule" and cracked his leather whip across the mule's back. The startled mule lunged forward and completely tore the two front wheels, axle and fifth wheel from the wagon, leaving Henry and the boys sitting leaning forward and almost on the ground.

Henry had one fine-tuned attribute—the ability to really address any problem by putting a good cussing on it. He didn't use any superfluous language, just stuck to the basics.

I fetched them on home for dinner in the pickup, and then Dr. McElroy decided he'd better help with the breaking if it was ever to be done. It turned out that the crop was such a grassy one that it took hired help to get it gathered. That crop was the only one Henry made at Osierfield; he went back to Alabama in the fall.

POSTSCRIPT
The Beavers Prepare a Sow

To Henry's credit, he knew how to slaughter a hog. Mrs. Beavers, to her credit, knew what to do with so much pork.

The sow didn't need shooting between the eyes; Henry bashed in her head with a chop axe. His wife and chillun followed by dipping the hog in a boiling syrup kettle of water, heated by a lightered knot fire, and rubbing her clean of the loosened hair with face bricks. She was quickly strung up and gutted, saving the lights, lungs and chitterlings, then split down the back with a chop axe. After this she was quartered and carried to town for grinding and mixing into sausage meat at John Henry's ice plant where there was a commercial sausage grinder. Naturally, the skull had been split, the brains removed for scrambled eggs the morn following, and the remainder of the head and jowls saved for hogshead cheese, nowadays called souse meat.

Henry's wife, due to habit, or necessity (Henry was stout) or ignorance, put all the meat into sausage patties, fried them in hog grease that she had rendered in a cast-iron cook pot over a hot fire and packed them in five-gallon crocks, covering the whole passel with more hog lard. The whole family ate pickled, preserved hog meat way into the summer, plus a few 'tators and greens when the weather warmed up.

TURPENTINING

Working turpentine involved taking oleoresin or "dip" from living pines—longleaf and slash in the southeast. Since the tar was used mostly by the navy and the merchant marine to caulk decks and tar lines, it was sometimes called the naval stores business. The industry originated in coastal North Carolina in the late 1700s, moved to Georgia after the big Carolina timber was cut, and finally into Florida and Alabama. Most of the pine stands were leased from farm and timberland owners and the going rent was in the range of one to two hundred dollars per thousand faces. This gave the lessee the right to work the faces for four years

I followed a cup-hanging crew of five or six men at Osierfield for most of one morning back in January of 1952. One man would approach a pine tree with a broad axe and chop off the outside bark then flatten the tree on one side. Another man stepped up with a blackgum maul, and as the first man held his broad axe horizontally, the maul man would hit it a strong blow, sinking the broadaxe into the living tree about a quarter inch deep. A third man stepped in and pushed a galvanized strip of tin called an apron into the tree, then the cuphanger placed a one-quart tin cup just under the apron, resting it on one 20D nail. Lastly the chipper followed and cut slanted streaks, running up at an angle on both sides of the cup, making a semblance of a cat face, hence the name faces or cat faces to describe the cuts.

A tallyman kept track of the work. The tallyman in this particular crew was Clay Porter, a very tall black man highly respected in the quarters. He carried a clipboard, paper and pencil, and as each man chanted out his tally call, Clay would make one pencil dot on his tally sheet beside the man's name, for the men were being paid by piecework, usually a few cents per face. Most times the crew was in sight of Clay but oft times they were at some distance. Clay, though, knew each man's tally call. They all differed; some hollered out their girlfriend's name "Oreen" or some railroad name, but never their own name.

Sometimes the tallyman carried a stiff, dry stick in his hand and would loudly tap on the tree if the work was not done according to his liking. It was called a tally-whacker and the crew hated to hear the sound, for it meant backing up and redoing some of the work. (It comes to mind that Mama told us boys to call our pecker our dickey but wife Mary called it a tally-whacker.)

A chipper, using a hack, which was about twenty inches long with a curved blade on one end and a counterweight on the other, would head into his drift of trees about the middle of March when the sap had started rising and put virgin streaks on the new boxes. The counterweights on hacks, cast-iron round weights with holes through the centers, varied from seven to three or four pounds. The heavier ones were used on virgin faces when the chippers were pulling through lightered or fatwood. Hackblades, scrapers, counterweights and shove-down irons were bought from The Council Tool Company, Wananish, North Carolina and came in different widths from 0 to 1 and 2. All other tools were made in the Osierfield blacksmith shop. Hacks and scrapers were kept at razor sharpness by using a cutter or three-cornered file stuck in a corncob or short green branch. These cutters were sharpened on an oval-shaped whetstone about six inches long and were the favorite combative weapon of turpentine hands in settling Saturday night misunderstandings.

Faces were chipped every other week from mid-March until mid-November and dipped on about the same schedule. The chipper and dipper knew that trees facing an opening and having a lot of lateral limbs would run more gum so extra cups were left lying near these trees. Some of the better chippers could put streaks on fifteen hundred to two thousand faces a day and the average dipper could dip thirty eight-gallon buckets of raw gum in a day. A fifty-gallon barrel of raw gum, when distilled at the fire still, would turn out about eleven gallons of spirits of turpentine and three hundred and thirty pounds of rosin, which solidified upon cooling.

Pine faces were worked upwards, beginning with the virgin boxes, about a foot and a half or two feet a year for the four-year period. As the faces approached the fourth year and were several feet above the original, they were called "snatch boxes" and if the operator went still higher, they were called "pulling boxes". Some operators went upwards nearly ten feet, which necessitated putting a long pole on the scraper heads.

Before 1900 most turpentine operators used a box axe that was about two and a half to three inches wide and eight to ten inches long on the blade to cut the boxes in bases of living pines. These cavities would hold three or four pints of crude gum and a good man could chop out sixty to ninety in the run of a day. Traditionally a crop of boxes was ten thousand faces but by the 1930s this had come down to six to eight thousand and even less.

Lige Wilson, known as Big Red, was part of the cuphanging crew. He worked for many years as the chief truck driver with the Dorminy-McElroy turpentine works, driving into the woods in a two-ton Ford flatbed to pick up the full barrels of raw gum. He kept two skid poles, about twelve feet long and four or five inches in diameter, in a rack under the truck body. He knew where all the drifts were and on reaching a barrel placement in the woods would back up close to them, pull his poles out then place one end on the ground and the other onto the back of the truck.

After checking the barrel lids to make sure they were secure, he tipped the barrel onto its curved side and by sheer manpower, pushed and rolled the barrel up the skid poles. Once the barrel was onto the truckbed, he rolled it forward and then rocked it back and forth to deftly stand it on end. This one man was handling around five hundred pounds with each barrel.

In the past turpentine operators had a cooper and helper who put together barrels from wooden staves and banded them with steel bands made in the local blacksmith shop. The operator would lay the completed barrel on its side and bore a bunghole with brace-and-bit then put several gallons of hot hide glue inside the barrel, rock it gently back and forth to coat the insides, and pour out the excess.

Turpentining was hard, hot, nasty work, for pine gum ran best during the hottest months. I knew of only one white man out of perhaps a hundred black workers in the woods, and he couldn't handle the work. In the 1940s a chipper earned about three dollars per thousand faces chipped and a dipper got a dollar and a half a barrel for his work. Hands in the woods subsisted on little food, usually a gallon syrup bucket with leftover biscuits, hoecakes, and a little syrup and fatback. Most carried a gallon jug of water, sweetened by adding a cup of cane syrup.

When Dr. McElroy leased new turpentine trees, he usually put a hot fire through the woods to help clear out brush and make it easier to walk from tree to tree. He once hired Fred Smith, who lived about five miles east northeast of Osierfield as the crow flies, to help him. Fred met Dr. McElroy on a windy winter day and was given two or three boxes of cordwood matches and a quart of good copper-stilled shine. That was Dr. McElroy's part of the deal; Fred's was to start walking eastward, strike a match every third step and toss it into the wiregrass. Dr. McElroy only stipulated that Fred was to turn up at the end of his walk with at least one pint of shine left.

"Make work" in the winter months consisted of "rucking" or raking around pine faces with a scovey hoe outwards to about three feet from the tree, to protect the tree from fire. Raw gum was highly flammable and if the cup and face caught fire it often killed the tree. The rakers got paid one or two dollars per thousand faces

Turpentine men seldom went to town; but after the Saturday morning cash payoff, Clay Porter carried most of the womenfolk to town in a covered pickup truck with his favorites riding in the cab. When Dr. McElroy closed his turpentine commissary in the mid-1940s, he hit upon a unique method (so he thought) of supplying his families with groceries. He'd get Clay Porter to haul all the women to Dill's Grocery in Ocilla and allow each to pick up thirty dollars worth of groceries for a month's supply. It turned out to be a miserable failure. I can hear him now as he took fancy canned goods from their shopping carts, saying, "I don't even allow my wife to buy such," instructing them to buy only iron rations—that is, grits, cornmeal, lard and fatback. The innovation lasted one month.

POSTSCRIPT
The Turpentining Mules

  We kept twelve to fifteen head of mules for plowing and pulling dip or turpentine wagons at the heart-pine mule barn at Osierfield. Turpentine mules were real savvy about getting through the woods between close pines. Seems they were able to judge the distance better than a man and could clear two trees by a scant few inches on either side without benefit of a gee or a haw. The mules responded to a dipper's cluck, drawing up close so that the dip buckets could be emptied, then they would stand still until there was another cluck or "come up mule." It took a pair of mules to pull one of the old wooden-spoked Thornhill wagons with four or five hundred pound barrels of dip on board. Later, when good wagon repairmen were scarce as hen's teeth, we went to rubber-tired wagons made in local welding shops and usually a single mule could pull one of these.

  Italy Williams, an old hand probably in his eighties, watered the mules twice a day, seven days a week. Uncle Italy, as he was called, had experienced a broken leg somewhere in the past and was left with a hobbling gait but it never stopped him from doing his task. He drew water for the mules, bucket by bucket, and poured it into a v-shaped trough made of two rough pine boards nailed on their edges, letting the water flow by gravity to the mules' drink trough. Morning and evening he filled the trough as many times as it took to satisfy the mules' thirst. Italy also rationed out unshucked ear corn morning and evening, taking care not to overfeed the mules so they wouldn't founder.

JOE KING AND HIS FAMILY

I first became acquainted with Joe King in 1946. At this time he was probably the oldest black in the turpentine crew and the patriarch of the King family from Dodge County, across the Ocmulgee River. Dr. McElroy moved the whole four generations south to Osierfield, including Joe's daughters, Martha, Mary and Jensie. Joe had turpentined, dipped, chipped or "pulled boxes" for all his life and knew nothing of other means of employment. He had only a rudimentary command of the English language, indicating his understanding or misunderstanding of questions directed at him with grunts and motions interspersed with "Ya-sur-no-sur." I admired him for his dedication to the work ethic, his loyalty to his employer, and his obvious love for his offspring.

The last was notable. I recall an incident under a tobacco barn in downtown Osierfield when the three girls got up a conversation involving the question of who among them Joe loved best. It was comical and tragic at the same time, for they all were loyal to Papa Joe and loved him. The conversation turned to violence with hair-pulling, wrestling to the ground, tearing clothes, and knocking each other on the head and face with tobacco sticks (about four feet long and an inch in diameter.) Blood was spilling and work at filling the barn with leaf tobacco had stopped. It ended with my having to break up the fracas. The girls didn't exactly kiss and make up but agreed to settle their differences after the barn was filled.

When the Dorminy-McElroy fire-fed turpentine still was operating at Osierfield, it was Joe King's duty and responsibility to leave his shotgun shanty on the north side of the railroad tracts, traipse over to the still and start the fire under the cookpot. The still consisted of a brick-lined circle about ten feet in diameter in which sat a cooking pot of pure copper. Raw dip was poured right out of the dip barrels into the still where it was distilled into liquid spirits of turpentine, the remains forming solidified rosin. Because the dip came from the cups in the woods, it contained pine bark, needles and pieces of pinecones, which had to be strained out before the stilling operation. Actually it would have stilled out with all this foreign material in but at a lower grade because the color would be darker. Spirits of turpentine were graded by color with the highest and most desirable clear grades called "window-white" and "water glass." They went down to "Nancy," "Mary," "Isaac," "George," and so forth, the darker grades named according to the skin color of slaves a way long time ago. The lowest, most discolored grades came from scrape, the solidified gum or rosin, which appeared on faces when the weather cooled.

Joe's job put him at the still around five in the morning to kindle the fire, but Joe had a problem. Seems Miss Lilly, his step-over-the-broom wife (it was legal and Dr. McElroy performed many marriages by this procedure), was a highly sanctimonious type of the "never die" religion whose persuasion included a young deacon boyfriend. In order to keep an eye on his wife after he went to work, Joe would spread several wheelbarrow loads of dip-impregnated skimmings around his shanty yard and set it on fire, thus illuminating his yard for to watch Miss Lilly after he had left.

The deacon wasn't so dumb, though. He approached the north side of the shanty out of Joe's sight, tapped on the shutter, and was admitted by Miss Lilly.

The "never die" religion was headquartered at Joseph Robinson's house at the mule barn. Meetings turned into a medley of drums, washtubs, pot and pan music along with a heap of shouts, "amens", and "praise Jesus" and bodily gyrations by the members. Nellie Williams used to say that to worship correctly one had to make a loud and joyful noise. That surely happened in those meetings and the intensity increased as the shine was imbibed, although not all drank. Their belief was simple: if you made enough noise and praised the Lord fervently enough, you'd never die. Whenever a sect member did die, though they might be into their eighties, the survivors would say so and so had lost faith.

Joe King had one boy as I recollect, name of Benjamin. He was a sho'nuff big, heavy, strapping son and always into some mischief—nothing as serious as drugs, rape, robbery, or gunplay, but continually stirring up trouble in the turpentine quarters amongst the rest of the hands. Once Joe encouraged Dr. McElroy and Mark Crawford, the woods rider, to give Benjamin a sound whipping to try to straighten him out. Benjamin meekly submitted to being tied twixt two pine saplings with leather belts while Doc and Mark Crawford lashed him. One whupped and one held a pistol on him, alternating the duties.

Seems this didn't deter Benjamin from his wayward conduct and so Mark and Dr. McElroy came again. At the time Benjamin was living alone in the Cooty house (later the pond house on the hill south of the depot.) Benjamin was laying up for them this time and as they knocked on the stoop porch and told him to come out, Benjamin fired three shots through the wooden front door. The rifle slugs went clean through the one-inch pine boards; I could still see light through them many years later. His firepower was obviously more than a .22 caliber rifle so Mark and Dr. McElroy hastily retreated and called the High Sheriff of Irwin County. Of course, by the time the Sheriff got out to Osierfield, Benjamin had taken off through the woods, which he knew like the back of his hand, and nothing more came of the altercation, as far as I heard.

After Joe was worn out turpentining, he didn't like to stay home by himself so when the cotton-picking truck turned up he climbed aboard with some helping hands and went to the cotton patch. Being in his eighties, he rarely picked over fifty pounds in a day but spent most of the time sitting on his sheet, shotgun in hand, protecting his cotton. He spent the whole day, "caint to caint," (caint hardly see near sunup to caint hardly see near sundown) in the field and subsisted this ten to twelve hour day on his sweetening water, well water sweetened with cane syrup. Lilly might or might not have put biscuits or corn pone, or on good days some fried sowbelly, in his bucket.

Late one evening, hearing a lot of wailing and crying in the quarters, I stopped and went into Joe's shanty. The daughters thought Joe had gone to the great beyond but were reluctant to check it out. Joe was lying on his back, his eyes wide open and staring toward the ceiling. I could not detect breathing or feel a pulse, so took two coins from my pocket, closed his eyelids and placed the coins on them.

ONE UNIQUE INDIVIDUAL

Rob Dixon came to Osierfield in the late 1930s, "stolen" from a turpentine camp in Marion County, Georgia. He was secreted away by Dr. McElroy and his daughter, Mary. Back then it was common practice to "steal" other turpentiners' hands, usually because they had built up a sizable debt at the previous owner's turpentine commissary and, unable to pay it, were held in bondage to secure the debt. The new turpentiner either paid the debt or helped the hand escape. Another story says Rob Dixon had killed a white man and was fearful of a lynching. At any rate, Dr. McElroy and Mary turned up near dark one evening, took Rob and his one croaker sack of belongings, and headed south to Osierfield. How they had heard of him I never knew.

Among Rob's belongings were two cast-iron dip spoons that had a metal extension for holding a wooden handle. Used to dip pine rosin from boxes cut in the pines, the spoons had been passed down to him by his father before the turn of the century. He was stirring the fireplace fire and dipping up ashes with one of them when I went into his shanty one cold winter day. I had never seen one, and on asking him if the tool had a name, he told me of its origin and use. To this day I have never seen another one in any antique shop or flea market.

Rob and I became good friends and exchanged a lot of personal intimacies over the years, but one day we came to a Mexican standoff. I'd told him to do some which-a-way about a task and he refused. I made some threats, fully intending to carry them out when he said, "White man, I ain't scared of you nary abit," and I enjoined, "Fool, I ain't scared of anything you want to try." We were standing about three feet apart looking at each other eye to eye; then he and I both slowly turned and walked away. Next morning it was business as usual and the confrontation was never mentioned again.

He was strange among the other turpentine workers and lived about a mile away from the turpentine quarters. The other Negroes respected him and in fact were scared of him. The tale hereabouts was that Rob had the Judas eye and could cast spells.

Because he was a loner and didn't get along at all with fellow workers, he was given a "drift" of his own (a few thousand cups) to chip and dip. He did this efficiently and thoroughly, so Mark Crawford had no complaints except, he confided to me one time, he was afraid of Rob and didn't allow him in his truck. Crawford kept his .38 Special loaded on the seat and a Browning unplugged automatic shotgun loaded with .00 buckshot propped on the floorboard of his truck, standard armament for a woods rider at the time since he was the final arbiter between the turpentiner and his hands.

Rob was an acute observer of critters in the wild and their habits. How I wish I'd listed some of his local idiomatic names for birds and animals. The only two birds names I can remember were "lord God" or "logcock" for the pileated woodpecker and "strike bird", the loggerhead shrike, called by us local boys a "French mocker" or "butcher bird" whose habit it was to catch its prey on the ground then fly to a nearby plum tree or barbed wire fence and impale the victims on a thorn. (The victims sometimes hung there for days; I once saw adult strikes repeatedly feeding a lot of young from a mouse impaled in a plum tree.) Rob Dixon kept a martin pole hanging with homegrown gourds for the martins to nest in. It was a habit learned from southeastern Indians who did the same. He was the first person, black or white, in the confines of Osierfield to try to get a colony of purple or "bee" martins to come to his home.

Rob kept a decrepit mule on hand for plowing the garden and pulling his one-hoss wagon to Osierfield, about a mile away. We always left him an acre or two in the short rows of the fields near his house so he could grow mule corn and fodder. He never bought any mule gear but picked up bits and pieces of cotton rope, collars, hames, belly straps, bridles and bits, which he put back together with haywire.

His mare mule subsisted on very little, which one could tell by looking at her protruding ribs. Rob would gather hundreds of citrons for feed and stack them under his hip shelter of the mule barn. He raised a few hogs, and he was probably one of the earliest practitioners of raising almost fat-free, lean-meat hogs. He gathered wagon-loads of pusley (Florida purslane) and fed it to his hogs along with the citrons, swill from the kitchen, and an occasional ear of corn.

Rob liked to hang strips of varying colored cloth on all approaches to his shanty. He shifted to poly when it came in vogue saying, "It don't take hardly nary bit of wind to make it flare out and quiver." This act alone put him in a separate class from all the other hands. I think he knew it and fostered their suspicions to say, "You bastards stay where you are and don't go messing around with me." I was a bit amused and perhaps also fascinated by his actions and promulgations but didn't push him except to ask, "Rob, why did you hang these cloths out?" He answered, "It'll keep the hawks away from my bee martins."

Miss Martha, his step-over-the-broom wife, died one day. The mourning for her demise was short, but when Rob's mule died twixt the traces (diagnosis: overworked and underfed), it caused Rob to go into a deep depression. He dogged me morning and night and all times between to get him another mule. About a year before we had gone out of the turpentine business and had been left with a lot full of fine working mules once used to pull dip wagons in the pine woods and to plow tobacco fields. They were eating us out of house and home and we had a forced sell to the only mule and hoss buyer we knew, who said, "I'll give you fifty dollars a head for everything in the lot." We said, "Sold." He counted the cash, loaded the fine mules and took off.

Well, I had this in mind when Rob and I went mule hunting in the late 1970s and fully expected to pay two or three times this price, due to the declining number of mules (a result of the abundance of tractors). We finally located a pretty good-looking mule down in Pearson, and the owner wanted three hundred dollars for the animal. I could see Rob's eyes sparkle as he checked her teeth, walked all around her, patted her on the flanks and rubbed her nose.

The astronomical price dumfounded me, but we agreed to pay it after I haggled with the owner for over half an hour. He was a good horse trader and knew Rob had fallen in love with the mule, so he had us between a rock and a hard place. In one last effort to redeem myself for my inadequate hoss trading I said, "I'll pay your asking price if you'll deliver this mule to Osierfield." He hesitated only a second before he said, "It's a deal."

There are so many tales concerning Rob Dixon that there isn't enough paper to put them on. He was my only steady employee; he looked after the cow fences, mended them when needed (always), and fed out hay to the cows in wintertime. Son Bubba and grandson Donnie, who called Rob "Bobbert," still remind me of the relationship we had and when things go amiss on the farm they always claim it's the fault of Pa and Bobbert.

POSTSCRIPT
Picking Up Pecans

Rob was married to Martha, sister of Miss Hattie White. I have a picture of Martha and Hattie sitting on the seat of Rob Dixon's one hoss wagon. They had contracted to pick up the pecans in a fifteen-acre pecan orchard situated about a quarter mile northeast of Osierfield. They are both smiling, their wagon wheels slanted in the four cardinal direction of the compass but proud to have a means of going besides walking. Fortified only by dinner from a bucket and well water, they'd just spent a ten-hour day picking up several hundred pounds of pecans and putting them in sacks.

The pecan orchard had been planted near the turn of the century, about fifty years before, and had many inferior type nuts in it. These two sisters had gathered up the nuts, keeping the different types separate under the trees from which they had been shaken—Columbians, Frotchers, Money makers, and a few Stewarts, the most desirable variety. I'd check in with them near sundown every evening and weigh up their sacks, paying them on Saturday for the week's work. They earned three cents a pound for gathering the pecans, and we were getting six to eight cents a pound for most varieties with a high of ten cents for the oilier and more tasty Stewarts.

Sometimes we made a little profit, sometimes broke even, and sometimes we came up short.

One day Ulysses Cummings turned up and said he'd cut down the whole orchard, pay us six dollars a cord for the short pulpwood and clean up and pile the limbs. We accepted but were busy farming then and couldn't see after the agreement. Ulysses downed the orchard, put the butt cuts into short wood for sale and, leaving all the small branches on the ground, disappeared. We hired a bulldozer with root rake to pile up the mess, then harrowed it and put it into loblolly pine. They are doing nicely in 1995—about eighteen feet high and growing. Harvest is still ahead, probably five years before first thinning, but it beats pecan harvesting.

JOSEPH ROBINSON
AND THE HIGH SHERIFF OF IRWIN COUNTY

Sometime in the late 1940s Dr. McElroy got several families of blacks to move to Osierfield from across the river in Telfair and Dodge counties to chip boxes and dip rosin from pine trees. One whole family came over—David, Joseph and Arthur, plus wives and younguns.

Joseph was by far the most intelligent of his siblings and was even up-to-date on current affairs. God only knows the source of this information, for he was without daily papers or television—in fact, had no electricity in his shotgun shanty. Joseph was also a mean artist and his specialty was cars. Most of his walls were graced with pictures of fancy cars in well-executed lines and living color—probably drawn with crayons his younguns brought from school.

Back in the middle to late 1940s and on into most of the 1950s there were over forty shanties in the Negro quarters, nearly all of them in the shotgun configuration. The living room, with fireplace, one sleeping room in line, and one shed on the rear where cooking was done on a wood, or sometimes kerosene-oil, stove. The shacks were hastily thrown-together frames sided with pine and battens. Most families garnered any cardboard they could find to tack on the inside walls so that some of the cold wind was cut out. There were no glass windows, only wood shutters swinging on two rusty hinges.

Many evenings on the farm as I delivered the hands to their shanties, I could pick up the appetite encouragement of frying hoecakes, patties of cornmeal, salt and pepper, and water but the discourager was the smell of burning hair in the fireplace to ward off mosquitoes. Theirs was a monotonous diet of cornbread, fatback and sometimes white-flour biscuits, supplemented by coons, cottontail rabbits, possums and squirrels, plus fish when they had time to catch them. Nearly all hands had a collard patch that grew and produced all year long.

Joseph was the champion dipper of all the turpentining quarters. He could dip and deliver more pine gum or dip than anyone else, probably earning only one to three dollars per five hundred-pound barrel of dip. It took a thousand cat faces to produce about three barrels of gum, so Joseph supplied his extra needs by a little bootlegging on the side. I don't think he ever drank but was ready to sell his fellow hands a little 'shine for fifty cents a drink on weekends. At one time his overzealous sales began to disrupt the ordinary course of turpentining. There would be no-show on Monday but turn up on Tuesday, stay sober and give it hell until Friday noon.

Dr. McElroy figured to give him a little trouble so he decided to put this liquor dealing back into proper perspective. He informed the High Sheriff of Irwin County, Dud Hudson, that Joseph got his delivery of a five-gallon glass demijohn on late Friday or early Saturday. I went along and sat in Doc's car with him and the sheriff, waiting for the delivery. The bootlegger turned up, opened his car trunk, took Joseph's cash, gave him the five gallons and dug off, all so fast it was hard to follow.

The High Sheriff told his deputy to run Joseph down and bring him back with the evidence. There ensued a desperate chase through palmettos, briars, bush and bramble, and the deputy came back empty handed.

"He outran me," he told the sheriff. Joseph had outrun the deputy while toting a five-gallon demijohn (forty pounds) on his shoulder. A few minutes later Joseph came up behind the sheriff and Dr. McElroy, whistling, and nonchalantly said, "Mr. Sheriff, I seen your car parked here and wants to offer my assistance to any crime that might have took place here."

Dud Hudson and his deputy knew Joseph had outwitted them. The sheriff says, "Joseph, how fast can you run?"

Joseph politely replies, "Mr. Sheriff, I has two speeds—as fast as I want to and as fast as I got to." We all had a good laugh and times went on.

DRINKING LIKKER
"Likker talks mighty hard when it gets loose from de jug."
— Joel Chandler Harris

Jimmy Lester Jinright of Osierfield was a hard and heavy drinker who was employed as a scratch foreman by Dr. McElroy. When Doc was not present, Jimmy Lester was sitting in the jaybird seat, cock of the roost, and underlings both white and black moved and spoke according to his dictates.

On evenings and weekends Jimmy Lester was one of the biggest bootleggers of shine whiskey in the environs of Osierfield. He kept a five-gallon charred wooden keg situated in the crotch of a narrow-leafed holly growing in a cypress sink about two hundred yards west of his house. It had a rubber tube running from the bunghole on the keg to a mouthpiece on the other end; midway along the tube was a clothespin that shut off the flow. Every morning Jimmy Lester visited this keg, put the lower end of the tube into his mouth, released the clothespin and by the force of gravity got himself a few gurgles of shine to face the day.

He got his stump likker from White Fabo over on the north side of the Ocmulgee River near Jacksonville, Georgia. He prided himself on transporting the five-gallon demijohns from across the river to the Osierfield farm without being caught by the High Sheriff or federal revenuers. He drove a WWII jeep, carrying about thirty gallons of shine liquor concealed under the hood, cushioned with croaker sacks to withstand the bumpy dirt road. He proudly told me that he'd disconnected the turn lights and stop lights on his jeep so that if he was followed from the rendezvous, the law would not know which direction he had turned. Jimmy Lester knew the back road routes like the back of his hand.

One time we were to build an overflow well on a pond in the Shelter Field Cut. Jimmy Lester figured it'd take most of the morning to complete the job so he siphoned out about two quarts of shine into a gallon jug. He was to do the bricklaying and I was to be his mud man, mixing the sand, mortar mix and water at about a three to one mixture and providing him with mud when he called for it.

Lester got at it with a passion, using concrete blocks weighing about forty pounds apiece. He took to hassling and sweating profusely after laying the foundation ring. He let it set for a short time, meanwhile taking a few gurgles from his jug allowing as how it was such hard work to lay and mortar the joints of the blocks, and on top of that to pour a watery mix into the holes of the blocks to stop water flow in case it seeped through the joints.

The well rose slowly; it took nigh on to twenty blocks per round and we went up about five or six rounds. Lester took his few gurgles at the end of each layer of blocks. It was around noon when we finished and he wiped his brow and took another slug of shine. "'Bout now," he said, "Fronnie Mae has my dinner ready and I have to answer the dinner bell."

Likker drinking notwithstanding, the concrete set, the pond filled, and the excess water in the spring flowed over Jimmy Lester's well, under the dirt dam and into the creek below, just like the doctor ordered.

Jimmy Lester was an avid bird hunter and kept two good bird dogs. About mid-winter of this same year he invited me to go quail hunting with him. The hunt started about sunrise on the old Hiram Mobley Cut. About two hundred yards east of Hiram's house we came to the family dump, in which sat an old abandoned kerosene cookstove with oven compartment and door still attached. Jimmy Lester swung open the rusty door with a loud screech and pulled out a gallon crockery jug with a corncob stopper, heisted it to his shoulder and took several good swigs.

"You want a sip to start the day?" he says.

He told me if I was particular about drinking after him, I could take a pint mason jar from the trash pile and pour some shine out of the jug. I picked up a jar, not worrying about drinking after him but most dearly wanting to see what came out of that dark jug.

What came out was clear and sparkling, with a ring of beads around the top of the jar denoting a high proof, probably at least one hundred. That was my first drink of shine. Not wanting to appear a sissy or an ungrateful bastard, I had poured the pint jar about half full and chug-a-lugged it down. For the next five minutes it was difficult to get my full breath as I coughed and spit. The shine hit my stomach and, minutes later, my brain.

Lester stood back, laughed and slapped his thighs at my predicament. When he hauled shine to the quarters to sell, he always cut it in half with well water and his dealers then cut it again, but I'd gotten the whole bang.

We wandered away, me staggering and falling in stump holes and not daring to take the safety off on covey rises. Drinking and hunting was routine, though, for Jimmy Lester, and he continued to knock down three or four quail every covey rise, shooting from his left shoulder and using a Winchester pump gun that sounded like an automatic in the rapidity of fire.

During the winters of 1956 and 1957 we cleared a branch (or intermittent creek run) to make way for the pond house pond. The turpentine workers, all expert axemen, did it all by hand using crosscut saws, axes and bushhacks—no chain saws. We put in hard labor getting the stuff cut down, piled and burned. Jimmy Lester was still on the place at that time, and it was a Friday evening, the night to howl on the farm. I had carried the handcrew home by pickup to the turpentine quarters, telling them I'd see them tomorrow for payday. They took this to mean I was heading towards my home in Fitzgerald and figured they wouldn't see me until Saturday.

Instead, I made a big circle and headed back to the pond site to check on the brush fires. When I rounded the curve at the Mobley Cut, there sat Jimmy Lester's jeep, tailgate down and on it a five-gallon demijohn of shine likker and eight or ten quart mason jars. Jimmy Lester was parceling out the likker to Crow for his weekend sales, Crow being one of his best dealers.

I didn't give a damn about their liquor dealings, but I had the headlights on and they couldn't see who was approaching. They split, leaving the five-gallon demijohn on the tailgate along with all the quart jars lined up. Jimmy Lester went off north through some young volunteer slash pines and Crow ran off south into the creek run. It took a lot of shouting to let them know who had come upon them but finally the two cautiously returned, all torn up from running through briars. Crow had lost a shoe in the boggy creek run.

We all had a good drink of shine, from Crow's share, not out of Jimmy Lester's demijohn. He still had more handlers to supply for the weekend.

TOBACCO

Most of the lower coastal plains of Georgia were settled by Tarheels in search of new stands of longleaf and slash pine to turpentine. They were also masters at growing flue-cured or leaf tobacco, one of the early exports of this country. When it was discovered that the coastal plain soils were well suited for growing tobacco, Tarheels were sought out and urged to come to Georgia as "demonstrators". They came in good numbers as late as the 1940s, sometimes subsidized by Chambers of Commerce, and bought up small farms, sowed seeds brought from North Carolina, and taught their skills to south Georgia farmers.

To prepare the fifteen by hundred foot beds a jo harrow, pulled by a mule, went back and forth across the bed until it was well worked then several more passes were made with a spike-toothed harrow. We didn't use a tractor for fear of compacting the soil. The final treatment was to meticulously rake the beds with stiff-toothed hand rakes, before sowing the sand-seed mixture. We always raked towards ourselves and left no footprints behind, kind of like painting yourself toward a doorway.

Bed-sowing time was between Thanksgiving and Christmas. Tobacco seeds are very, very small, much smaller than turnip seed, and a few seed heads on a tobacco plant will yield an ounce of seed, which would sow over a hundred square feet of bed. To prevent their being sown too thickly we crawled under old barns and collected half a washtub of really dry, pulverized soil and mixed it with an ounce of the seed. There were only one or two old men entrusted to the sowing. They'd dip about a gallon of the sand-seed mixture at a time out of the washtub and, with backs bent, slowly hand-sow the seeds in a back-and-forth motion. This couldn't be done when any kind of wind was blowing, for the seeds were light and would pile up downwind. Some growers had the hands go barefooted until the whole bed was sown. They'd then put on their shoes and begin pressing the seeds into the topsoil, one stomp at a time. After this the beds were never walked on again until it was time to pull the plants.

After sowing, we stood two inch by six or eight inch sideboards edgeways on the sides and ends of the beds and drove a row of two-foot stobs into the ground down the center. Then we stretched wire from each sideboard over the middle stobs. Over the wire we stretched cheesecloth, three to four yards wide and over one hundred feet long, anchoring it on #6 finishing nails tacked onto the tops of the sideboards. The cloth had to be tight because if a heavy frost came or rainwater froze on the cloth, it would sag and either burn or kill the tender plants.

Since the seed had been only pressed into the top of the soil it usually took root and sprouted within a week, turning the beds a bright yellow-green. Within another week or ten days the plants would be an inch high. At this point Pa-in-law would special-order a ton or two of powdered sheep manure, and, after removing the cheesecloth, workers standing at the sides of the beds hand-sifted the manure over the young plants. Doc admitted the sheep shit didn't have much nutritive value but he thought it tended to warm up the beds.

After the manure application the beds took on a distinct brown color but the stuff slowly dissolved and permeated the soil and then suddenly the plants took off. I can still smell the sheep manure and would know it in the dark. It has a distinct smell, not unpleasant like mule and cow crap. Tobacco plants really got "TLC," more so than any crop on the farm.

Meanwhile, the fields were streaked off in rows with a plow shovel, then Otis Austin laid off the rows by sighting on one stob in the middle of the field and another, topped by light-colored corn shucks, at the far end. He'd line up the two stobs, cluck to his team, watch the stobs between the sides of his mules and lay off a row straight as a rifle barrel.

When the furrows were opened, it was time to put on guano, a specially formulated 3-9-9 mixture that contained a good amount of cormorant and gannet droppings gathered on the cliffs and islands off the coast of Peru. We spread the fertilizer with a bright red-painted K-P knocker, a wooden box mounted on the plow stock, which rolled on a notched cast-iron wheel, newly purchased at John Henry's Hardware for thirty-five dollars. The machine kept up a steady knockety-knock as a lever hit the wheel and dribbled the guano into the furrow.

One morning we had a hilarious moment. All the mules that had usually pulled the K-P knocker were busy, whereupon someone said, "Old Popeye is still in the lot. I'll fetch him." This was done and Popeye was backed up to the machine, and the singletree hitched onto the loggerhead. No one thought for a minute Popeye would show his ass, for he'd put in many years in the quiet of the turpentine woods pulling a dip wagon. But when the plow hand, Sam, clucked for him to "gitup" it took only a few turns of the knocker wheel following close behind his shanks to panic the mule. Popeye took off like the proverbial scalded cat, crossways over the tobacco field with Sam trying his best to keep the brand-new, expensive machine upright. He was doing his best, but it wasn't good enough; we last saw Sam, Popeye, and the K-P knocker leaving the field in a cloud of dust. Sam was outrun by the mule, but he never turned loose the plow handles even when the knocker turned on its side. Sam soon appeared holding only the two plow handles, all that he could salvage. He presented these to Dr. McElroy and it took until almost sundown to locate Popeye and fetch him back to the mule lot. We all had a mighty good laugh and it was back to the hardware for another knocker, but not for Popeye to pull.

The last two weeks of March, tobacco plants were pulled by hand from the beds, one at a time, and carried to the fields for transplanting. We used two mule-drawn New Idea transplanters driven by a hand who sat on a mule seat atop a water tank. The plow lines to the mule ran between two plant droppers who sat side by side above a steel sword that opened up the furrows. As the plants were dropped, two slanted steel packing wheels on the back of the machine packed them tightly into the soil.

It took an old worn-out mule to pull the transplanter at a slow even gait, and only women were dexterous enough to place the plants evenly into the open furrow. Two worked together on a single row. They'd make a few bobbles at first then fall into a slow, steady count, which proceeded into a sort of chant. After they synchronized the chant, the plants took on a uniform spacing, about one foot apart, that could amaze an uninitiated soul and make him think a cogged machine had automatically dropped the plants. After a few near-perfect rows they'd begin to talk woman-talk, interspersed with hilarious laughter, all the while continuing the tedious job of spacing the plants as if it were a game. The women had a little help from the rhythmic clickety-click of the water feeder that shot about a half cup of water into the furrow just as each plant was placed; it was the only watering the plants would get. The women were so good at their work that it was hardly necessary to have a follow-up man walking behind the planter with a pegged stick and a handful of tobacco plants—the skips were that rare. Plant droppers were respected by their peers, myself, and anyone who appreciated work that was done the old-fashioned way. The women stayed at it for eight or ten hours a day, most of it spent sitting on cold steel seats, with their hands wet. They went home at midday, built a fire, fried some cornmeal hoecakes and a bit of fatback, washed it down with well water and were back at work by one o'clock.

We'd pray for a good steady spring shower and cloudy weather to set the plants before the sun got too hot around mid-April. Once the plants are set tobacco will grow really fast if the environment is favorable. We've stuck Coke bottles level with the tops of some plants and seen that the tobacco had grown nearly two inches by the next day. This was without any of the present-day herbicides, fungicides, or pesticides; we added only a mixture of some Paris green, cornmeal, water and a little cane syrup around the plants to kill the cutworms and mole crickets.

The fast growth was partly due to frequent plowing. Using a two-inch shovel on the Hammon stock, along with a twelve to fourteen inch sweep, a good plow hand and a gray mule could plow so close as to actually see the growing plants hump a little upwards. We sometimes plowed as often as twice a week and at times seemed to be fighting against our goal of fast growth. I think I finally convinced Dr. McElroy that we were plowing too often after pointing out to him a healthy tobacco stalk growing from a crack in the concrete sidewalk of a local seedsman.

Under good conditions the tobacco reached nearly head high by the first week in June. When the plant matured it had eighteen to twenty leaves, each about a foot wide and two feet long if was good leaf tobacco. Those at the bottom yellowed and were called sand lugs because they drooped and a good amount of sand stuck to them. North Carolina tobacco buyers always kidded Georgia farmers about the amount of sand on the bottom leaves and swore they had a small mountain of Georgia sand outside their Winston-Salem cigarette factories. For the six weeks or so of harvest about three leaves per stalk per week were cropped off the plant as it matured upwards, beginning with the lower leaf tobacco, then cutters, followed by the long, mid-stem leaves, and finally tips, the very top leaves.

We'd begin preparations for harvesting near the first of June by building eight or ten tobacco sleds. The sled runners were made of two narrow planks, about two inch by four inches, sloped off the forward ends so they wouldn't dig into the ground and on top of them sat a floor of boards with a frame running around the sides and ends. Croaker sacks were stretched over the framework and attached to the boards using soda water caps and shingle nails. We nailed a two by four inch crosspiece on the front of the runners and bored a hole in it for the loggerhead. The finished sled didn't look like much but it did the job for one season.

Putting in tobacco by hand was a big operation requiring close to thirty workers. In the field eight or so croppers snapped the leaves off the stalk then two sled drivers loaded it onto the sleds and carried it to the barn. There two men off-loaded the tobacco and the barn work began as eight handers handed the tobacco leaves to one of the four stringers. The stringers tied the leaves to sticks that were about an inch in diameter and four and a half feet long. The sticks had to be stout because a full stick of tobacco with twenty-five to thirty "hands," made up of three green leaves each, probably weighed at least fifteen pounds. Once the tobacco was strung onto the sticks two more workers were responsible for hanging the sticks in the barn. Each twenty by twenty foot barn could hold fifteen to eighteen hundred of these sticks on tier poles and one of our sixteen by sixteen pine log barns would hold about a thousand. We'd begin at good daybreak and promise the hands a full day's wages if we finished two barns by noon. For their day's work croppers earned four dollars and barn workers three.

By sunup we had the croppers in the field, mules and sleds ready to start. It took a bit of persuasion to get the croppers going for heavy dew had settled on the tobacco leaves that time of morning and they didn't cotton to wading in. I'd have to demonstrate the procedure, which they already knew better than me, by cropping all the leaves I could hold under one arm then tossing them into a sled. "This is the way to do it," I'd say and usually they'd follow. I think they wanted to see me thoroughly wet and miserable at the beginning the day. Some took off and got very far ahead, then waited for the slower croppers to catch up. Son Bubba, at age eight, was a sled driver. His job was to cluck to the mule to get the sled moving (later on to let out the clutch of a super A Farmall tractor and pull the sled forward). He needed some assistance at the end of the rows to induce the mule to make the turn and head back to the far end.

Thus it went until a welcome cry came from the barn: "We've got enough. Stop and rest." Croppers would then sit back in any shade they could find and let the barn crew catch up. For six weeks we cropped, until finally we topped the stalks and broke out the suckers, or lateral branches, to give more nutrients to the tips or top leaves. All hands, arms and fingers were black with tar from the leaves. Fortunately, it could be easily washed off.

Cooking the tobacco was my job. The earliest cooking barns were fired by a furnace that burned castaway pine slabs from a local sawmill. Later, we tried stoker coal, kerosene and propane gas. The heat traveled through a myriad of one and a half foot flues spaced about two feet apart that led finally to the smokestack on the opposite end of the barn. To cure the tobacco the inside temperature was raised up to a hundred or hundred and ten degrees Fahrenheit, for coloring the leaves, then rapidly increased to about a hundred and sixty-five degrees. Many barns caught fire, usually due to pine sticks falling on one of the hot flues. The cooking was complete after five or six days when the stems were cooked or dried enough to withstand packing; the tobacco at this point had been reduced to a fraction of its green weight. A stick of flue-cured tobacco was beautiful, the leaves golden brown, and it smelled good enough to eat.

Leaf tobacco emerged from the cooking so brittle that it would completely disintegrate at the touch. So you had to leave the sticks hanging for a day and night to wait until the leaves "got in order." Dr. McElroy said they had to feel like a maiden's silk drawers. I wasn't too sure about the feel but knew the hanging leaves had to be limp and pliable, else they would crumble and turn into powder. Sometimes we pumped water onto the dirt floor to raise the moisture. It was a fine line to call; if the leaves were too moist, the leaf tobacco would sweat and mildew when it was packed into sheets.

When the tobacco "got in order" the sticks were removed from the barn one at a time, hauled to a packhouse and stacked in layers nearly head high. In a few weeks its color changed to a deep golden brown, the smell getting better all the while. Finally the leaves were removed from the sticks and the leaf tobacco stacked on a sheet of croaker sack material, stems out and leaf tips in. We tried to get between two and three hundred pounds on each sheet, packed down by a weight so heavy it took two to four men to lift it.

Finally the sheets of tobacco were loaded onto a truck and carried to auction. Whole families turned up for the cry of the auctioneer as he neared their farm's crop. If there was a good-looking daughter in the family, she got all spruced up, dressed fit to kill, and stood or sat near the family's first sheet to be auctioned. Two warehousemen, accompanied by twelve to fifteen buyers, preceded the auctioneer and started the bids in a sing-song jargon. Each sheet took only seconds to sell and the whole assemblage passed along at a steady rate. Following the buyers was a mathematical genius who could figure odd sheet weights and odd cent prices instantaneously, rarely making mistakes.

Growing the tobacco was at least a nine-month's job, but selling it and getting your cash was, at most, a half hour wait.

POSTSCRIPT
Foot Racing for "Dopes" or Cokes

Now comes to mind our foot races from a tobacco barn, about three hundred yards southwest of town, to the general store at Osierfield. We always promised the hands from the Negro turpentine quarters that if they'd finish the two barns by noon, or whatever time it took past this, we'd call it a full day and pay a full day's wage. To do this the workers had to start before dawn to empty the barns of the last week's cooking, stack it in the packhouse (in this instance the Depot) and then arrive in the field near sun up.

After the green leaf had been cropped, carried to the barn, strung up and placed in the barn for coloring and cooking I'd challenge the cropping crew to a foot race to the Osierfield store. At the time I was twenty-five years old and never smoked or drank except for a few beers. I promised to buy soda water for any or all that beat me running. Maybe, one time, I beat all eight of them and didn't have to ante up for the bill. As time went on I'd have to pay for two or three soda waters and in the end, a few years later, I'd have to pay for all of them. Anyway, it was a challenge and who can turn down a challenge in their youth? It was great fun, and at a nickel, a dope didn't severely wound the promoter.

THE WISDOM AND FOLLY OF EAR MARKING LIVESTOCK

Up until the 1950s, Georgia had no fence laws and the open range system prevailed. Farmers turned their animals out in the fall and gathered them up again in the springtime before planting. It was always possible to identify the livestock because farmers in Georgia had for two hundred years marked their stock with slits cut in both ears. In the spring when the animals were rounded up, most neighbors returned any animals not of their own mark. Some few altered the mark thereby adding stock to their farm.

Our mark on the Osierfield farm for both yearling cows and hogs was a swallow fork and slit in each ear. Putting in the marks took some good strong help. A couple of men would throw the animals to the ground and hold their legs while I rushed in with a razor sharp Shrade-Walden pocket knife, grabbed an ear and, pressing the sides together, cut a swallow fork in the ear from base to tip then quickly cut a straight slit in the underside of the ear. The process probably took less than ten seconds and blood flowed freely, though it clotted in a few seconds and healed in a day or so. There was a lot of squealing from the hogs and mournful bleating from the yearlings, but their protests subsided as soon as their feet were turned loose.

Ear marking took the place of the branding iron used out west, and identified the animal for the remainder of its short life. Sometime in the 1950s it was advertised in the Farmer's Market Bulletin that personal earmarks could be registered to insure legal ownership of disputed stock. We chose not to register ours, probably in case they caused an expensive wreck on the highway. During the open range period livestock had the right-of-way on the road and if a driver hit one, day or night, he was liable for the price of the livestock and had to fix his own vehicle. It usually turned out that the stock farmer claimed his herd bull or sow to be registered stock and a very valuable animal.

I had my own experience with this in the late 1940s when Mary and I were returning to Athens in our twenty year-old Model A Ford. As we approached Hawkinsville in Pulaski County a huge sow appeared dimly in the headlights. The brakes wouldn't slow our speed enough to avoid hitting her, so I stepped on the gas and tried to center her between the two wheels. We hit her a little off center and the Ford tilted to the right, both left wheels leaving the ground, and then plopped back down. We, and the Ford, lucked out, but I felt certain the impact killed the sow. I knew there was a registered Hampshire hog farm nearby so I didn't look back. Dr. McElroy had taught me that if you hit an animal, chickens, turkey or what ever, including dogs, continue on your way and put some miles between you and the stock owner.

He told me once of plowing into a whole flock of chickens, killing half a dozen, then backing up to apologize to the lady who owned them. She was irate and wanted to charge him two dollars per chicken. That was high-priced chicken meat in the 1930s but he went along with her, shelled out the cash and began picking up the dead chickens whereupon she says, "Those are my chickens and I wanted them alive, not dead, so I get to keep them." She did.

We once missed our registered herd bull from the bunch of cows kept in Ben Hill County. He was a purebred Hereford or "white face." Finally, on up in the morning, we heard that a huge bull was found dead that morning in front of the gate at the local abattoir, or slaughterhouse, when the butchers came to work. The people who had hit him on the highway somehow got him loaded up or dragged him to the slaughterhouse, which was only about a mile away. We didn't ask any more questions and didn't claim him. On foot the bull weighed eighteen hundred pounds or more and must have really messed up the front of someone's vehicle.

Once in the 1950s Claude Young , Dr. McElroys's scratch foreman, saw that a 150-pound shoat was missing from the hog fattening pen. He told Doc he was pretty sure the hog had been taken by a man living on Brant Freeman's place, about a mile north of Osierfield. I drove up there with Dr. McElroy who confronted the man. He protested that he was innocent of the charge; he didn't have any hogs with a swallow fork and slit in their ears and was not a hog stealer. Doc drew his pistol and said, "Let's look in your hog pen." We did and found the hog completely earless. The man had cut off both ears of the hog with his straight razor, even with his head. As Doc raised his pistol, the accused let go a fart, the length of which I'd never heard before or since, and begged for mercy, promising to have the hog back in the proper pen by sunset.

Sometime in the 1970s, a young fellow hit one of our Black Angus brood cows on the public road near the depot. A black cow is difficult to see at night even if she does weigh upwards of a thousand pounds. The driver and a friend of his, who knew me, walked to the depot to let me know what had happened and I carried them back out to the scene of the accident. The cow was lying in the road with a broken hind leg, still alive. The car had both headlights knocked out, the grill was in terrible shape and the hood all buckled up. The owner began hollering and shouting about what it was going to cost me to get his car back in presentable shape. His friend, Junior Slacks, said, "You said you'd keep your cool and talk this thing over." I told him we had liability insurance but this didn't stop his harassing and threats. It was past my bedtime (about seven-thirty in the evening) and I was beginning to lose patience. I slipped a six-shot .45 caliber pistol from the door pocket and rapidly emptied it just over his head, close enough to intimidate him and just far enough above his head to miss him. The two took off like scalded cats, and I returned to the depot and got into bed.

In about thirty minutes I was awakened by a telephone call from the sheriff. He said, "A fellow is here who wants to swear out a warrant to have you arrested for attempted murder."

I told him, "Mr. Sheriff, those guys interrupted my sleep and you know me better than what they claim. If I'd intended to kill him, he'd be laying in that road with at least five holes in him. They interrupted my sleep and I just wanted to get back to it without listening to any more shouting." That was the last I heard of the matter. Farm Bureau paid seven hundred dollars for car repairs and Bubba strung up the cow and skinned her out. We decided to put it all in hamburger meat since she was a bit aged. It made some beautiful, good tasting meat but Mary said she wouldn't touch this meat from a dead cow. I told her I'd love to be around when she ate a live one.

SCREW WORMS

Cochliomyia hominivorax, the screw worm fly, appears bluish or bluish-green and is about twice the size of the common housefly. The adult fly lays masses of shiny white eggs on bloody wounds made by wire cuts, nail scratches and branding marks; navels of newborn animals are especially vulnerable. The eggs, numbering as many as two hundred, hatch in twelve to twenty-four hours into the tiny larvae called maggots. They attach their heads in the fresh wound leaving their tails exposed for breathing. Maggot-infested wounds smell terrible.

The maggots complete their development into flies in five to seven days then drop from the animal's wound and crawl up on low vegetation to dry, expanding their wings within a few minutes. The adult flies mate in two more days and by the time they are five or six days old begin to fly around looking for animal victims. This short life is no exaggeration and keeps a steady supply of blowflies on hand in warm weather.

It's been estimated that in 1956 screw worms cost the livestock industry twenty million dollars a year. Screw worms were giving us fits on Osierfield farm during the fifties and sixties. It was almost a certainty that any calf dropped would get screw worms in its navel, their bloody, moist umbilical cord having attracted the blow flies. Any animal husbandry expert could have told us we should keep the herd bulls in a separate pasture and control-breed the brood cows so as to have them drop most of their calves in the winter months when the screw flies had migrated south. We were just thick-headed enough to think the bulls should run in the pasture year round.

One morning Dr. McElroy and I were having breakfast together at one of the Greek stands. There was a big breakfast crowd in the cafe when the screw worm problem came up. I was relating to Dr. McElroy some book learning acquired in Athens entomology courses, and commented that if we could somehow keep the blowflies from breeding and laying their eggs on flesh, we'd have the problem whipped. I had no idea at the time that efforts were being made to irradiate male flies and cause them to be sterile.

He listened politely and then said, "Young man, you need some educating." He proceeded to tell me maggots spontaneously appeared on a wound when blowflies "blowed" it or buzzed over it. He'd been taught this at the Atlanta Medical College, later Emory University, and firmly believed it, shades of Aristotle. Dr. McElroy said, "I'm going to prove you wrong." He signaled a veterinarian, Dr. Stewart, over for confirmation of this story. Dr. Stewart completely agreed with Dr. McElroy about how maggots came about, whether out of ignorance or acquiescence to Dr. McElroy's superior knowledge I don't know. Both men were way off track and would not listen to my so-thought prattle. It was very embarrassing and burned in my mind for some time.

Sometime in the late 1950s our herd bull got screw worms around his penis and deep into the scrotum. He was going down fast and had a big swelling around his penis. Jimmy Lester Jinright diagnosed the problem and said, "If we don't get him up and treat him, he's had it for this world." We reinforced the cattle catch pen with new-bought, strong pine boards and lured the bull into it with generous offerings of sweet feed laced with molasses. We slammed the gate shut behind him then I climbed onto the high fence and dropped a three-quarter-inch hemp noose around the bull's neck. With the remaining twenty-foot length of rope I quickly made a few circles around a catchpole buried deep in the ground. The bull, weight of fifteen to eighteen hundred pounds, hit the ground snorting and bellowing, whereupon four of the biggest, strongest hands from the quarters grabbed one leg each and spread-eagled him on the ground. I rushed up and began pouring the A-1 screw worm medicine into his wound, swabbing it deep to kill all the maggots. The liquid was of a bright red color, highly acidic, and when it hit raw flesh the bull came from amongst us. He reared up, bellowing something awful, knocked a couple of us down and promptly tore our strong pen to splinters, making a four by six foot hole in the side of the barn where before there had been none. The bull still had the heavy rope around his neck as he raced for the pasture.

Jimmy Lester said, "I'll sick Butch onto him." Butch was a pit bulldog known to be the best catch dog in the country and

I'd seen him bring many yearlings, cows and four hundred pound hogs to their knees. When Lester shouted for Butch to "catch," Butch outran the bull, leaped up and grabbed his right ear. The burning medicine must have gotten sho`nuff hot by then for the bull started shaking his head right and left. Along about the third switch of his head the bull threw Butch aside, casting him ten or twelve feet through the air. Butch had found his match and came whimpering back to his master, shaking his short tail.

That big strong rope, all twenty feet of it, trailed from the bull's neck until he wore it through about a month later. None of us wanted any part of him, and Butch sure didn't. The bull got over his treatment. He regained his weight and vigor and fathered many more fine calves.

GROWING SWEET POTATOES

One of my fondest epicurean memories of growing up in south Georgia is of heading for the oven of the Southern Comfort woodstove after school and pulling out a still-warm sweet potato and a hunk of corn pone or leftover biscuit. The sweet potatoes were baked in their skins after being well greased with a dip of hog lard. If Mama or Granny had churned lately, there would be a molded saucer of butter waiting in the icebox and a cut with the knife would produce a good pat of real butter. The taters don't taste as sweet now as in days gone by. I fear the plant scientists have gone the route of trying to produce a potato that will outgrow the others, pound per acre. By the way, the name "yam" is a misnomer. A yam is a tropical root and our southern ones are true sweet potatoes.

In the 1930s Uncle Warren Saunderson and Paw Scott Walker grew the best tasting taters in the county. At that time, harvested taters of all sizes were "banked" over the winter. We'd dig a hole in the ground, line it with six to eight inches of dry pine straw, pile the potatoes in, cover them with successive layers of pine straw and dirt and cover it all up with a few sheets of old roofing tin to protect the potatoes from rain. A narrow trench was left in one side of the hole, just wide enough to crawl in and get a mess. When Mama or Granny sent us younguns to the tater bank, we were always cautioned to pack plenty of straw back in the trench hole to keep the taters from freezing. In March we'd uncover the bank and separate the good eating taters from the smaller ones that were used for seed. The eating potatoes were then laid on dry sand beneath the house. Paw Walker had built the house high off the ground for just such purposes, as well as to discourage termites. The small potatoes, sometimes cut into even smaller pieces, were taken to the tater patch. Furrows had previously been opened with a shovel on a small scrape, bolted onto a Hammon stock pulled by a mule. Manure from the horse and cow lot had been scattered by hand in the furrows. This fertilizer, along with the compost provided by the previous crop, supplied all the nutrients a tater would use.

In a week, with the weather warming up, the seed potatoes began to sprout their leaves and put on good roots. They were then pulled from the beds and transplanted in the field, much like any truck crop. The seedlings were usually hand planted on a raised bed thrown up by the mule's plow. To plant the potatoes, one person led, poking holes three or four inches deep in the beds with a pointed stick, and another person followed, dropping in one plant per hole then pressing the hole tight with his foot.

At Osierfield we'd always grown enough sweet potatoes for our own use and for the hands in the turpentine quarters. Sometime in the 1950s Dr. McElroy decided to grow a few for the market. We bedded up the eleven-acre Fred Deese Cut, a field of Tifton upland that was pebble soil and one of the best producing in Georgia. We had to buy a few plants to finish it, for we were dropping them from a tobacco transplanter, trying to space them about one foot apart.

Lord-a-mercy, did those potatoes produce, away beyond our fondest expectations, near forty bushels per acre, and each bushel of sweet potatoes weighing about fifty pounds.

We began to dig them in the fall; old timers say taters taste better if they are picked after the first frost. When the first few rows were put on top of the ground, Dr. McElroy decided we needed to head to the Farmer's Market in Tifton to purchase a hundred bushel baskets with lids for about twenty-five cents each. Before it was over we made two more trips for baskets.

Usually the harvested potatoes were put into curing houses, where they were dried by artificial heat to draw out about twenty per cent of their field moisture, making them last longer for the table. But Dr. McElroy pronounced, "We'll air dry them," so he had the hands gather and fill the bushel baskets and wire on the lids on, then leave them sitting in the field for over a week or until a shower was predicted.

He and I dragged along the rows in his Mercury (he'd foregone the big Chryslers), he counting baskets on the left and I on the right. We'd tally up on each round, noting how many baskets we had, and the daily count was pretty nigh the same during the entire week we counted.

When rain was predicted, we picked up the baskets of potatoes and carried them to an unoccupied tenant house where we unloaded them, trying not to stack them too high. Lo and behold, nearly fifty baskets, sitting there innocently with their tops wired on and ready to be counted, were found to be empty. Someone had lifted the taters and left the empty baskets. Doc says, "I'll catch the sons of bitches." He had several hands in the quarters who would tell all for a pint of bonded likker. But this one proved a hard nut to crack, and he never did find out, maybe because the informers in this case were also the snitchers.

After the taters were stored, Doc confounded me with the directive, "Boy, you got time on your hands." So for the next few weeks I loaded up as many baskets as the pickup truck would carry and began peddling them to grocers within a fifty-mile radius of Osierfield at three dollars a bushel. It went well for a couple of weeks, until everyone and his brother began putting their taters on the market. We dropped the price to two and a half a bushel and finally to two dollars and still had a five-room house full of sweet potatoes. They began rotting, so we put a foot of pine straw in the five rooms, dumped the baskets on it and then paid hands to sort out the best ones about once a week. The peddling soon came to a halt as store-keepers started complaining, "too many taters rotting before I can sell them."

We'd turned a bunch of fattening hogs on the tater patch after the digging and then decided to dump several hundred bushels out of the ill-fated storage to feed them further. We had put up an electric fence to keep the hogs in, but they quickly tired of the tater diet and were continually tearing out to supplement their feed.

This was my first experience with perishable goods and, thank goodness, my last.

ROOT DOCTOR

Arthur Robinson was a stuttering, hunch-backed individual, looked down upon as the village idiot even by his own black race. He stayed to himself and meant no harm to any living soul. I first met him in the late 1940s while I was working in the summers on Dr. McElroy's Osierfield farm and attending college in Douglas, Cochran, and Athens in the winter.

I was riding by Hiram Mobley Cut one afternoon when I saw Arthur stooped over, resting on his knees and digging furiously in a hedgerow. Arthur heard the pickup truck, rose to his full height, and began to run off as fast as his shuffling gate permitted. I hailed him, "Arthur, come here, there ain't no harm in me. I just want to talk to you." Then he stopped, standing with a subservient expression on his bowed head, probably expecting some sort of bawling-out over trespassing because, though he lived on the place, he feared he'd strayed too far from home.

I said, "Arthur, I haven't met you yet, but I want to talk to you and learn something about roots." I'd heard he was the local root doctor—an eccentric oddball, a strange near-hermit, yet having knowledge of the superstitions harbored by his race and somehow curiously respected by them, especially when they were in trouble. They said he could cast spells, ward off demons, and, if he was willing, could give you a number to play on Cuba or the weekend lottery.

Arthur's specialty was roots—all kinds and all shapes. I can't correctly name all the plants in his hedgerow, but clearly remember his special interest in smilax roots, the evergreen type that kept its leaves in the wintertime. Some folks called it cat briar or bamboo root. There was also Quercus, the oak family, briars, black cherry, sumac, gallberry, man of the earth vine (really of the Ipomoea morning glory tribe) and others. But Arthur was most expert in catbriar roots. These came in all sizes—I once was presented with a globular root weighing thirty pounds that had been pushed from a hedgerow by a bulldozer operator. We didn't have sang or ginseng plants this far south but catbriar root kind of took its place.

The roots' magic didn't come from eating or chewing them—-they were usually secreted in a side pocket so that their power was carried with you. Shapes of the roots were very important, especially shapes akin to the human anatomy. Then, you had to really, truthfully, imagine a situation—fantasies were ok—and put your heart into it as you rubbed the root. Arthur told me about his philosophy and methods, and what miracles he could accomplish if his patients would just listen to his dictates. I never knew him to charge for his services but rather, to him, it was like preaching the Gospel and converting his listeners to his way of thinking, thereby saving their souls.

MEEKS HARPER'S BEAR

Neighbor Meeks Harper used to bear hunt down around Homerville, Clinch County; seems there was an open season on bears at the time. There was a good population of bears in and around the environs of the Okefenokee Swamp then and people who kept bee yards were eternally fighting wild bears that wreaked havoc with the hives. A wild bear has a predilection for wanting their share of honey and before settlers arrived were accustomed to finding a bee tree then tearing into it with jaws and claws.

Once Meeks shot a mama bear then caught her cub, fetched it to Osierfield and made a plumb pet of it. Meeks and the cub regularly turned up at Miss Julia's store at Osierfield where Meeks would honk his horn and request curbside delivery of two six-ounce Cokes. He took them in on the driver's side and quickly handed one to his bear, which now weighed upward of one hundred and fifty pounds. The bear would feverishly grab the coke in his forepaws and upend it, swallowing most of the contents though spilling a lot too. Meeks would chug-a-lug his before the bear got through, for the bear was getting a little aggressive and wanted more than one Coke.

Once Meeks' pet bear broke his chain and climbed about fifty feet up a solitary horsetail pine tree. He wouldn't come down, so Meeks hired a bulldozer from Ocilla, about ten miles away, to come out. The bulldozer was unloaded, and the driver raised the blade and slowly pushed the pine to ground level where the bear could be caught and rechained.

I don't know how long Meeks kept that bear, but I remember him as a big ferocious animal that had opinions of his own and actions to follow. I was a bit scared of him. Once I carried my son and daughter to see Meeks' bear on his homeplace. Meeks had the bear chained to a tree in his side yard. During our visit, one of Meeks' sons showed off the bear for entertainment. Bubba told me later the son teased the bear with a green tomato, all the while wearing a bandage on his arm where, the day before, the bear had given him a cut requiring fifteen to twenty stitches to close.

Such was life in Osierfield.

POSTSCRIPT
Gathering Honey

    Bears are not the only creatures that go to some lengths to gather honey. When people discovered that the sweet substance was good on cornbread or biscuits, they began building artificial boxes and keeping bees. The boxes were about two feet long and a foot-and-a-half high, filled with racks of trays of manmade honeycomb. The queen bee from a swarm would locate these and by her pheromones entice a whole swarm to follow her into the hives and set up housekeeping. In the process, a passel of honey was produced for the taking—it didn't involve cutting down a hollow blackgum, or whatever, and then having to smoke out the bees with powdered sulfur and a slow fire.

    I've tried the latter route with both good and very bad results. Once in the 1950s a couple of guys and myself robbed two or three trees on the Osierfield farm and secured several gallons of pristine gallberry honey with nary a bee sting. Then one in the group said he knew of a bee tree about three miles away in Ben Hill County.

    Have you heard about how temperamental different swarms of bees can be? Some are sweet and docile and then again some swarms are mean as hell. The Ben Hill County swarm was of the 'mean as hell' temperament, and as soon as I cranked the chain saw and began the felling cut in the blackgum, hundreds of bees attacked my bare face and neck. Sometimes I don't know when to quit when a set goal is in sight. I swore to myself that I'd drop the tree before quitting, as the other two guys ran to the hill. The bees laid into me and gave me dozens of stings. I could hardly see well enough to drive home, and the next morning it would have taken a couple of toothpicks to prop my eyelids open enough to see. I still have a picture of myself that morning, and my swollen face and neck were really unhumanlike. This occasion put me in a mood to dislike bees, honey and anything connected to the likes of them.

DYNAMITE

In the 1950s anyone, barring none, could buy at John Henry's hardware store in Fitzgerald one stick or a fifty-pound case of dynamite, plus percussion caps, and fuse in fifty-foot lengths. No one ever asked what you intended to use it for or why you needed it. John Henry tried to keep at least a case at the downtown store and a good store of cases about a mile out of town in a dry, locked magazine.

There were many uses for dynamite—mostly for shooting stumps on the farm, but also for ditching and blowing water holes for cattle. To identify stumps needing to be blown, a plow hand would break himself a bundle of gallberry bushes, leaves left on, and carry them along as he plowed. When he hit an underground stump that knocked the plow out of the ground, he was to stick one of the gallberry limbs nearby. After he finished a field, I'd go in with an iron rod and try to find the hidden stump near his flag, punch a hole under it and set off a stick of dynamite. We got out many tons of lightered stumps that mule plow hands had been going around for nigh on to a hundred years.

I remember first using dynamite alongside Jimmy Lester Jinright to clear the pastures on the north side of standing stumps. We'd tamp a slanted hole under the lightered stump with an iron rod, which was tapered on one end to a sharp point and swelling in the middle to about two inches. Dynamite sticks were a uniform one and a quarter inches in diameter and eight inches long. We'd put a percussion cap with about two or three feet of fuse into a hole we'd punched into a stick of dynamite and tamp the stick down as far as we could. Then we'd light the fuse and run like hell to get behind a big tree or under a pickup truck. The fuse, which had a core of black powder, was supposed to burn pretty uniformly at about one foot per minute.

Occasionally we'd have a misfire and, after waiting about five minutes, Lester would say, "It's all safe. Go and pull it out of the hole and we'll recap it." I did this on several occasions until one morning a set-up didn't blow and, as usual, Lester told me to go pull it. I dutifully rose up and started walking towards the stump and had taken but a few steps when the shot went off and showered me with wet earth. I belatedly became wise, real quick.

I'd been on the job only a few weeks and harbored suspicions that Jimmy Lester was jealous of me, having probably surmised I was getting ready to take his job as scratch foreman on the Osierfield farm. I felt a little badly about this for he seemed to be a decent sort of guy with a fine wife and two pretty daughters. Fortunately, he moved over across the county to a farm Dr. McElroy owned and the dynamiting was left up to me.

Happily, I fell under the acquaintance of a real professional dynamiter who made his living blowing stumps from the ground for Hercules Powder Company. He allowed as how he'd be glad for me to spend a day with him, watch the action, and ask any questions. First he told me, "If you want to live to be an old man, cut off the fuse square with a sharp pocket knife and insert it gently into the cap." This was the most sensitive part of the operation. The next step was to make a hole in the stick of dynamite about one inch from each end and pass the cap and fuse gently through the hole. Then the stick was bent carefully so as to be able to push it into another hole you'd made with your pocketknife about three inches down the stick. The dynamiter once more admonished me to push the fuse into the cap gently.

"Don't twist it," he said, "a little grit in the cap could ignite it." Then the fused dynamite was tamped into the hole previously made under the stump. He told me at least two or three times to push the charge in with a wood stick, nothing else. Then he said to pack mud or clay into the hole to keep the explosion underground where it would be most effective in pushing up on the stump. He'd already told me to use plenty of fuse, a minimum of three to four feet. Fuse was cheap and its length would become very important if you stumbled getting away. He told me to cut the end of the fuse on a slant to expose the black powder core, light it and then hastily get to safe cover. He further told me to stay undercover for a full minute after the blast for rocks and lightered chips occasionally flew one or two hundred feet into the air and could get you on the trip down. Lastly, and very important, if you had a misfire, stay away for at least one hour before gently digging out the dirt around the charge with your hands and a stick and placing another charge. This made me wonder where Jimmy Lester got his know-how.

The dynamiter had become really proficient after many years at this job. He'd get most stumps out with one stick of dynamite and rarely used more. I never did hear a window-rattling boom on his shots but only a muffled "umph!" then the stump rose a foot or two above the ground and rolled out on the surface as if some giant had pushed it from below. The dynamiter's expertise let him live to a ripe old age and enjoy his full retirement.

We occasionally blew one or two hundred yard trapezoidal drainage ditches with ditching dynamite. To do it we punched two or three foot holes in the earth twelve to eighteen inches apart, and dropped a stick of dynamite in each one, sometimes using as much as a whole case in a line. After the holes were covered, I placed a cap and fuse in the last hole. When the fuse was lit the whole line would blow out almost simultaneously, the percussion from one stick setting off the ones next to it. After the explosion the blown-out dirt would fall down evenly on each side.

My friend's son, Johnny Crenshaw, was enamored of explosions, so after I became very confident with dynamite we put on shows. Once I tied four sticks of dynamite around a tall dead pine, then set it off and watched the big pine splinter into thousands of pieces and crash loudly to the ground. Sometimes we tied a charge to a corn stalk and got away about a hundred yards before it went off with a loud boom. Another trick was to put about three sticks, fused and capped, into a weighted sack and throw it into a pond. It would burn underwater and go off with a thundering roar, making a high geyser and killing a lot of fish in the process. One of these charges loosened a stump in the bottom of the pond and blew it onto a tin roof, making a dent about a foot deep—which stopped this type of show.

Forty years ago, scarcely a day would go by at Osierfield when we didn't hear the thunder of a dynamite explosion, usually some farmer blowing stumps, but oftentimes the High Sheriff of Irwin County blowing up a liquor still. Nowadays, the nearest thing to a dynamite blast is the sonic boom of a jet turning on an afterburner.

THE GREEK STANDS

Nick Pope ran one of the "Greek Stands" on Sherman Street. I ate breakfast there many a morning 'twixt four and five a.m. in the fall when it was necessary to be up early to haul cotton-picking hands to the field. These itinerant workers wanted to start early, believing the dew setting on the open locks of cotton produced more pounds at weighing up time. Why the Greek establishments were called stands I don't know even now. They were basically restaurants though they stocked a lot of fresh fruits and vegetables; I can remember large bunches of bananas hanging upside down from meat hooks in the ceiling.

Nick served a good breakfast plus all the java a guy could drink. For thirty-five cents customers got two eggs, grits and more grits, and biscuits or toast, plus cane syrup for the guys with a sweet tooth. Sausage or bacon was fifty cents, and though I probably could have afforded it, and would have enjoyed it, I followed the dictates of my tight Pa Walker in managing one's financial affairs and usually opted for just the eggs, grits, and biscuits or toast. Nick's chief competitor, Bill Pope, ran the same type of establishment. Bill's Greek Stand was just down East Pine Street from our five-story building, the largest brick building in town. Bill Pope was also a Greek and, I heard, a cousin of Nick's.

There were no tables or booths in their restaurants. You sat on a swivel stool at the marble-top serving counter, put in your order, then in a few minutes saw it slide down the counter right before your eyes. It was not like the modern fast food eateries stockpiled with hamburgers and such for the drive-in window trade.

Bill Pope offered the same menu as Nick but also sold salt mackerel by the wooden barrel-full or by the fish. These mackerel, I think king mackerel, were sun dried and then placed head down in liquid brine where they would keep for months. Bill Pope would reach into the barrel where the forked tails were sticking above the surface of the brine and pull out one or as many as a customer wanted. The Greek Stands also had wooden barrels of soda crackers free for the taking. If you couldn't afford the higher priced things on the menu, you could fill out your hunger pains with all the soda crackers you could hold.

The most high-fashioned of the Greeks was Joe Pappas who operated the New York Cafe in the first block of East Central Avenue, just a block down from the center of Fitzgerald. His establishment was considered a really first-rate place for south Georgia. This meant a private table with bright oilcloth spread over it, decent silverware, a real cloth napkin, and a varied menu to order from. Back then we thought it really sophisticated and the food, cooked in his gas-fired oven, scrumptious. I've since eaten in some rather high-class restaurants, but the food seldom tastes as good as Joe Pappas' victuals. He even accommodated my Grandpaw Walker by baking him a possum with sweet potatoes after Paw's wife died. The New York Café was for special meals though, and Bill and Nick Pope's restaurants drew the daily breakfast and lunch crowds.

Nick Pope had an apprentice, or actually indentured servant, named Paul Simultaneous. I knew Paul's last name meant, 'taking place or operating at the same time,' according to Webster, but, in this case, it was a Greekish moniker that Nick gave him to go along with the anglicized Paul. Paul didn't know any English, but Nick kept prodding him in both English and Greek and Paul became a valued employee. Paul quickly learned to follow instructions from Nick like preparing "homemade chili" at twenty-five cents a bowl. Nick would holler, "bowl of chili" in Greek and then I could hear the hand-cranked can opener taking the lid off a tin of Armour's Chili and Beans and the slosh of the contents being poured into a sauce pan for warming.

Many of Nick Pope's dishes were homemade though and he really put on a show getting his ingredients ready for the noon meal. Between breakfast orders he was steadily chopping up Irish potatoes, onions, and chunks of beef with a meat cleaver for his Irish stew. He'd put it to cooking at five or six in the morning and let it simmer till just before noon. The only seasoning I saw go into it was salt and pepper, but you only had to get one taste of it to know he'd added several more spices and herbs. During mullet season his specialty was a deep-fried mullet split down the middle and served up on a long platter with fried potatoes and freshly sliced vine-ripened Georgia tomatoes. The fish dinner was an expensive one, priced at a dollar, but Nick wasn't stingy with the portions, for he'd serve a pound and a half of mullet with the head cut off.

The Greek Stands also sold bonded liquor by the half-pint and pint. All the Greeks were honest, hardworking-at-long-hours persons and didn't lower their dignity by handling shine or stump liquor. You could put in an order for the legal liquor at the food bar and have it delivered behind a partition near the rear of the stand. Nearby stood a wooden barrel for disposing of empties. On Saturdays, especially, the barrel would be empty in the morning and near full by closing time.

The Greeks also offered home delivery of liquor for the more timid customers, both ladies and gents, delivered to your door by bicycle and hidden in a brown paper sack. Last week a young man in his seventies told me that the delivery job had been his and related the fact that a lot of those deliveries were to some rather prestigious addresses. He still remembered what Bill Pope told him: "If you don't come back with the cash, it comes out of your wages."

When old Nick Pope died, I went to his wake. George, his beloved son, had the keys to Nick's stand on Sherman Street so he went there and came back with several cases of cold beer which we consumed by one or two in the morning, taking turns toasting Nick, our departed friend and benefactor.

Bill Pope's stand was torn down sometime in the 1950s. During his years in business he had made a slit in the plaster wall between two lathing boards, deciding this was a safe depository for all the silver dollars he took in trade. The slit was about eye level between the two adjoining studs and was hollow all the way to ground level. Over the years he'd deposited his silver dollars, one by one, till the hollow contained hundreds of the cart wheels. When the wrecking crew started tearing down Bill's place, coins piled out in a huge mound onto the floor. I don't know of the disposition of this hoard but hope his survivors shared it.

The Greeks, all of them, ran a tight ship. They'd toss out a recalcitrant customer onto the street if he disturbed the tranquility of the place and started to hurt business. They didn't need a bouncer—they were in charge. Most wore white aprons, full length, hanging from their necks and, though they were the proprietors, they worked as hard as anyone else. I fondly recall the smells, yes, especially the smells. They were exotic restaurants wafting strange, pungent smells onto the streets outside. I miss them dearly and often wish to be back in time when the Greek Stands were in their heyday.

POSTSCRIPT
Preparing Salt Fish

I long ago learned to appreciate salt fish, probably due to my familiarity with it at the Greek Stands. A few years ago I was delighted to see fried salt mackerel on the breakfast menu at the world renowned Sea Island Cloister Hotel but, in biting into the fish, found it had been taken fresh from the brine, battered and fried and served with grits. I tried to stomach the fish, a bite at a time with a sip of water but had to push it aside. Apparently preparing this dish correctly was foreign to the chef.

This isn't a cookbook but a few short words on correctly preparing, cooking, and serving salt mackerel is in order. The night before you plan to cook salt mackerel wash off the brine, lay the fish on a cutting board and slice it into strips about an inch wide then put it in a dish and let a slow faucet run over the fish to wash the salt out. Putting in a clean face brick will help absorb more of the salt. Next morning pour off the water and shake the pieces in a paper bag of corn meal. Lastly get a Fry Daddy full of peanut oil to very hot, then pick up each piece of the fish with tongs, dip it into a bowl of beaten eggs and drop it into the boiling peanut oil one piece at a time so they don't stick together.

Nowadays the salt mackerel are hard to find. D. Alec White keeps me informed of the arrival of a shipment at the Food Lion.

A HIGH CLASS AND EXPENSIVE TRAIN WRECK

Sometime in the 1960s, when we were living in the old pondhouse, I was offered an unlimited amount of Tanqueray Gin and Chivas Regal Scotch whiskey coming from a couple of railroad boxcars derailed while passing over Hunters Creek, about three-quarters of a mile east of Osierfield. The manifest consisted of hundreds of fifths and quarts of the above-mentioned brands now scattered across a couple of hundred yards of Hunters Creek, its muddy bottom and for some distance along its banks.

The word quickly spread and many of the local citizens, both black and white, converged on the scattered wreck and began picking the ripe cherry. Before the railroad officials put an armed guard on the spillage, hundreds of cases of unbroken bottles were ferreted away by any means of conveyance available. Many more cases were secreted up and down the creek to be picked up later.

Local entrepreneurs started out selling their ill acquired gains for five dollars a bottle. By the next day, though, the price fell to three dollars per bottle; there was so much on the market that Osierfield couldn't absorb it all. Lessons are learned from many places and different situations. I learned I couldn't handle half a glass of 96 proof gin mixed with iced tea even if it cost just three dollars a bottle, cash on the barrel head and delivered to my door.

The aftermath of this short story was that several high-ranking railroad officials and some of the wrecking cleanup crew lost their jobs when they were found stashing several intact cases in the trunks of their autos or in the backs of pickup trucks. None of the locals were ever prosecuted, just the railroad-connected folks who ought to have known better.

The rumor still persists, some thirty years afterward, that one can dig around in the mud and find intact bottles. I might just check things out during our next severe drought.

RIDING THE RAILS

Growing up, one of my fondest desires was to ride a rail car. I could remember when they were hand-powered by two men pumping up and down on handles, using the center point as a fulcrum. Eventually a one-cylinder gasoline engine replaced the hand-powered cars. The rail cars, or motorcars as they were sometimes called, had stout oak handles fore and aft to permit their removal from the main line. A guy could lift one end off the track and then walk around to the other end, pick it up and set it off the track.

The opportunity to ride finally came in the 1970s. A rail car operated by the section foreman and his crank boy stopped on a pass track which ran a full mile through the farm at Osierfield. I begged to get aboard and promised the two we'd stop in Douglas, Coffee County, for a steak dinner on me. Their destination was Nicholls, about fifty miles down the line. They were in constant touch by hand-held radios with what was coming north on the main line and after getting the all-clear, they threw the switch onto the main line and we screeched off south at about forty miles an hour. It was mid-summer and the "monkeys" (rising heat waves) shimmered above the roadbed. It was a wild ride—the motorcar lurched from side to side like a ship rocking over ground swells when approaching land. Staying aboard meant holding on to something tied down.

The break at Douglas was welcome. The crew talked about old times when communications weren't so precise, and they might meet a fast passenger train or special freight head on. Moving quickly, they would brake and haul the rail car off the rails as the on-coming train whooshed by. Our trip, although exciting, was not so eventful as that. After making the return trip, the crew deposited me near my pickup truck parked on the north side of the farm. I was exhilarated by the ride and looked forward to bragging that I'd made a hundred mile round trip on a rail car.

A few weeks later a couple of quail hunters related to me their tale of riding the rails. Seems they were hunting along the railroad right-of-way near Osierfield. As they walked west toward their truck, parked over a mile away, a slow-moving coal train returning empty cars to Kentucky or West Virginia started moving off the mile-long pass track.

They quickly thought, "If we hang onto the side ladders we can jump off near our car where the pass track joins the main line." They jumped on and climbed to the top of the side ladder and then got inside the coal car so they could ride in comfort until the time came to jump off. It so happened that by the time they reached the main line the train had rapidly increased its speed, moving near-on thirty miles per hour; jumping off was not a good prospect. They had a quick ride to Fitzgerald; but the coal dust that had settled in the car commenced blowing and by the time the ride ended the black stuff covered them entirely except for the whites of their eyes.

The train slowed at Fitzgerald's Westwood, about a mile west of town, to change crews. The hunters climbed off, completely black all over and spitting coal dust. They say they spat coal dust for three days after. On hitting the ground they got to a telephone and called a taxi from Fitzgerald. Three times a taxi showed up but each time the driver said, "You all cain't get in my car with all that coal dust on you."

The last cab driver allowed he'd call a friend of theirs and was good to his word. Shortly, a friend turned up in his pickup. "You guys have to ride in the back," he said.

POSTSCRIPT
Laying Rail

In later days there was a section foreman and a crank boy who supervised about ten miles of track. The section crew at Osierfield was led by Tom King who looked after the track from Osierfield to Fitzgerald. His job was to replace worn or rotten cross-ties, drive a spike through the rail plates into a cross-tie then shovel granite ballast to settle the ties and make a good resilient roadbed.

Section crews also had to lay rail where needed. I ignorantly thought Bethlehem Steel in Pittsburgh molded curved rails for negotiating the curves, but found out later that the section hands manpowered thirty-foot long straight sections into a curve. They worked as a team, and used many rhythmic chants to guide when to push, shove, rest and then go again until the curves were accomplished in a gentle, easygoing fashion.

Back then they were handling forty to sixty pound rails per three-foot section of rail or between twelve hundred and eighteen hundred pounds per thirty-foot section. The rail line through Osierfield in the 1990s has one hundred and forty-pound ribbon rail standing over the cross ties nearly a foot above the plates. Sections of ribbon rail eighteen hundred to two thousand feet long are brought in on flatcars and welded. Now one can no longer hear the clickety-clack of the truck wheels passing over the rail joints.

SAM DAVIS, OFFICIAL WASP NEST REMOVER

All us locals called him Sam Spade. Back in the 1940s and '50s when we began putting leaf tobacco into the curing barns, the womenfolk called on Sam to precede the barn crew to the barns and remove all the active wasp nests. He had come from across the Ocmulgee River where he had once been shot in the face with a load of birdshot, leaving half his face scarred. Sam still spat up fragments of bone in the time I knew him. Nevertheless, he was a faithful employee most of the time.

He did smell like a goat but in retrospect methinks this had little or no effect on his ability to remove wasp nests.

He'd begin the operation by rubbing the fingers of one hand under his armpit then reach for the wasp's nest and gently, slowly, pull it by its supporting stem from the wall or rafters of the stringing sheds. All the while the wasps were standing on their noses buzzing and carrying on something awesome. After he carefully broke the nest from its anchorage, Sam took the nests, one at a time, and slowly walked away from the tobacco barn. To the best of my knowledge he never got stung or bitten. I think now his slow, deliberate, motion kept the wasps calm.

You can do the same with a swarm of thousands of honeybees. Just break off a succulent piece of honeycomb, then back off and chew and suck on it to your heart's content. The secret is to make slow, slow, deliberate movements; never slap at the bees or wasps, or make loud slapping noises around them. Very few can do this when hundreds of bees cover their hands, arms, and face; but if you manage it, the bees will accept your movements as their own and not pay any attention to what's going on. Who is going to be the brave or foolish knave to try this theory of slow motions? Not I, least from a cold start—maybe after a few sips of bourbon and creek water to fortify myself.

Growing up, we thought it was good fun to pitch water and kerosene-soaked wads of cloth at wasps' nests and then try to outrun them. We had much better success if the kerosene-soaked rag was tied on the end of a long fishing pole and set on fire. Paw Walker caught up with us after we had tried this one day and promised a thrashing to the next boy coming near to setting his house on fire. He was a man of true promises.

The wasp larvae in its circular tube is prime fishing bait just before it reaches maturity. I've seen many fishermen turn up with several big circular nests of larvae and no other bait. They always catch a string of warmouth, stumpknockers, or shellcrackers.

I never thought to ask them how they got their wasp nests.

DOG DAYS

This morning, November 8, 1994, I talked with Shelby D. Aycock who helped farm this place for nigh on twenty years then bought a place or two of his own. He got all he owns by hardscrabble work and perseverance. Shelby related to me the significance of "dog days" in the 1940s, but this morning couldn't recall most of it, except to say it was a "festering time." The old folks bought a special powder at the country store for making a salve to put on sores, scratches, cuts and boils that wouldn't heal. He recalls one of the ingredients was black gunpowder. It was a time when everyone was in the doldrums, and there were many things a person shouldn't do. Fact is, the list of don't-dary-do things far outstripped those you should do.

Some said dog days started when the Dog Star, the bright star Sirius in Canis Major, or sometimes the bright star Procyon in Canis Minor, came showing best, now often reckoned from July third to August eleventh. Others say they are a period of from four to six weeks between early July and early September, the sultry, close part of summer.

I recall, also, a period of stagnation and inactivity when leaf tobacco wouldn't color and cook out right. Gnats were terrible, it took both hands to fan them away. I've seen many south Georgians, when both hands were needed, as in cleaning a mess of fish, poke out their bottom lip and blow hard, directing the stream of air upwards to blow the gnats from the eyes. It took two different blows, one for the left eye and one for the right, and you had to do it every few minutes.

During dog days, we knew that summer was coming to an end. The old swimming hole had dried up, we'd swayed down all the young pine saplings near home, swung on the big wild Scuppernong vines till they were worn out, hobbled around on the sides of our bare feet due to stone bruises. We could almost hear the school bell ringing.

I think, perhaps, dog days are a curse of living in a semi-tropical climate and the only way one can combat or avoid them is to move northward. A friend and author, James Willoughby, is to move northward. A friend and author, James Willoughby, who turpentined in Florida and south Georgia for nigh on sixty years, once told me it was a great and earnest wish to accumulate enough "scratch" or wherewithal to stay in Georgia upon retirement—but above the gnat line.

He settled in Thomaston, north of Macon and south of Atlanta, which I hope is gnat-free.

WELLS

I'm not talking about oil wells here, just surface wells for drinking water and watering livestock. At one time there were over forty hand-dug wells on the farm—some still exist. The best drinking well was at the Cooty House. The well was between thirty and forty feet deep, which was where the most palatable water was found. Wells this deep had many streams of seepage coming in and yielded buckets of water that would frost a gallon jug in mid-July.

I once took on the job of digging a well. Here in south Georgia you start with a pair of hole diggers and a short-handled shovel. Stake off or visualize a round or square hole into the earth three or four feet in diameter, then start digging, throwing the dirt as far away from the hole as possible—it will have to be thrown even farther out later on. You get through the first two feet of sand and pebble dirt in a hurry—that's easy. Then the real work begins when you hit the red Georgia clay.

Using a short-handled shovel, I probably got down close to six to eight feet deep the first day, at least to the point where I could throw the dirt out of the hole without a lot falling back in. The next step was to put up a three-poled affair with a well tackle and thirty to forty feet of rope hitched to a good ten quart bucket. At this point it takes another man, a mud puller, to lower the bucket down to the man in the hole who fills the bucket with clay. The man on the surface pulls it up on a voice signal or when the well digger yanks the rope. This is back-breaking work for both men although the digger probably gets the worst end of it. He is in a stifling narrow space, hence the short-handled shovel. Water is steadily trickling down on him and the deeper a hole gets, the hotter the air. The only light is diffused sunlight. This doesn't present a problem for the first ten feet, but after that he is working in half-light or less. The only time the well is well-illuminated (excuse the pun) is from around high noon until two or three o'clock in the afternoon.

My well had gone no farther than about twenty feet when

I began hitting rock formation. We stopped digging there and built a brick or concrete well curb, then erected the permanent well tickle apparatus over it. After that, we dropped a twenty-foot section of PVC to just a few inches off the bottom and attached a foot valve that prevented water flowing back down, so that the pump would stay primed. Then we turned on the Sears Roebuck pump and let it run for several hours. The water was clayey and milky at first then began to get more and more clear.

We'd heard from several old timers that if we put a catfish in the well, he'd prosper and help clean anything that might grow on the walls. We dropped an eight-inch catfish in, and within a couple of years he must have weighed six to eight pounds and had grown to almost twenty-four inches.

Well, at one time some of us thought we detected an off-flavor in the water we were drinking. I went out and found that the wooden cover over the well had been knocked aside. Wondering what might be down twenty feet, I went to get a flashlight and, lo and behold, spied a big ole ugly tomcat all swelled up floating on the surface. I drew him out and disposed of him and we all went to gasping and spitting for the next few days.

We pumped the well dry, refilled it, then pumped it dry several more times, in the meantime pouring a gallon of Clorox bleach into the well. We had saved our purifying catfish and reintroduced him into the well after the pumping was done. After a while, we began cooking and bathing in the water again but still not drinking it. That went on for several weeks, then finally we began drinking the water, being sure no more critters could enter the top of the well. No one experienced any health hazards, and life went on.

Though a few families in the turpentine quarters shared a community well, most had their own. The quarters were located in Norfolk Loam areas where a surface well needed to be dug only eight to eighteen feet deep to get water. In the wet season, water rose in all wells to the surface of the ground. Then users carried a bucket and pan with handle to the wells and just dipped the water, which was milky white, up from the surface at ground level.

There was an eight by ten foot well at the Prospect Church farm in Ben Hill County, dug by some hands for watering tobacco plants. The well was even with the ground surface and lined underground with railroad crossties. It seems that one time Dr. McElroy forgot where it was situated and backed his firetruck-red, four-door Chrysler into it. The car's big shiny chrome grill alone must have weighed half a ton.

The big car fell backwards into the wide well, hood and grill pointing skyward and the doors pinned shut so Doc couldn't get out. As the water rose in the car, Doc lowered a front window and yelled, "Get Lowe Bryant and his wrecker out here in a hurry." Some of us cranked up and rushed to the Ashton schoolhouse, where the only telephone within miles was located. We were connected after the operator said, "Number please."

Luckily, Lowe was there and responded in about fifteen minutes. He hooked onto the Chrysler bumper with his tow truck and winched Doc from the well with no damage to his Chrysler. The biggest altercation came when Dr. McElroy heard Lowe's charges.

Doc says, "What do I owe you?"

"It'll be fifteen dollars cash," Lowe answered.

Doc yelled, "That's a hell of a price for five minutes work. You son of a bitch, you caught me in a bind."

Lowe commented, "Doc, you should have agreed to the charges when you were stuck in the well! Not after I pulled you out! I'm ready to loosen the cable and let the Chrysler back into the well."

Doc knew he didn't have a bargaining tool so peeled off the cash to pay Lowe Bryant.

One more well story. One Christmas wife Mary had given me a gold-tipped Waterman fountain pen. It was a big fat beauty with the rubber tube reservoir for liquid ink built in the barrel. The reservoir was filled by placing the whole tip of the pen into a little trough molded into the glass ink bottle then pulling upwards on a little lever on the side of the pen. You filled the trough by tilting the ink bottle upside-down, lid screwed on tight, of course.

One day I was drawing water for hog mash when the new pen slipped out my shirt pocket and plunked into the well. I saw it splash about ten feet from the top. I immediately said to three or four folks standing around, "That well isn't going to claim my pen." They asked, "What are you going to do about it?" We didn't want to pump or draw the well dry for the water was needed for the hogs. I took the well bucket, filled it with brickbats, slowly lowered it to the bottom of the well and tied the chain securely to a post. Then I shed my shoes and most of my clothes and began lowering myself into the well amid shouts of "You're a fool, you're gonna drown yourself." I got to the water level, took a deep breath and followed the well chain to the bottom. When my ears popped loud, I knew I had gone past the fifteen-foot depth and in a few more pulls I reached bottom and found the pen.

Before going back up, I decided to give the folks upstairs a little show. I always liked swimming under water and could stay down for at least two minutes, so I sat on the bottom of the well for over a minute slowly exhaling a stream of bubbles. It was an effective show, for wells spooked most guys and few wanted to go down even when it was dry.

POSTSCRIPT
Anthony Hines, Master Mason

One day I accompanied Dr. McElroy to Ambrose and was introduced to Anthony Hines, a master mason. "Antny," as he was called by his many friends, was over eighty years old and had practiced bricklaying, mortar and cement mixing for over sixty of those years. Dr. McElroy told Antny, "This boy will be here to pick you up at sunrise in the morning."

When I picked Antny up the next morning, I brought with me an ample amount of sand from our local sandpit, dug shovel by shovel, and a few hundred bricks and brickbats or pieces of bricks. We loaded up his tools and mudbox and headed toward Mystic to build two well curbs for Dr. McElroy who needed a well in the shelter field for watering mules and hands.

My job was to hand Antny bricks, mix the mud and carry him hand-drawn water from a well half a mile away. Antny let me go early to look after other chores as he finished the brickwork and plastered over it. He spent the sun's last light embellishing his work with fancy figures. He would produce whatever the customer ordered but was at his best when he could just build a good well curb and finish it any way he wanted.

Antny's artistic sense was expressed in a sideline he developed. He made an exceptionally good tombstone using a brew of local sand and mortar mix and embellished them with careful figures and flourishes. He made the designs with metal stamps borrowed from his collection, gently pushing them into the mortar mix just before it was set.

For a complete tombstone, his fee was reasonable, according to the times, about three dollars or thereabouts. This sounds cheap but that's all he asked and he had a waiting list of customers, at least in his mind. He related to me that they were of three classes—them that would pay cash on the barrelhead, them that would pay next Saturday, and them that would pay when they got the money.

A lot of his work, I know, has weathered the elements and still looks good after over forty years. The local blacks admired him and hung their star on his star. Not long ago, Bubba and I decided to save some of the history of Osierfield farm by hauling one of Antny's well curbs, built nearly sixty years ago, to the new pond house yard. The wide base of the curb had been started at least four feet below the surface of the ground and tapered to a three-foot square at the top. While Antny might have gotten carried away, the curb still stands in good shape. He didn't want, he said, to come back fifty years later and find it tilted out of kilter.

GUANO

A USDA yearbook in the 1920s says the consumption of guano for fertilizer in the United States was around 4,756 tons in 1900 and by 1921 had risen to 37,570 tons. Guano, or bird excrement, is rich in nitrogen and phosphate. The nitrogen content of the guano of seafaring birds may run as high as ten to twelve per cent of total weight and phosphoric acid may run as high as twenty to twenty-five percent. Guano had a pleasant, never forgotten smell.

Chile exported untold thousands of tons of "soda," or Chilean sodium nitrate, until just before WWI when the Germans became proficient at extracting nitrogen from the air. Guano contributed the nitrogen portion of this Chilean mixture. At the time Chile had laws on the books, and enforced them, as to how many pounds per acre or how many inches of guano could be shaved from marine birds' excrement each year. Nowadays farmers use chemical fertilizers, and guano is a thing of the past, except to old timers. The term, however, has been carried over to the present day as in, "How many pounds of guano did you put to the acre to produce two bale per acre cotton?"

Guano used to come in two hundred-pound capacity croaker or hemp burlap sacks. Paw-in-law Dr. McElroy was growing upwards of five hundred acres of cotton in the late 1940s and early 1950s and found he could get a big discount if he ordered carload lots. He dealt with the C.O. Smith guano company in Douglas, Georgia, who delivered fifty to sixty ton loaded carboxes directly to a railroad siding in Osierfield

The railroads wanted to keep their carboxes in almost constant use and charged demurrage when one sat for more than twenty-four hours at the siding. Dr. McElroy didn't intend to pay these extra fees, so we'd gather up the strongest-backed crew from the quarters, along with two mule wagons, the turpentine two-ton dip truck and various dilapidated pick-up trucks to off-load the guano. I'm talking about two or three carbox loads, with fifty to sixty tons per car, the discount being better as the ton order increased.

Two men, called back loaders, would grab the ends of a two hundred-pound sack of guano and place it on the back of a "toter." All the toter had to do was carry it to the carbox door, step down and place it on the conveyance. We unloaded just a couple hundred feet from two competing country stores and, invariably, bets came up among the customers as to who could place on his back such and such poundage, stagger to the door of the carbox and deposit his load onto the wagon. All in the crew could easily tote two hundred pounds; most could make it with four hundred pounds. A new record was set one day when Arthur said, "Lay it on me, I'll tote six hundred pounds out of the carbox or die trying." He proceeded to do this and won all bets.

My load was a steady two hundred-pound sack.

GOING FISHING IN LAY-BY TIME

Lay-by time in mule farming days was that looked-forward-to time, in mid-July in south Georgia, when a mule farmer had his corn crop laid by. This meant that a final plowing had been done, leaving the corn free of weeds and grasses and shoring it up against a strong wind until it was ready for snapping in the fall. The peanut crop was laid by in late August or early September, just before the vines met in the middle. This also was the last cultivation until the peanuts were ready to dig in September-October. When the peanuts were done, it was truly lay-by time—no more plowing and cultivation and a rest time for the mules, unless a guy fooled with tobacco.

Lay-by time, people said, was when a one-hoss farmer had a crop laid by, his wife knocked up and the cow had gone dry. Nothing to do but rock on the piazza. It was a time of joyous celebration on old-time farms. Time to go to the creek to muddy fish, cut watermelons, and have barbecues and sings. It was a time for some serious drinking after putting in endless ten-hour days looking at the south end of a northbound mule.

During lay-by time, I'd go with the hands to the creek to muddy fish, carrying a bunch of scovey hoes to muddy up the potholes, causing the fish to come to the surface for oxygen. We scooped up what we could and then went grabbing for the remainder, getting down on our knees in the creek water and feeling for movement under roots and stumps on the creek bank. Most often we caught big cat, stumpknockers and suckers, and threw them on the banks for the womenfolk to put into a wet croaker sack. We often threw out various species of water snakes too and an occasional cottonmouth moccasin. All snakes were quickly dispatched by the women, using scovey hoes and sticks. I never knew of a person being bitten. The hands put strong credence in their belief that "a snake cain't bite under water," which was surely erroneous, for snakes grab their prey under water.

Some resorted to gathering unripe black walnuts, scraping away the green skin and throwing them into the deep potholes of receding creeks. I don't remember what the walnut skins and hulls had in them to make it a toxic mixture, but when the walnuts mixed with water, fish rose to the surface. Nowadays fishery biologists use Rotenone which, when injected into the water, will kill most fish and immobilize the remainder. When the method is fine-tuned in an expert's hands, it can kill off overproduction of bream, which lay fifty to sixty thousand eggs at a time in the warm months, and leave the big bass, called trout in south Georgia, unharmed.

One of the more sophisticated methods we used to gather fish was a shocking machine, readily available at telephone companies for about fifty cents. On cranking the handle a strong direct current was sent by the batteries or magneto into the receiver, producing a ring. We took advantage of this electrical source by stringing the electric line of the old telephone from the bank or over the side of the boat and into the water. As we cranked, the electricity would flow into the water and stun any nearby fish, which we then scooped up.

Lay-by time also offered the opportunity for some mischief and we often applied these telephone generators to that cause. A few uninitiated participants were invited to hold hands as someone turned the crank, sending electricity first through the electrical line and then along the human chain. They quickly discovered that it was unwise to be on the end of the line for the voltage created was direct, not alternating, and the last person on the line felt the strongest shock.

MAKING SAUSAGE

Hog-killing started according to weather conditions, usually in late November after peanut picking. Dr. McElroy gave each half-cropper or good turpentine worker a free hog every fall, the weight and size depending on family numbers. It was the custom.

We had built a fancy concrete-floored pen with a sprinkler system overhead, and it was there that I was taking care of my special duty to shoot the hogs just above the eyes into the brain. I'd shot over twenty head of hogs without mishap, each hog instantly slumping to the ground without a squeal while the hogs yet to be killed continued to eat alongside their fallen mates. All of a sudden Miss Marie Swinson, who lived over two hundred yards away, came a'running and hollering out of her house, yelling, "I've been shot." Seems one of the .45 caliber slugs had ricocheted and penetrated her house, falling on her while she was resting in her bed. This wisely stopped the shooting of hogs on a concrete floor.

After each hog was shot, one man grabbed its ears and another slit its jugular vein so that the hog would bleed out. Being careful to keep the hog from dragging on the sandy ground, several men carried it over to the scalding pot. A fire of lightered knots, resinous knots from virgin pines, was roaring under a hundred gallon cast iron syrup kettle full of water. When someone could pass a finger through the surface of the water less than three times, the water was the right temperature for scalding the hog so that the hair could be removed. Too hot would set the hair, but just right made it easy for the women to remove the hair, using a facebrick to rub across the skin with forward and backward strokes.

When the hog was scalded, the beautiful clean, white carcass was hung from two strands of wire looped over one of the shelter beams. The hog's hind legs were cut to explose the Achilles tendons, and then a piece of hardwood stick about fifteen inches long and carved to a point on each end (a gatlin stick) was inserted so that the hog could hang nose down in a spread eagle position. As long as the tendons were properly exposed and the gatlin stick correctly placed, a four hundred or more pound hog could be safely hung for gutting. After it was hung, the hog was incised from the tip of its snout down to the anus so that the organs could be removed. Especial care was taken not to split the duodenum; its contents would contaminate the meat.

After it was gutted, the hog was placed on a wooden table and halved with a chop ax and then quartered with butcher knives. The two hams and two shoulders were the choice pieces, followed by the two sides or middlings, all bound for the smokehouse or to town for grinding into sausage. Some chose to rub a generous amount of table salt deeply into their hams, shoulders and middlings, then pack them in a salt box for curing.

All quarters of the hog were trimmed of excess fat, which, along with the sowbelly, was rendered into lard for frying. Literally no part was wasted except the contents of the intestines. The intestines themselves were several times washed and saved as chitterlings. The liver and lights, or lungs, so called because of their lightness, were put into a liver pudding and even the pancreas, or sweetbread, was eaten. In old times the ileum or small intestine was cleaned thoroughly and used for sausage casings.

The entire head was saved; the cranium was split open and the brains removed, providing a great delicacy when scrambled the next morning with a few barnyard eggs. The two halves of the head were then boiled for a couple of hours on a cookstove until the meat fell off. Everything, including the tongue and lips, were highly seasoned and made into hogshead cheese or souse. It contained a gelatinous substance and when molded or put into a container with a lot of weight on top, would form a block hard enough to be sawn into slices as needed.

The skin was cut in small pieces and fried to a crisp for adding to cornmeal. This mixture baked in a cast-iron frying pan produced cracklin' bread, which is especially good with fresh garden vegetables or with cane syrup after a meal. As I said, no part of the pig was wasted and likewise, when you savor a can of Vienna sausage, you are eating all of the hog's organs.

I used to have the job of sausage-press operator. A generous amount of ham or shoulder meat plus a little fat was carried to John Henry's ice plant where he kept a commercial meat grinder for the public. The grinding produced as many as three No.2 washtubs of ground meat, which was brought back home, seasoned with salt, red and black pepper, and sage, and thoroughly mixed by hand. A sample was parlayed to Rosa, a forty-year-plus cook of the domicile, who promptly fried a few patties. She sent out the samples for taste analysis and all in the crew tasted her culinary offering. Someone would say, "It needs more pepper" or salt, or sage, and sometimes none of the above. When there was a consensus of opinion that everything was in perfect proportion, the mixture was transferred to the sausage press in five to ten pound lots and hand-cranked to press it through a spout into the sausage casings.

We had two sausage presses on hand, and honestly, they were so sturdily built of cast iron that they couldn't be worn out in a lifetime of cranking. They were cylindrical and about one foot high, not counting the eight to ten inches of cranking mechanism on top—an upright shaft with spiral grooves and a horizontal gear, turned by the handle. They weighed about fifty pounds and sat on short, one-inch legs with holes in their bases for anchoring the press to a table. One model was made by Chop-Rite Manufacturing Company of Pottstown, Pa and the other by Enterprise Manufacturing of Philadelphia. The latter one still has its original paper label with the following print:

This machine is unique for many purposes
1. fruit press
2. lard press
3. sausage press

8 qts. No. 35

After the press had been thoroughly cleaned, an interchangeable plate was placed on the spiral shaft—the solid, flat plate if pressing sausage and the perforated one if squeezing fruits or pressing the last liquid fat out of fried pork skins. The cylindrical top was swung back, ground meat put in, then the top swung back and locked. There was a round spout about six inches long on the bottom side that tapered from two-inch to three-quarter-inch diameter on the small end. The spout was the only part of the machine not made of cast-iron but more often aluminum or stainless steel. The sausage casing was slipped onto the spout ready to be filled with the sausage. We tried using the ileum as in old times but it repeatedly ruptured, so we bought manmade casings. The press was anchored on one of the ten-foot worktables and often I'd crank out a ten or fifteen-foot sausage without a break. I cranked slowly and the womenfolk guided the full sausage down the length of the tables, tying them with cotton string every three or four feet. The long ones had to be drooped over broomsticks suspended from two loops of haywire hanging from the tie beams in the smokehouse. All in the family saved broom and mop handles to use.

 Parts of the hog that were to be smoked were taken to the smokehouse. Green oak or hickory was burned outside and then, when the wood was reduced to glowing ashes, brought into the smokehouse and placed into a hole in the middle of the floor. Smoke from the ashes preserved and flavored the meat hung in the smokehouse. An old black man of my acquaintance, who worked a one-hoss farm in Thomas County, always smoked his hog meat with chinaberry wood—said his pa and grandpa did the same. The smell of chinaberry wood is obnoxious to me, but this fellow relished it. Mother-in-law Thelma would get up during the nights when meat was being smoked to check it, not trusting the job to anyone else.

 Sausage and smoked meat from a hog were precious commodities on the farm, representing an investment of time and money and providing food for the families. It is no surprise that smokehouses were about the only structures on an old-time farm that had a padlock on the door.

POSTSCRIPT
Making Mash for Hog Slop

Dr. McElroy liked to slick up his fattening hogs by placing about twenty or thirty wooden turpentine barrels around a well at headquarters. We'd fill the barrels three-quarters full with shelled corn, put in one can of Red Devil lye and then stir with a boat paddle. In warm weather the corn swelled and begin to ferment in a few days. A good smell emanated from the barrels; and when we poured the swill into a wooden trough, the hogs would fight over it and eat their fill, all the while squealing from the hot mixture. This was 1940s animal husbandry but it produced a good-looking hog. I'll venture that the animals didn't have any intestinal worms to bother them; and since they had already been drenched with burnt motor oils and fuel oils, probably they didn't have any lice either.

SETTLIN' UP

Most white and black half-croppers or sharecroppers were anxious to divvy up the proceeds of the crop come fall and expected a financial settlement with their landlord or landlady. Settlin' up might go like this.

"Well, Bip, you've done well this year. After deducting your share of the guano, seed, labor of gathering, etc., and adding back your labor in tending and gathering the crop, you've come up in the black." Meaning there is something left over in cash. Usually the hands accepted two to four hundred and fifty dollars cash settlement and promptly invested the whole shooting match in a good used car that might last through to the next fall A few wished to dispute the figures, saying they had been charged too much for this or that.

Whereupon Dr. McElroy, backed up by his bookkeeper, Miss Maude Meeks, said, "I just remember that you didn't get charged for such and such items." The account was then refigured and the results always came out with a cash payment less than the original settlement. Some hands were pretty proficient with their pencils and writing tablets but mostly good memories served them. Joe David Brown in *Southern Folklore* stated, "We'uns that caint read or write have a heap of time to think and remember, and that's the reason we'uns know more than you'all."

Fred Deese had a second figuring in mind one fall and told Dr. McElroy, "Doc, you say it's all in, the deducts and the credits and everything what-so-ever" (one of his favorite expressions, thinking it sounded a bit sophisticated). Doc scratched his head and Miss Maude pondered what was coming next. What was Fred up to? He was up to upping his settlement.

He again asked Doc the same question about whether everything was accounted for or not and, getting another affirmative answer, Fred dropped the bombshell. "Doc, I still have two bales of seed cotton stored in the Cooty house!" Whereupon Doc McElroy exclaims in great surprise, "To hell you say! You are just going to cause a lot of trouble for me and Miss Maude for now we've got to refigure your whole account."

DEEP SEA FISHING

After the death of my father-in-law in 1955, I approached his widow, Thelma D. McElroy, with the idea of taking the farm crew deep-sea fishing as a small reward for their having gathered another successful crop on the Osierfield farm. By then I'd become acquainted with the Crum brothers at Carrabelle, Florida, who had a couple of forty to fifty foot boats and were in the business of chartering boats for fishing. I knew the boat would cost a hundred and fifty dollars for a full day's fishing out in the Gulf Stream, so I timidly asked her for the three hundred dollars to cover boat rental, lodging for the farm crew, at one or two dollars a night at a fish camp, and food.

Man, howdy, this was an interesting experience. None of the guys had ever been out of sight of land, and we were set to motor out almost due south for thirty or forty miles into the Gulf of Mexico! We usually got up six to eight hands or half croppers for these trips, straight from the farm—three souls in the cab and the rest on the back of a pickup truck.

We would get settled in the fish camp cots, walk to a good seafood restaurant for supper, and turn in early, for we departed soon after sunrise and a good breakfast. The Crum Brothers furnished the boat, cut bait, and heavy saltwater fishing reels. The reels were loaded with something near fifty-pound test line, for one never knew when he might hook a fifty or hundred pound jewfish, a type of grouper.

We had to steam out several hours from St. Marks or Carrabelle to deep water of six to eight fathoms beneath the hull. Captain Crum depended on his long experience and did not use a depth finder or Loran, just the compass in the binnacle and his pocket watch. When he found a good fishing site, the Captain would slow the boat and get his deck hand forward on the starboard side, where he lowered a cotton line weighted with a good-sized hunk of lead that had a hollow in its bottom packed with a glob of Octagon soap. Crum's deck hand called out the depth each time he brought in the swirling lead line and looked closely at the glob of soap in his weight. Both he and the captain were checking to see whether sand was sticking to the soap, indicating that the boat was over a rock bed, the favorite feeding ground for groupers, red snappers, and the likes. When the lead man hollered out that they were over rocks, Capt. Crum reversed the engine and tried to back up to the exact spot the deck hand had located, and prepared to drop anchor.

Then the deck hand came aft, baited our hooks with mullet he'd already cut up and, in a few seconds, we were letting off the reel brake and hearing the line sing off towards bottom. Each line had a couple of hooks on wire leaders, plus two or three ounces of lead. We were instructed to feel for the line slackening as the lead hit bottom, then to make a few quick reels upwards to get the baited hooks off the bottom. If the site was a hot one with a lot of hungry fish below, the action took place immediately. When a fish bit, we would feel a hard bump that would almost snatch the rod from our hands, and immediately we had to lay the rod over the deck railing and began furiously reeling in, keeping the line tight to prevent the fish from escaping. On one trip out, in the 1950s, we caught so many fish in the six to twelve pound class that, after selling them on the dock, we had enough money left over to pay for the trip.

Shelby Aycock was a dyed-in-the-wool, ardent fisherman. Once he became seasick before the boats left the dock and lay on the deck all during the trip out. But when the captain cut the motor, he got up enough courage to get up and, holding on to the railing with one hand, he fished with the other. Handicapped as he was, he outfished all of us.

Son Bubba went on one of these trips with us. Sometime into the fishing, Bubba yelled that he'd hooked a really big one, and we could tell by the bent rod that he had hooked a real monster. We all laid down our rods and watched the action. He had the big fish within eight to ten feet of the surface and we could clearly see it coming up through the clear water when an eight to ten foot shark struck it, severing the head from its body just behind the gills. The head was brought on board and weighed in at eleven pounds.

When in the U.S. Navy, on board the tin can, *Perkins*, I often fished from the fantail of the destroyer near the Marshall Islands and in deep waters off the Ryukyu Islands, southwest of Japan. A couple of Navy cooks I'd befriended furnished me with cut bait in the form of meat scraps from the galley. They'd bake or fry some of my catch, once even trying the meat of a four-foot long barracuda. I expect we sometimes had better fare than the officers in the ship's wardroom.

Once on a return trip from the Gulf Stream I asked Capt. Crum if I could steer us back in. He readily accepted the offer and, after watching me keep the boat on course for a few minutes, lay down and was soon snoring. Before he fell asleep, he had simply told me to keep a due north compass heading and to wake him on making a landfall.

The farm crew kept giving me apprehensive glances as they looked ahead, seeing nothing but empty sea for miles ahead. None of them had ever before been out of the sight of land. I had previously "conned the helm" on the *Perkins* for countless hours, even through a couple of typhoons, without mishap and, by comparison, the churning Gulf Stream was easy as paddling a boat on a farm pond. Capt. Crum slept heavily for nearly two hours as I adjusted our course by a couple of degrees and brought us back into Carabelle.

I've tried trolling from boats off the Atlantic coast, mostly for king and Spanish mackerel but it's tiresome pulling in the fish as the boat steadily moves ahead. I really prefer bottom fishing in the Gulf. I guess I'm an old-fashioned, sit-on-the-bank creek fisherman, matching my wits with the fish below. You never have any idea of what's going to strike your bait, but when the captain cuts the motor and the boat gently rocks to and fro, the serenity of the scene, and even an occasional nibble, are worth the trip.

Where have all the fish gone? I don't think simple sport fishing has done them in. It's greed and modern technology. When boats' captains can, with the aid of Loran and global positioning, and depth finders, put their boats within a few hundred yards of a wreck or artificial reef, they are taking unfair advantage of the Finny Tribe. This modern equipment, along with two to three hundred-foot trawler nets, has decimated the oceans' fish. It's about like hunting mountain goats from helicopters.

FLYING

From the time of my first flight, my interest in flying was intense. In 1944, while in Navy boot camp at Bainbridge, Maryland, I was supposed to be standing at attention for Saturday morning inspection when a huge, four-engine Martin flying boat roared down the adjacent Susquehanna River. I could not resist craning my head to watch it skim over the water and roar into the sky. 'Bout then a Navy Chief Petty Officer tapped me on the shoulder and told me to put my rifle over my head with my two hands and to take two laps around the drill field. It was a huge field and one lap was close to two miles.

In the early 1950s, Glynco Naval Air Station was still in existence down near Brunswick on the coast of Georgia. In the fall hurricane season, huge dirigibles from Glynco came directly over the Osierfield farm, going inland to escape the high winds preceding a hurricane strike on the coast. The sound of the engines is one I still cannot compare to any other. They flew low, probably around two or three hundred feet above ground, trailing their mooring lines just over the treetops. Through the open windows of the gondola, the crew was clearly visible. We often hailed them and got return shouts and waves as the dirigibles lumbered on in their slow plodding way.

Sometime in the mid-1950s, Brother Jack was stationed with the Navy at Dobbins Naval Air Station, just northwest of Atlanta. He purchased a used Aeronica Chief, a light side-by-side aircraft covered with fabric. He once flew it nonstop to Osierfield and landed on a dirt road west of the farm. Because of the wind direction he had to land the plane downhill and he later told me he thought it would never stop rolling. When it finally came to a stop, he got out, picked up the tail, pointed the aircraft uphill and then taxied back up to the top. There we both picked up the tail and pulled it into a gate opening so as to clear the front end of the traffic on the main road.

His first concern was to refuel, and when I told him there was no aviation fuel at the Fitzgerald airport, he wanted to know if I knew the way to Douglas. I assured him I did know the countryside well and it would be no problem. Yes, I knew it from a pickup truck but not from the air and we promptly got lost. He had noted the general compass heading, and we spent some anxious minutes watching the fuel indicator bump between zero and a little above. Finally, on locating the airport he flew straight in instead of making the usual left-handed turn.

Alas, there was no aviation gasoline at Douglas. We finally cajoled a local flyer to carry us into town, where we purchased ten gallons of white Amoco fuel. We then made an uneventful flight back to Fitzgerald, following the railroad tracks just a few hundred feet below us. I can vividly remember Jack getting into the traffic pattern, pulling the carburetor heat on, slowing the engine to a slow idle and watching the slowly windmilling wooden prop as we approached the ground.

After his visit, Brother Jack got back to Atlanta without getting lost. But one Sunday morning shortly thereafter, he filled up the tank of the Aeronica Chief for a flight over the city. A fill-up would give him three and a half to four hours flying time, and he figured on being up for about one hour. Lo and behold, a ground fog rolled in beneath him, completely obliterating any sight of the terrain below. Back then the only instruments consisted of a altimeter, fuel gauge, and a little ball floating in liquid in an inverted cup, the turn and bank indicator, which told the pilot whether he had the wings level or not. This meant that Jack was flying blind without any indication from instruments to tell him where he was.

Well, Brother Jack began climbing to clear any towers that might be sticking up into the sky, all the while making gentle turns so as not to get too far from the landing field. He sweated this out for over three hours before finally seeing a small hole in the fog. He dove the aeroplane groundward towards the hole, broke into the clear, found the field and watched the tower for a safe or "come on in" landing light. He told me that he taxied up, put the little plane in the hanger, and promptly put a "for sale" sign on it.

In spite of Jack's adventures, I had vowed to get my wings. The opportunity came when Bill Robitszch found a 1946 Taylor Craft for sale for a few hundred dollars up in Griffin. The owner agreed to fly it down. He didn't quite make it to the airport but was shy about ten miles and crash-landed in a cornfield. There was no major damage, for the corn stalks had cushioned the landing. The owner had had enough of flying and sold out for a figure substantially lower than he first asked.

Before I bought the aeroplane, I began taking flying lessons at the Fitzgerald airport. A licensed instructor would fly down from Cordele and give three or four of us one hour of instruction each Sunday afternoon. He started my instructions in a J3 Piper Cub, painted in the familiar yellow, a tandem-stick controlled plane with dual controls. I can remember only one hour in this aircraft, but distinctly recall that on the approach for a landing, when one pulled the carburetor heat, the engine would always backfire and sound if it was going to quit.

The instructor warned us, "There are two things you cannot recover from, runway left behind and altitude lost." He also reminded us that if we hadn't reached a safe altitude on take off, to lower the nose for a glide as the engine stopped and don't try to bank left or right for a return to the field. He stressed the importance of this, saying that many pilots had been killed by a stalled plane because the pilot had lowered a wing and ended up diving straight in. He even said if big trees are ahead, continue to glide straight and if you still had any control, try and put the fuselage between two tree trunks. He continued, " you'll probably rip off two wings but it will slow the plane down to where you'll probably survive."

Finally after about six hours of lessons, the instructor told me to taxi over the side of the grass strip and without any prior warning, stepped out from the back seat and said, "It's all yours—take it around the field."

Man! Was this what I'd been waiting to hear! I promptly taxied to the end of the runway, held the brakes and "ran up" the engine to check out the right magneto, then the left, then back to both. I confidently pushed the throttle all the way forward and sailed down the runway with the tail held high, got up flying speed, then gently pulled back on the stick and was instantly airborne. I believe I even let out a whoop of joy, but the enthusiasm quickly dampened when I looked back and thereby was reminded that the instructor's seat was empty. The feeling was probably a lot like that of some students whose instructor tapped them on the shoulder, produced a black-painted broomstick and promptly threw it out an open window saying, "You have the only control stick and I'm depending on you to get us down."

I climbed up to six hundred feet, made a pretty good left turn without skidding to one side, flew the downwind leg, and made another pretty good left-handed turn into the final approach. About this time I nearly chickened out and was thinking of putting off the landing and going around again. But with the ground fast approaching, I remembered what the instructor had told me about alternately looking out the left window, then straight ahead; it helped immensely with depth perception, judging the distance between the landing gear and the ground. As I pulled gently back on the stick, the landing gear touched ground and after a few short bounces the plane came to a stop. Then, with plenty of runway ahead I gunned the engine and flew the flight pattern again, landing this time with a few higher bounces. Then I taxied up to the instructor standing on the side of the field amidst cheers from my fellow students.

Boy, oh, boy did I feel like a professional pilot, but in ensuing years after hundreds of take-offs and landings, and a few lucky escapes from serious trouble, I look back and realize how dumb and green I was about piloting. The instructor wrote out my student pilot certificate right then and there, permitting me to fly anywhere, observing visual flight rules, i.e. visibility of a thousand feet and a ceiling of a thousand feet or more, as long as the pilot was alone. Passengers were not permitted.

We all soon broke that rule. I'd carry Bubba to the far end of the grass runway, in the pickup truck, go back to the hanger, rent a J3 Cub and taxi down to pick him up. After we'd flown near an hour, I'd again leave him at one end and pick him up later. I put in many hours flying with a student permit until wife Mary said she was going to give me whatever it took to qualify for a licensed pilot certificate.

Getting my pilot's license required driving to Tifton on a Sunday morning, renting a Piper Tripacer with instructor, and going through three hours of instrument flying with my half of the windscreen blacked out by black sheet. This was a new and frightening experience. I also had to fly a triangular course of at least a hundred miles, touching down at least twice to get my logbook signed.

I picked Dublin and Cordele and back to Tifton for the flight. Feeling real confident, I left the flight line and ventured over the farm at Osierfield for a few buzzings of the folks below. After a few minutes of this I thought I was back on the compass heading, but was soon hopelessly lost. I got down low enough to read some highway signs and finally reached Dublin, landed, got signed off and proceeded to Cordele, again getting lost en route. Naturally, I didn't tell the instructor this, but he surely knew after checking the proof clock for air time.

The time finally arrived when my instructor told me, "I believe you are ready to take your check ride with the FAA inspector." We took off southwest of Tifton, went through a bunch of maneuvers and were flying along on a level course when the instructor reached forward and pulled the throttle back until the engine was idling. He said, "You'd better look for a landing site." I promptly lowered the nose, put the plane in a normal glide pattern, and began gently circling. He knew exactly where we were but wanted to see how I'd react. Suddenly I spotted a clay agriculture strip with a couple of planes parked on the end. I made one more short gliding turn so as not to come up short and greased the plane in for a "dead stick" landing.

After the forced landing, the FAA guy said, "Good" and told me he was satisfied. "Take us back to Tifton." I promptly gunned the engine, stomped the left brake and put the nose wheel about three feet into soft plowed ground alongside the narrow dirt runway. He said, "Cut the engine" and my mind said, "Oh hell, I've played it now." We both got out, pushed the plane back on the runway and returned to Tifton. He promptly signed me off as a licensed private pilot, never mentioning the bogged down nose wheel.

I soon began to be interested in trying stunt flying. I got all my information from reading instruction manuals and then taking to the air alone to try them. I'd been taught how to recover from a spin during pilot training; just stomp in the rudder pedal on the opposite side from the direction you are turning or spinning and lower the nose. To purposely go into a spin, slow the plane down by climbing steeply or pulling back on the throttle. When the ship begins to quiver or nearly stall, kick in the rudder right or left according to which way you wish to spin.

The first time I spun one alone I climbed to over three thousand feet, wanting plenty of altitude for recovery. I timidly let the plane revolve around its axis for about three spins before recovering. It's an exhilarating experience. The plane is falling almost straight down, and the sky and ground are going around in circles.

Later on, gaining more confidence I'd let the plane spin five hundred to a thousand feet down before recovering. This purposeful spinning and recovering destroyed an old fear I'd had for many years. We boys all grew up hearing that if a plane and pilot got into a tail spin, that was the *coup de grace* of a fatal dive, ending in a fiery finish.

The next stunt I tried was the inside loop, really very easily rendered. Just drop the nose, get up maximum speed, pull all the way back on the stick and, as the nose goes over the top, cut the power; gravity will take care of the rest. This is also most exhilarating as the sky trades places with the earth. Another trick was called the chandelle. You flew along fast and level, pulled back on the stick till the plane stood on its tail, then kicked in right or left rudder, causing the plane to "wing over" and head back in the direction from whence it came. I also liked to do a maneuver called the sideslip, used to descend rapidly without increasing speed. It took opposite rudder and aileron control and was a favorite tactic of old barnstorming pilots, who had to get over high trees at the end of a runway then drop down quickly into a small short field.

I liked to carry the children and their friends for short hops. One night I even took them to look at Christmas lights, though I never did cotton to night flying. If Bubba was flying with me and I started anything out of the ordinary, he'd take the yoke away from me and put the plane back on straight and level flight. But my youngest daughter, Donna Raiford, quickly learned the up and down controls and would often grab the yoke, pull back hard and cause us to go straight up, then she'd quickly shove it all the way forward and put us in a quick dive. She'd shout with glee when going through these motions. Donna's favorite flight on a Sunday morning was to fly to the coast, the steady drone of the engine putting her to sleep until I killed the engine as we landed on the beach. She would then get out and wade in the ocean for a while before we headed home.

I once left Fitzgerald airport with a full tank of fuel and in bright sunshine, heading east towards Osierfield. After I was in the air I saw that a ground fog, formed near ground level and extending over two thousand feet into the altitude, was moving towards me rapidly. I foolishly went into it and quickly reached zero visibility. Before going into the fog I had set the stabilizer for a gradual climb and increased the throttle setting, then I watched the turn and bank indicator to keep the wings level. I emerged over the top into bright sunshine and flew in circles for over two hours before seeing a hole in the fog. I promptly dived through it, recognized a highway and flew along it under the fog at about a hundred and fifty feet above the ground. After I got on the ground, I put the plane back in the hanger, where it stood for several weeks. Now I knew how Brother Jack had felt!

Another time, I headed west to Arkansas in the slow Taylor Craft, which wouldn't go over ninety miles per hour flat out. At about four thousand feet over Crystal Lake, a valve broke its stem and flew into the head of the engine, causing the whole plane to shake. I found it would idle at only about a thousand RPM's. I barely made it back to the airport where I rented a Cessna 150 and started out again.

All went well; I stopped at Jasper, Alabama and had no more trouble till I came in sight of the Mississippi River. It looked so interesting that I shoved the aerial chart onto the floor and began following the river northward. After fifteen or twenty minutes, I tried to get back on course but didn't know where I was until I went down low enough to read "Steele" on a watertank; I'd wandered into the bootleg of Missouri, though at the time I didn't know it. Sighting an agriculture strip below, I greased it in and nonchalantly walked up to some men I saw to ask for the shortest route by compass to Searcy, Arkansas. I didn't tell them that I wasn't sure what state I'd landed in.

They gave me the heading I'd asked for, not telling me it would carry me directly over a Strategic Air Command field. Suddenly, here comes a B-52 Bomber directly towards me. The pilot turned sharp left with smoke pouring from all six engines; at the same time, I turned hard right and we passed each other, rather close. I was happy when, a short time later, Searcy turned up ahead.

Once I had the Taylor Craft parked at Fernandina, Florida airport while visiting Little Cumberland Island. Jim Kilgo expressed a desire to fly home with me over the Okefenokee Swamp. We had reached the east side of the swamp when air pockets in the blustery wind began bouncing us up and down, over a hundred feet at a time. I could see Jim's hands and arms getting whiter and whiter, and he finally asked to head towards Fitzgerald by way of the shortest route. He was a game one, though, and went up with me the next morning in some smooth air. In one of his books he writes of seeing a pair of red-tailed hawks tumbling end over end in front of the plane. They were copulating in the air, clasped together.

On which note I'll end. I once thought flying was as exciting as sex, but subsequently changed my mind. If you've been promised some loving, take him or her up on it. Remember, though, your loved one might have a change of heart, but that plane will still be sitting in the hanger when you next want to take it up.

FUNERALIZING

In the country, we still refer to the barbaric custom of making a big show of burying the dead as "funeralizing." It's been that way for eons and probably will not change across future eons. I have attended countless funerals, either as a pallbearer or friend of the deceased, both black and white.

Once I was asked to help in building a coffin. 'Twas on the front porch of the Cooty House here on the farm where Hardy Scott and Mary resided. Seems they had lost an infant boy, carried full term, and wanted to bury him properly, but didn't have the where-with-all to do it in the customary fashion. Claude Young, the half-cropper in the 1940s and 50s, and scratch foreman, asked me to turn up at the Cooty House to help. We all called Claude "Yander" though not to his face. He got this sobriquet from his oft repeated response when asked the whereabouts of such and such a person. "Why, he's over yander there siding cotton in the Hiram Mobley Cut (or elsewhere), that's where you'll find him."

Yander wanted me to help in the coffin making, so I turned up at the Cooty House with saw, hammer, and nails. Yander was already there and pronounced we were going to fix up a coffin for the recently departed Scott. Back then we all used leftover boards from a barn or other unused building. To get things off in the proper direction, he said to Hardy and Mary, "Bring the little pickaninny out here on the porch so as we can measure him for size and length and not waste sawn lumber."

They complied, the dead one was measured, and we began sawing and hammering to put the coffin together. We allowed a few extra inches in the coffin's length, just in case we'd mismeasured; Daddy always told me, "Measure twice, saw once."

Together we produced a decent looking box. Claude thought to make it a little more decent by directing a bystander to go over to his house and ask his wife, Miss Beulah, to send back the most worn bed sheet she could find. The bystander was back in a few minutes with a freshly washed and ironed bed sheet. Claude took the sheet and draped it over the casket, trimmed it with his pocketknife and proceeded to line the casket with the white sheet. Mary said, "He'd rest better on a cotton mattress." She allowed that she'd go to the nearby cotton patch, which came up almost to their front door, and pick some cotton. She quickly produced it, and the cotton was placed in the coffin, the sheet was laid over it and tacked down with upholstery tacks someone had produced. I don't remember any words being said; Yander and I just nailed on the lid of the coffin and pronounced the job done. It didn't cost the Scotts a penny, but I rest assured it was done with dignity and proper respect.

Otis Austin and wife Mary also had a stillborn youngun when they lived on top of the hill across from the "New Pond." They had foregone all the usual funeralizing customs and cost by digging a shallow grave on top of the hill and placing over it several peanut plow points, worn out digging points of half-inch steel about three feet long. The grave stayed intact for several years until we began turning the peanut land a foot deep to bury the past year's debris. Some plow hands uncovered the grave site and skeleton.

Some indignities to the deceased happen sooner rather than later. Do you remember going to the old time funerals when, near the end of the service, the parson reached over, picked up a handful of dust or dirt, sprinkled it over the coffin and said something like, "Ashes to ashes and dust to dust?" Then the funeral directors slowly lowered the casket on canvas straps into the grave, sometimes all the way to the bottom, which always tore at the heartstrings of the bereaved family. Well, I heard of one time when the director let down the casket so that it was about level with the ground, then it seems the straps on one end of the coffin malfunctioned, letting one end slip downwards while the others held. The result was that one end fell to the bottom of the grave hole with an accompanying loud bump and the casket was left standing upright. Whether the bereaved thought this a bad omen or whatever, there were moans and cries of anguish. I wasn't an eyewitness to the debacle but a friend, whom I trust to tell the truth, was.

I believe undertakers now leave the lowering of the casket till all folks have left the burying ground. Used to be, they'd leave the loose earth right near the grave site for easy shoveling, then they went to putting an artificial grass carpet over it, and now use a backhoe to dig and a front end bucket to carry away the soil.

In 1984 dear Mother died way out in Fort Worth, Texas. Sister decided to have her cremated and turned up at Evergreen Cemetery with a pretty little box adorned with an artificial rosebud. She intended to scatter the remains over the family plot where our father was buried. I wasn't up close enough at the graveside service to see what went on, but on returning home Aunt Lucille Walker called on the telephone crying, "What a shame it was to see your Mother's bones lying all over the ground." I agreed to hurry back to the cemetery, carrying a yard rake and a container. Sure enough, there were many bones, some two inches long, lying all around. I raked them up as best as I could and put them back in the rose box Sister had left with me. I'm positive she up-ended the box thinking there would only be ashes and dust within.

Once I was a pallbearer at Mr. Arthur Woodard's funeral. Just as we got him from the hearse and under the small tent, a hellacious thunderstorm developed directly over the grave site and torrents of rain began to form. This wasn't a gentle summer rain but a real lightered floater or frog strangler of a rain. Lightning was flashing all around and thunder had the ground shaking. Water was flowing from the eaves of the tent into the burial hole in a steady stream when someone went over to Lois Woodard's car and pounded on the window, saying we were ready to finish the service. She and Mrs. McElroy answered, "Go ahead and get it over, we aren't going to get out in this weather." Some wit said, "The size of a man's funeral is completely dependent on the weather."

I've been to some funerals where family members get carried away and lean over and kiss the corpse, stroke his or her hair and begin pushing the coffin cart every which away. For these reasons and a host of others I've requested in my will to be buried on the farm, unembalmed, and in a cheap wooden coffin—fact is I think I'll get about building it myself.

"DAD" DIXON

August 11, 1995 - John Dixon came by this afternoon late. We all called him "Dad," even when he was only fourteen or fifteen years old. Now he had a whole lot of gold shining across all his teeth, a sign of affluence. He was driving a '68 customized van and was fresh in from Miami with a light-skinned woman sitting beside him and more light-skinned younguns in seats behind. I said, "Dad, I hear the Cubans have taken over down there." He grinned and said, "We even have a Cuban mayor." I tried a few Spanish phrases on him and he immediately took up on it. He told me that Miami is a dangerous place to live. There are few killings a week in his neighborhood twixt blacks and Cubans. "Dad" told me, "I always felt safe at Osierfield; all us got along except for a few Saturday night cuttings to settle an argument, and then not to the extent of killing off one of our own."

"Dad" was one of Rob and Martha's "yard chirren." Rob and Martha didn't have any children of their own but always kept a bunch of younguns under their roof. Seems "Dad" Dixon was Pearlie's son and Clyde "Crow" Foster was his dad. When the children moved in with Rob Dixon and Martha Dixon, they assumed the last name of Dixon, a proud name from the patriarch of Marion County.

"Dad" reminded me of many old times, like when I carried him to the farm at Mystic for work in the fields. There was a cheap soda water on the market at all the country stores, bigger than any of the rest—nigh on to fourteen or sixteen ounces. He swore he could drink three of them without stopping so another guy challenged him to put up or pay off. "Dad" said, "Put your money where you mouth is—then I'll show you." Three big soda waters were put before him and he promptly up-ended each one and chug-a-lugged all three.

When he worked for Dr. McElroy, he had been driven to do his duties, was half-starved, and had to be completely subservient. He recalled the big change in the Osierfield farm operation after Doc McElroy died. He still worked hard and long hours but in a different atmosphere. He remembers working from sun up to sun down, never drawing a large wage but respected and thanked for his good work ethic and dependability. "Dad" was a good field hand, put out to his utmost, smiled constantly and was easy to get along with.

Occasionally a person, black or white, got wanderlust in his or her soul and, after working on the McElroy-Hopkins farm, decided to emigrate. When the farm became mechanized, more left to find work elsewhere. I told the whole batch of hands that all were welcome to stay on the farm rent free, along with free water and wood, but that I'd not accept the responsibility of keeping up their houses. All but three or four families moved, most went north and a few south.

Over the years I have had visits from many of them besides "Dad" Dixon, on good terms and equal status. Their employers have treated them fairly, realizing how valuable employees are who learned the work ethic at an early age and were eager to stay in the work force. They used to get three dollars a day, cain't to cain't; now they are offered close to forty dollars for an eight-hour day. Some of these guys and gals talk of returning to the farm but that's sweet and nostalgic talk—I couldn't afford them and besides they wouldn't want to sweat it out as in the past. I can say truthfully that I wish them the best: health of good quality first, second, wealth, at least in their minds, and last, the time to enjoy it.

GLORY BE, ALL THE COWS ARE GONE

No more fence patching, no more cow shit on the shoes tracking into our houses. No more fussing, fretting and cursing those dumb animals when trying to make them go somewhere they don't want to go. No more cows tearing down fences and ravaging a pretty, growing crop. No more cursing us by our neighbors for the same reasons. No more threat of litigation by neighbors for damages done by our cattle. No more calls from the railroad folks saying our cows are on their right-of-way and that they've killed a few.

Their favorite time for breaking out always fell on a weekend when often only one of us was present to try getting them back in. A hungry cow will tear up the best of fences during the crop-growing season to get to a change of diet—usually growing corn. One time Doc McElroy's herd of cattle got into an old carbox full of Chilean Nitrate placed on Esbon Faulkner's place. The cows liked the salty taste of the Nitrate, a side dressing for corn and cotton. They licked their fill of the substance and fifteen or twenty died.

We have spent many a day, dawn to dusk, trying to bait the herd into a lane leading to our cow barn and then have a couple of big bulls begin fighting and tear a whole side of heavy lumber fencing off the barn, through which all the herd follows. Then again, in the winter, a whole herd of cattle can be led over most of the county by blowing the truck horn to assemble them and showing them a few bales of hay on the pickup truck tailgate.

In wide-open pasture where several bulls are foraging they'll usually keep a good distance from one another, the dominance of, usually, the older bull taking preference. But in a confined space all hell breaks loose. This is when it's dangerous to be amongst them. I've been knocked down and trampled by angry cows on many occasions and have just barely reached the top rail of a board fence before a yearling crashed into it.

Sometime in the 1950s Brahma bulls were imported from India. In their homeland they are considered sacred by the Hindu.

Animal husbandry experts thought a Brahma cross with existing breeds in America would put new genes into our cattle herds and they have. The true-bred Brahma is white or grayish-white, has a large frame, conducive to putting on more flesh, and massive shoulders, with a huge chunk of meat at the base of their necks. They are very omnivorous in their choice of forage, eating a lot of leafy plants, such as palmetto fronds, that our standard breeds pass up. They were brought in to breed for heat tolerance and can stand the tropical or sub-tropical heat of Florida and south Georgia.

Brahma bulls, pronounced 'Bremmer' in south Georgia, look formidable with beady, stare-you-through eyes, very long, drooping ears and the huge lump on their shoulders—kind of like a bovine bulldozer. People that keep the breed pure say they are docile animals and even safe for children to be around; I've seen a huge one of over three thousand pounds saddled to ride. In spite of their gentle nature, purebred Brahma bull riding is a favorite in the rodeo circuits; a lot of it is pure hype, due to their formidable looks. I might have it a bit off, but I hear the rodeo bulls are mad to begin with due to a tight cinch encircling their penises and a fighting desire to get loose from the constriction. I have also witnessed bullfights in Texas and Mexico with the Brahma bull up against a man and a horse.

Brahmas are also excellent jumpers of any obstacles in their paths. In previous times serious and heavy buyers, mostly meat packers or owners of local abattoirs, sat in the front seats at stock sales with only a two foot high cinder block wall separating them from the sale ring. The early Brahma bulls thought this height no problem and promptly jumped into the rows of buyers, who hastily scattered like a flock of poults when a chicken hawk flew over the barnyard. Livestock barn operators hastily installed an iron fence, about two feet higher than the cinder block walls, to protect their buyers. After several Brahma bulls succeeded in topping this, more height was added. Brahma bulls weren't mean and seldom, if ever, hurt anyone—they just wanted out from close confinement.

This particular skill of the Brahma bull can be put to more romantic purposes. I've seen a neighbor's Brahma walk up parallel to a six-foot fence, nimbly jump over, without the benefit of a starting run, and promptly mount and breed several heifers before their own brood bull knows what's going on.

A fond remembrance is of attending a cattle sale at the Old Fort Worth, Texas Cattle Exchange, then ensconced in a huge spread west and south of Fort Worth. It was held in a very attractive, tile-roofed, sale barn built along Spanish architectural lines. One of the things that amazed this south Georgian was that at least a quarter of the buyers were pure Indian but wore the traditional, ten-gallon hats. Take an Indian with a wrinkled face from countless moons, plus a stern countenance, place a ten-gallon hat on his head, and he becomes a serious competitor.

When we quit turpentining, I thought Rob Dixon would be a good prospect for looking after the cow-herd. I furnished him with a well-worn International 504 diesel tractor to carry out his duties. I went through several sessions, demonstrating the many gear shifts of this machine. The only ones he picked up on were reverse, same as "back mule," and road gear—the fastest speed a tractor of that vintage could muster—about ten miles per hour. I've many times seen him racing across an open pasture in road gear, bumping out of the seat a couple of feet high when he crossed bull diggings, holes where two opposing bulls had a stand-off.

Sometime in July in the 1960s, five huge brood cows, weighing over a thousand pounds each, entered the space beneath the hay barn in the shelter field and accidentally pushed a strong gate shut behind them, thereby denying themselves a way out to the green pasture and water. Uncle Rob Dixon, just by chance, rode by this shelter on his rounds and discovered the carcasses of about two and a half tons of beef cows lying dead.

He came over to the depot to report the foul mess to me and said he couldn't stand the stench to pull them out, one by one, and to drag the carcasses over into the adjacent woods for buzzard bait. I gave him verbal hell about this, reminding him it was his job to look after all aspects of the cow herd's welfare. He was steadfastly adamant in not being up to the stinking task. After some more stinging rebukes, I figured I'd better set an example; e.g.. no task is too difficult to overcome if one sets his mind to it.

I proceeded to the cow barn and began hitching a tow chain just above the hoof of each animal and dragging the carcasses off to the woods. The large animals had reached a state of putrefaction so far advanced that with each pull a leg and hindquarters on one side of the animal parted from the remainder, so it took quite a few pulls to get most of the dead animals from under the shelter. It was a nasty job I almost backed away from but figured someone needed to do it. I came as near puking as never before with the stinking smells. The stench from their remains stayed around for months.

One time when Grandson Donnie was in about the fifth or sixth grade, he was riding with me in the pickup truck through the south pasture. There we discovered eight or ten huge brood cows lying dead under a big persimmon tree. A violent thunderstorm had just passed through and one bolt of lightning had gotten the tree and all the brood cows near it. They looked peaceful but were inert and the only thing I saw out of the ordinary was many droplets of fresh blood over much of their hides.

I was terribly chagrined by the sudden loss of ten thousand pounds of beef and thought I had to say something. "The God-damned crazy sons-of-bitches oughta have known better than to congregate under that one tree." It came back to me a couple of days later when Donnie's teacher called and said Donnie had repeated the same words verbatim in his part of a show and tell session.

Other cow herd owners will attest to the oft times ridiculous, non-sensible acts of cows. One of those times came in 1955 when we had to move two to three hundred head of cows from the north pastures to the south pastures. During the late summer we'd gotten our first paving, some shining black macadam separating the two pastures. The old brood cows act as leaders; if you can get them to follow your truck then most of the herd will follow. Well, the first few balked and stepped back from the new paving but finally leaped out on it and raced across. All of the old herd cows and the brood bull followed but, lo and behold, about thirty yearlings stayed on the north side baying and bawling and refusing to cross. We had traffic backed up east and west and I was completely befuzzeled. Uncle Rob said, "Keep your cool—them yearlings ain't never seen any paving." Well, the stand off lasted for over an hour when finally one mother cow after another recrossed, the highway and led her calf across. Yes, just her calf—and it took some time for every mother to cross over. Old cow herders use the trick for matching mother and calf. Say you separate twenty brood cows and calves for sale; the cows are put in one pen and the calves in another overnight. A cow with calf by her side will always fetch more than the two separately but if they are all black and about the same size, there's no way to match them up. So the following morning one cow at a time is let into the calf pen where she will immediately go to her calf, which will commence suckling; she will not permit a strange calf to suckle. This is about enough for cows and I know about half of it sounds like bull.

MORE WAYS TO SKIN A CAT

Natural wisdom sometimes outsmarts the expected or educated approach. The following several stories demonstrate this truth.

Some years ago according to Eugene Harper, Superintendent of Ben Hill County Schools, an itinerant painter passing Harper's school noticed the faded sixty-foot flagpole in the front school yard. He walked in the Superintendent's office and made an offer to repaint the pole for one hundred dollars. They haggled for a few moments and the painter dropped his price to seventy-five dollars. At this point, Superintendent Harper asked, "When can you do it?" and the painter replied that he could start right then.

Harper thought this to be a wonderful opportunity for his students to witness a steeplejack in action as the painter climbed to the top of the pole and painted it all the way to the ground. Classes were dismissed and the students filed out to watch the show.

The painter hauled out a five-gallon bucket and stirred up about a gallon of aluminum paint. He then walked over to the pole, unhooked the halyard and lowered Old Glory to the ground. He carefully folded the flag and placed it some distance from the pole so as not to have it splattered with paint. Producing an ordinary bath towel from his van, the painter attached it to the rope halyard then dipped it in the five-gallon bucket. He raised the paint-soaked towel to the top of the pole and began to switch the rope back and forth until the pole at the top was painted all the way around. Then he lowered the rope a bit and repeated the process, continuing in this manner until he reached ground level.

Gene, seeing he'd been bunkered, sent the students back to their classrooms. The painter saw the pained expression on Gene's face and said, "I'll let it dry for a short time, then put on a second coat to make the job last longer."

Another story involves a gentleman whose Cadillac had been damaged in a parking lot when someone backed into the front door. The metal was buckled but not dented and no paint was cracked. The Cadillac owner pulled his car into a body repair shop and leaned out of the window to summon the shop foreman and ask him if he could fix the door. "Sure," the foreman said. "I'm really busy right now, but I'll stop and do the job for fifty dollars or you can leave it and I'll fix it for twenty-five by tomorrow morning."

The gentleman opted to have it done right then, assuming the body man would take off the inside door paneling and hammer the door back out with a rubber mallet or some such tool. He watched as the body man walked over to the bathroom and returned with a wet towel and a plunger. After wiping the door with the wet towel the man slowly pushed the plunger onto the deepest part of the buckled door and then quickly pulled back on the handle whereupon the door metal popped back into shape.

The Cadillac owner was chagrined to see how easy it had been and began to haggle. The body man pulled up his knee and said, "I can it put back into the same shape it was when you brought it in." The haggling ended right away.

No haggling occurs in this next story, just plain clever thinking. A trucker new to a route approached an iron river bridge that seemed to have a low clearance. On getting out of his cab he saw that his truck body was indeed about four inches too high to clear the cross truss. He asked a local hayseed how far it was to a higher clearance down river. The man answered that it was about thirty miles, but said, "I'll get you and your truck across right here for five dollars." The driver took him up on the offer so the local walked around the truck and let air out of all the tires thereby lowering the truck enough to let it pass. "You can pump the tires up again about a mile down the road," the hayseed said to the driver.

A similar problem confronted me one day when I was carrying stringing sticks to the tobacco barn. I had loaded up nearly five hundred sticks, enough to finish the stringing job and their weight lowered the whole truck frame five or six inches, almost flattening the springs. I drove into the hip shelter of the barn and the sticks were unloaded, but when I began to pull out someone shouted, "The cab isn't going to clear the tie beam." After I verified that this was true, I looked at the tie beam supporting the roof and knew I shouldn't tear it out. The prospect seemed to be digging trenches for the tires to follow in order to lower the truck enough to drive out.

About then Big Jim Henry, who weighed in at about three hundred and fifty pounds, shuffled over and said he thought he could solve the problem. He lowered the tailgate, sat down heavily on it and brought the whole truck low enough to clear the tie beam by about an inch.

A man once said, "Simple answers to complex questions are a sure sign of intellectual mediocrity." But who can fight success?

RED NECK SHOW

This morning in the Wal-Mart parking lot there were four huge semi-trailers with tractor attached. All the trailers had Colorado license plates. One contained Jimbo, the giant steer, six feet tall, twelve feet long, and weighing over thirty-five hundred pounds.

Another holds Willy the Whale, thirty-seven feet long and weighing thirty-two hundred pounds. He's a sperm whale. This tanker truck had its engine idling—must be circulating the water Willy rests in. What do you feed a tanked whale?

Yet another houses Geronimo, the world's smallest horse. His trailer was as large as the others. They must carry a lot of hay for Geronimo or else maybe it contained a whole herd of little Geronimos.

Last, but not least, was a trailer load of the "world's largest and longest snakes." Guiness Record book suggests this may be a reticulated Python from Indonesia or an Anaconda from Brazil. I'm a bit concerned about the welfare of the critters, yet am sure they are probably well fed and watered for the owners want them to last a long time.

There was a wooden ladder and viewing platform at each trailer, but no admittance price posted, so I guess the cost of a look is negotiable, according to how brisk business is. My curiosity is up; I will have to spend some dollars to satisfy it. Like Mama always said, "Curiosity killed the cat, but satisfaction brought him back." I'm going to pick a slack time to go into the trailers, for this is red-necking to the nth degree and I don't want too many witnesses to my act—my red-neck leanings are already suspect.

PART III
FIELD NOTES

ODE TO SWAMPS

From an early age on, swamps have intrigued me. There is a diversity of life in this ecosystem found nowhere else. I find quiet and serenity there, and probably a sense of serendipity, for when I wade into a swamp seeking one thing or another, something more unusual or more pleasing and unexpected often turns up.

My first experience in south Georgia swamps was as a boy sometime in the late 1930s. On a regular basis we followed the old ditch that drained the southwest side of Fitzgerald into Minnie's Millpond, a mule scrape-pan built dam full of pond cypress and cattail marshes. Every few years a steam shovel and operator redug this ditch to facilitate the town's drainage. We followed him closely for he turned up a myriad of water moccasins whose heads we promptly bashed in. Looking back, I know that ninety-nine percent of these were banded water snakes, terrible for their musk but completely harmless.

On long afternoons of exploration we were thrilled by the constant flushing of wood ducks as we rounded a bend in the creek. There were a lot of bends in the creek; back then the steam shovel operator tried to follow natural drainage patterns and avoid straight, ugly channels. We boys knew the birds only as summer ducks, for they bred here. We preferred to call them "squealers" for their call on flushing.

We could also expect that at our approach, a solitary great blue heron would laboriously take wing with a loud guttural squawk. He might have been my favorite, due to his enormous wingspan and his love of swamps. Things come to reality though. On one camping trip my part of the meager fare was two drumsticks of a great blue heron. Fried in hog lard after being coated with corn meal, salt and pepper—it wasn't too bad for the evening meal.

One's ears would ring with the oft repeated and plaintive "Peter, Peter, Peter" of the tufted titmouse as his calls echoed through the swamp. The swamp was a favorite habitat for the titmouse because, being a hole nester, he could find numerous nest holes in rotten black gum and willow stumps, previously hollowed out by downy woodpeckers. Nowadays the titmouse sometimes nests in bluebird boxes.

Another sound, sure to be heard, were the calls of the pileated woodpeckers—either its usual call, or more often, its distant drumming on a signal tree, a sound that resonated throughout the swamp. Though I thought then that the bird was tapping the tree for food, I realize now that those peckerwoods were not seeking grubs but probably establishing territory.

In the springtime, especially, we would see the spotted sand-piper. He'd take off with rapid wing beats, part sailing, part flying, just over the surface of the water. He didn't fly too far, so we could count on flushing him again around the next bend. He had a predilection for nervously pumping his tail up and down, a trait that makes it easy for an observer to identify him.

Hooded warblers, the male wearing a mask, were there in good numbers, particularly on the millpond's upper edges. Another of the warbler tribe, the prothonatary, or golden swamp warbler, with its piercing "sweet, sweet, sweet" calls was omnipresent. Like the titmouse it favored the swamps, in part, because of the numerous nesting cavities previously hollowed out by downy woodpeckers. We also encountered barred owls, hearing them call even in the daytime and adding greatly to the wilderness feeling.

Birds dominated the swamp; animal inhabitants were few, although we once found a stump with four cute ring-tailed coon babies nestled in the hollow. Surely the sow coon had to swim out and swim back to the mainland to nurture them. The red tree rat, or golden mouse, also lived in the swamp, nesting in his dome-shaped nest.

Wading along, watching the birds and animals, hearing the continual croaks or "strumming" of the banjo frog, looking overhead to see white ibis circling, flushing sora and king rails, watching red deer mice jump from their nests and swim to nearby trees, watching heads and snouts emerge, not knowing whether they were big turtles or alligators—it is an unmatched, exhilarating way to spend an afternoon. Swamp wading, though, ain't for the timid souls but for the explorer, seeker of new knowledge and exciting experiences. It does help to know that gators always swim away from you; they're never aggressive unless some fool has been feeding them.

Swamps from time immemorial have been unfairly characterized as dark, sinister, unhealthy places to be avoided at all costs, but they are pleasurable places and I find peace and contentment there.

HUNTING PEARLS IN FRESHWATER CLAMS OF HOUSE CREEK

In 1540 Hernando de Soto and his soldiers spent a good deal of time in Georgia, ostensibly in search of gold. He found only minuscule amounts, but he is said to have extorted a modest store of freshwater pearls from a legendary Indian queen while there.

When I was a boy, House Creek, dividing line between Ben Hill and Wilcox Counties, was a pristine subterranean spring outflow, not contaminated by agricultural runoff or fertilizers. We used to find pearls in good numbers there in the freshwater mollusks or clams. Whether we learned of their existence from the old folks or found them ourselves by happenstance, I do not recall. We spent hours opening the elongated clams in our search for the pearls. I can well remember a flat-sided spirits of turpentine bottle, then found in most medicine cabinets, that I filled most nearly full of these jewels.

The clam beds had thousands of inhabitants, almost touching one another. We split open the clams with our Barlow knives and then ran a finger along both sides of the bivalve halves, feeling for hard bumps where the mollusk, in the same manner as the saltwater oyster, had taken in some bit of foreign material and tried to overcome the irritation by laying on successive layers of mother-of-pearl. After searching for pearls, we'd toss the remaining two halves back into the creek for use by fish, turtles, coons and the like. The pearls were rarely perfect spheres and those that were tended to be rather small. Still, they exhibited all the iridescence and natural beauty of mother-of-pearl. We agreed the search was as exciting as panning for gold around Dahlonega or in the Klondike. Monetary value was of no concern. It was exhilarating just to know real pearls did exist in the freshwater bivalves of south Georgia.

I've since done a little research on fresh water mussels and their habit of harboring and nurturing pearls. The bivalve produces irregularly shaped pearls that may be white, pink, yellow and red to steely blue, their color and luster determined by the part of the shell's interior to which they are attached. Many of the pearls are literally rainbow-hued in some fossils from Jurassic or Cretaceous deposits of one hundred and thirty-five to one hundred and eighty-one million years old.

The best of freshwater pearls are thought by some to far exceed in beauty those from saltwater oysters. One exceptionally fine pearl, found by a man named Carpenter near Paterson, New Jersey in 1857, was bought for fifteen hundred dollars by Tiffany's. As DeSoto's experience proved, early inhabitants of this country appreciated the beauty and value of the pearls and used them as wampum. Caches of them numbering many thousands have been found in Indian burial mounds. In later times, entrepreneurs found they could cut beautiful and long lasting mother-of-pearl buttons from the shells of mussels. Sixty pearl-button factories were located along the upper reaches of the Mississippi around the turn of the nineteenth century. The search and mining of mussel beds eventually devastated those located in the Mississippi River.

House Creek still flows clear and steady, but all that remains of the clam beds are a few long dead, empty bivalves. The House's many tributary streams, such as Little House Creek, drain a lot of farm and pasture land and the runoff has polluted the water and killed the mollusks.

POSTSCRIPT
Bowen's Mill

House Creek was dammed up at Bowen's Mill where stood the grits mill run by Uncle Billy Smith. Farmers brought their shelled corn from miles around for grinding into grits and meal. The force to grind the corn was supplied by water running through a long chute extending from the earthen dam to the mill house. As the water poured out of the chute it caused an upper millstone to turn against a lower, stationary, stone. Water ground grits and meal are thought to have a better taste than corn ground by an electric or diesel motor and a system of belts. I think this is a bunch of baloney but old folks swear by it. I believe that the lure was standing on the milling floor as miller Smith slowly opened the chute gate by the hand crank, hearing the surge of running water, and then as the heavy mill stone began spinning, feeling and hearing the entire millhouse pulse with life. One could actually feel the floor trembling. Uncle Billy used to invite us boys to stick our palms under the spout leading from the millstones, gather a handful of corn meal, almost too hot to hold and to relish it raw..This mill on House Creek was the last to operate in Ben Hill County and relied, in part, on the steady supply of water from the big springs called The Boils about two miles south of the site. It was operating as late as 1941, but shortly thereafter, the dam broke and was never repaired.

BIRD WATCHING

At about age eight, in 1934, I began to collect miniature reproductions by the master bird painter, Louis Agassiz Fuertes, whose paintings had been printed on a stiff two by three inch card. The bird was depicted on the front in living color and a description of the bird's habitats, range and diet was printed on the back. They came with packages of Arm and Hammer baking soda, which was used in biscuits and peanut brittle, as deodorizer in wooden iceboxes, and as a good toothbrush powder. Doubtless, housewives of the time found many other uses. There was one card to each yellow box, which was emblazoned with its familiar logo— a red circle enclosing a hefty bent arm with the hand grasping a hammer. Many boxes of the powder in my grandmother and mother's cupboards went missing as I surreptitiously took them behind the barn, poured out the contents, and destroyed the boxes, causing the ladies to go the store, buy another box and wonder where their supply had gone. I was determined to garner a complete set or as near to it as possible but never got beyond twenty or thirty different cards before going into the U.S. Navy in 1943.

On return in the spring of 1946, I found that my bird cards had either been sold off or bartered by my three younger brothers for things more to their liking. I replaced a part of this collection in the 1970s when I won an ornithological quiz on Sapelo Island and received as a prize a number of the cards, provided by ornithologist Herb Kale, packaged in old-time waxed paper envelopes. They are now collector items.

As a youngster, I carried the cards into the woods in shirt pockets or short pants pockets in warm weather when we didn't wear shirts. One day, I wandered into the nearby woods and, hearing a loud scratching in the leaves, became awfully curious as to what bird or animal might be making the big noise. I was inclined to think it was something much bigger than it turned out to be. After several minutes of careful stalking, I came on a male and a mama bird. I had my cards handy and recognized the birds as a pair of jorees, the old-folks' name for roufous-sided towhee. Without the cards I might have thought I was looking at two different kinds of birds, although I had a vague hunch the two were kin even before checking. A few minutes later a beautiful tiny Maryland yellowthroat with his distinctive black mask, came along, accompanied by a dull, yellowish-green bird of the same size. We had nicknamed it "tweet" but it is now known as the Northern yellowthroat of the warbler tribe. These observations, at close range, set me on fire and I promised myself to continue this sport, to identify every creature in the woods and fields, and to learn all I could about their markings, habits, differentiations and the whole shooting match.

EARLY NATURALISTS

Robert Norris and I first met when we had an unexpected encounter in the woods south of Fitzgerald in 1938. Norris may have a different version but mine is this.

I loved to get into the woods early morn when birds were waking up, talking to one another and displaying themselves. I had proceeded southwest of home with my BB gun in search of specimens I couldn't identify from the Fuertes pictures on Arm & Hammer baking soda cards. I heard strange noises from a second growth thicket and began stealthily approaching to see the birds. Just then, Norris came growling and hissing out of the underbrush, reminding me of the black bears inhabiting the area that were blamed for Paw Walker's loss of fattening pigs. Norris chased me homeward for a few hundred yards. Somehow I managed to hold on to my gun during the chase.

Norris was a star high jumper and football player in high school but was also already seriously studying birds and sketching them. We began birding in the woods behind my home and soon became close friends. I was so enamored with Norris and his knowledge of birds that I missed very few, if any, of these get-togethers. My repertoire of bird identifications rapidly increased as he pointed out minute differences between sexes of the same bird, all the while introducing me to new species. Before going birding with Norris I had known the common birds: mockers, thrashers, bluebirds, robins, crows, and blackbirds, but was inclined to call all small birds "tweets." Norris began teaching me ecology in the broadest sense. I learned to recognize both spring and fall migrants, amazed at what came through our woodlands and thickets in migration. He also taught me that different birds liked highly specific habitats in their travels. In the few seasons I was under his tutelage we became so adept at identifying microhabitats that we named one the "Worm Eating Warbler Thicket" because we found this elusive warbler in almost the identical spot for several springs running. Today bird habitats are so fragmented due to man's wholesale destruction of their preferred sites that it's difficult to find much continuity.

Norris' interests included mammals so we set trap lines behind the dam at Minnie's Millpond (nowadays Lake Beatrice) five or six miles south of Fitzgerald. We baited the mouse and rat traps—the spring type—with cheese sometimes and also with halves of raw peanuts. Even apple slices attract a wide variety of rodents, including rice rat, two species of deer-footed mice and shrews, one type of which was the smallest North American mammal. We sometimes set as many as fifty traps in late evening after we'd trotted out to a site on the backside of the dam.

The pay-off came early the following morning when we jogged out in darkness eagerly anticipating what we might find in the traps. Norris was in top shape physically and usually jogged well ahead of me, then rested until I caught up. All this took place in the winter months while we were in school, but we were always back in town for the eight-thirty bell.

Lake Beatrice was our favorite stomping ground. Often we'd wade the shallow west side through a huge cattail marsh, continually flushing sora and king rails, birds that took wing ponderously as we waded in. The rails were new to me, and I'd never have known this was their favorite habitat unless Norris had shown me. Norris liked to bellow, "Eureka, I have found it," as he came upon something interesting. When he shouted these words, I'd automatically speed up my pace, knowing that on a lucky day, it would behoove me to be in sight for some rare or unusual bird or mammal was present.

Norris was an exceptionally good artist at age fifteen. He worked in watercolor, beginning with a penciled outline of the bird on a small canvas board. He would add a perch, paint in the background, and then begin painting the bird, looking at a fresh-collected specimen or, in most cases, painting from memory; he had an exceptional memory for field marks. For all that, he set a one-hour goal per painting and rarely went overtime. Norris accepted an offer to illustrate a "Birds of Georgia" by Marie Reddy who was to write the narratives for each species. He once generously offered me as many illustrations as I cared for before shipping them, and I timidly accepted three: belted kingfisher, yellow-shafted flicker or yellowhammer, and a group of wild turkeys feeding. Alas, the turkey painting went missing from a biological exhibit in a glass case in Baldwin Hall, University of Georgia, but I am still the proud possessor of the first two, now hanging on the living room wall. Norris had also become interested in sculpture and molded and shaped several good busts. He was a perfectionist and wouldn't do mediocre work.

On field trips Norris carried a collecting gun and an old Army canvas bag. With his experience and expertise in high jumping, he took farmers' fences as a personal challenge and refused to climb over them, but instead backed off, got a good running start and hurdled them, pack, gun, and all. Once he misjudged and hung an ankle in the topmost strand of tight-pulled barbed wire then crashed down on the other side with torn trouser leg and a badly cut ankle joint. Although it bled for the rest of the day, he completed the whole length of the trip as if nothing had happened.

Once Norris, his brother, Charles ("Chops"), and I decided to walk out U.S. 319 to the Ocmulgee River, upwards of a thirty-mile round trip. U.S. 319 was a dirt road then, lined for many miles with farmers' fences and untreated cypress fence posts. We located close to fifty active bird nests, mostly bluebird, but also several species of woodpecker, the great crested flycatcher and screech owl. We didn't carry lunches so we helped ourselves to blackberries, huckleberries, plums, and an occasional raw ear of corn, courtesy of some farmer who had planted up to the highway, and washed this all down with creek water.

On a trip to Milledgeville to attend a Georgia Ornithological Society meeting, we hitchhiked—I was barefoot as I recall—and got to Macon shortly before dark. We decided to seek a place to spend the night. Pay-for lodging was out of our reach; we both carried only a few dollars, and expected to come home with a little change. The abandoned building we chose to spend the night in was heavily infested with huge wharf rats, and throughout the night we took turns sleeping while one kept the rats at bay with a stick. In the morning we walked to the north side of Macon and quickly caught a ride the rest of the way to Milledgeville. Norris was to give a short talk on a bird observation and borrowed the tie Mama had insisted on me carrying. The trip home was made in record time, due to the many kind motorists on the roads then.

Though this story is in the past tense, the days in the field with Norris are strong in my mind. (I can recall almost verbatim those conversations of fifty years ago yet have difficulty remembering the ones I had a month ago— I believe this is a common affliction with septuagenarians.) Sometime, along the way, he shifted his interests from fauna to flora. A mutual friend told me that Norris had bent the barrels of his collecting guns in a vise, making them useless, and vowed he'd never shoot another bird. Norris is still very active in botanical endeavors and is considered to be among the top botanists in the country. Recently Norris donated his pressed flora collection to Georgia Southwestern College in Americus and is continuing to add to the already thousands of plants in it. In his customary fashion the specimens are artistically arranged and accompanied by his neatly written notes.

DR. FRANCIS HARPER, OLD-TIME NATURALIST

Robert Norris once casually mentioned to me the fact that Dr. Francis Harper somewhere up in New Jersey was desirous of obtaining herpetological specimens, frogs, snakes, salamanders and turtles, from south Georgia. During his 1912 introduction to the Okefenokee Swamp as a member of Cornell University's expedition, he had been enraptured by the tales of the swamp folks. Albeit they had different names for a lot of the critters, he was amazed what details of natural history they knew regarding the animals inhabiting their swamp.

I wrote to him in 1941 and received meticulous instructions on how to preserve specimens and send them on to him. It amounted to going to the local pharmacist, obtaining a supply of formaldehyde (used in the embalming trade and by a few unscrupulous butchers who would spray it on hanging meat to make it keep its fresh red color longer) of forty percent strength and diluting it with tap water at a ten to one ratio, thereby producing formalin. One just plopped the small specimens into the solution. I usually thumped them on the head to immobilize them and before they recovered they would be dead and preserved. If the specimens were large, I was to get a hypodermic syringe from somewhere and inject copious amounts of the fluid into their bodies. I had to be careful for the stuff was hell on the hands, eyes and olfactory senses.

I first contacted Dr. Harper when I was fifteen years old and, after sending the first Mason jar of specimens to him, watched the mailman each day, eagerly anticipating a response, hoping the well-packed jar had reached him intact. The letter finally arrived and he said, after correctly identifying all the specimens sent, "You are to be commended on preserving these specimens and putting them in my hands." He further instructed me on proper methods of preservation, the intricacies of scientific labeling, and correct recording of collection sites geographically. Boy-oh-boy, I felt as important as any member of a National Geographic or American Museum of Natural History expedition to darkest Africa.

I swore to myself I'd do my dead level best to search far and wide for new specimens, both for his satisfaction of what was living hereabouts and for my own, for I dearly wanted to know the names and habits of the critters inhabiting our area. Most of my spare time was spent in searching for new animals and herps and learning how to identify them. I read everything in the local library by William Beebe, Ola Johnson, and particularly Raymond Ditmars' book, *Reptiles of the World.* I kept the latter book checked out so often I don't believe anyone else knew it was in the library. Meanwhile, Dr Harper would pass along suggestions in every letter he wrote to me. "It would be interesting to keep a record of any local names of amphibians or reptiles that are in fairly general use in your part of the state." Or, "At this season you might find gopher turtle eggs by digging down a few inches in the mound of earth just in front of one of their active burrows."

Although I joined the US Navy at the end of 1943, we continued to correspond. In his letter of March 13, 1944, he addressed a collection I had sent him earlier. "The real prize is the rainbow-colored darter," he wrote. "I doubt if that species has ever been collected in the Coastal Plain of Georgia. Fowler (Henry W. Fowler, Academy of Natural Sciences of Philadelphia) has not yet made it out, but thinks it may even be a new species." Fowler did describe the darter as a new species of fish and named it *Poecilichthys hopkinsi* or Hopkins Darter. The name has since been changed to *Ethestoma hopkinsi* and is still a valid species in 2000, although it has since been collected in much of the Savannah River drainage and is now commonly called Rainbow or Christmas Darter. The original, or type specimen, was collected in Osewichee Springs, Wilcox County, Georgia in August 1942.

I finally met Dr. Harper at Brevard, North Carolina in the middle or late 1960s. He and his wife Jean arranged a ride over there from Chapel Hill where they were then settled. We talked on two afternoons, mostly about his beloved Okefenokee Swamp and our admiration for the old time settlers there. After his stint as a naturalist in Cornell's reconnaissance of the swamp in 1912, he was so enamored with the inhabitants, both human and herpetological, that he returned many times over the years, often bringing his family to camp in tents. He made lists of all known plants, animals and birds as well as recording the songs, chants and hollers of his friends.

Before the two afternoons were over (he was walking with a cane because of falling from a tree, breaking his collar bone and several ribs, this while in his late seventies) I asked him and wife, Jean, to step outside so that I could take their likenesses for 35mm colored slides. He agreed to this. Afterwards Miss Jean said to me, "I'm very surprised that Francis permitted this, he doesn't like to be photographed." Apparently he'd made an exception, probably due to our long correspondence, which lasted from 1942 to 1970.

By the way, Mary Jean Sherwood Harper was a teacher with excellent credentials, having been chosen as tutor for Franklin Delano Roosevelt's children. She had a personal relationship with Franklin and it probably, behind the scenes, helped immensely in the federal purchase of several hundred thousand acres of the Okefenokee Swamp as a wildlife refuge when he became president. The government bought a large portion of the swamp from the Hebard family of Philadelphia. The family had cut much of the virgin pine and cypress timber in the swamp and then sold their acreage for about two dollars per acre.

On November 21, 1972, the Chapel Hill newspaper announced: "Dr. Francis Harper, zoologist, author and editor, died Friday, on his eighty-sixth birthday at his home at 311 McCauley Street here." He chose not to leave his library and field notes, letters, and unfinished manuscripts at Chapel Hill but bequeathed them to the University of Kansas. I treasure my bound copies of *The Mammals of the Okefenokee Swamp Region of Georgia*, which he had written and his annotated *Bartram's Travels*. He sent these and numerous other papers over the years inscribed, "M. Hopkins, Jr. with the regards of Francis Harper in appreciation of your good contributions to our knowledge of Georgia zoology."

THE RED-HEADED SCORPION

What was known to me during my growing-up years as a red-headed scorpion was in actuality a broad head skink, or red-headed lizard. The adult male, over twelve inches long, has thick muscular jaws and, during breeding season, a glistening orange-red head. To a youngster it presented a formidable sight and something to be reckoned with in the wild. It was as poisonous as a rattlesnake, we were warned, and when we saw one, we bashed in its head with a stout stick or shot it with BBs and .22 caliber scattershot. In fact, until I was a young man, I gave this reptile wide berth and was a bit, maybe two bits, scared as hell about what harm one of this species might inflict.

As it turned out, John Crenshaw, an Atlanta man, told me of their harmlessness. They were docile, he said, and had no toxic qualities at all. Crenshaw was book and field-trained as a herpetologist and though I was highly skeptical of his description of the reptile, I trusted him enough to experiment with it. I caught several of the big males, was bitten once, looked for real trouble and found none.

Crenshaw, with whom I worked at the time, received a cage of adult collared lizards at Emory University Field Station in Baker County in 1950 from out West, and encouraged me to reach in and pet one. It promptly took my forefinger in its jaws, clamped down and wouldn't let go, the whole while spilling my blood onto the floor. Old folks had warned me not to mess with turtles—they'll latch on and hold until it thunders. I was not sure whether the same was true of lizards but the warning ran through my mind for a bright sun was in the sky with no chance of a thundershower. Crenshaw proceeded to pry open the ill-spirited lizard's jaws, enabling me to get loose. I decided then, "Don't trust newfound friends and oracles; they might put you on the wrong road home." The collared lizard's bite turned out to be of no consequence.

After that I handled broad head skinks, but not without goosebumps up my spine and in other unmentionable places. You had best look out for a good bloody bite from their strong jaws if you try to constrain one of any size. Let him go or keep him, and don't worry too long about the consequences. To tell the truth, though, I'm still scared as hell to capture a full-grown one, as that early imprinting still presses hard on me. With a bit of bravado, and perhaps bourbon, I will quickly grab a large, red-headed scorpion, unconcernedly fondle him, hoping to hell he doesn't possess hidden poison to do me in.

TEKTITE

Older dictionaries fail to mention such a phenomenon. My latest volume says "Any of several kinds of small glassy bodies, in various forms, occurring in Australia and elsewhere, whose exact origin is unknown." One of the "elsewheres" is Osierfield, Irwin County, Georgia. I was circling the farm in a pickup truck one hot day in 1955 when Hardy Scott, a plowhand, hailed me. His Super C Farmall tractor had broken down in a field of cotton he was working. While we were engaged in fixing his tractor, one of us dropped a bolt or nut into the loose sand beneath the tractor. When we dug around, shifting sand, we came up with the glassy material, but thought it to be the bottom of a coke bottle that had survived a melting hot fire.

I carried it home that evening and cleaned and washed it. I just happened to hold it up to a strong light and noticed that it glowed a golden color. The unknown object rested on a hall closet shelf till 1958 when a neighbor, C. M. Copeland, noticed it and said "We ought to send this to our state geologist, Garland Peyton." Peyton acknowledged the gift or donation of the tektite December 1958 saying, "Inasmuch as these objects are rare and arouse a great deal of interest, the specimen will be a very fine addition to the museum."

They did display it prominently and tastefully with a bright light showing through the tektite. It remained in its case in the Department of Mines and Geology building for years and then went missing. It was not found until 1997 when Robert L. Humphries discovered it in a museum in Cartersville, Georgia.

Approximately thirty-five million years ago these pretty pieces of glass rained down from the heavens in only a few places in the world. The tektites found in Georgia are called Georgiates. The Osierfield specimen is the only one to have been found outside of Dodge County. It is particularly interesting because it is nearly a perfect circle and very flat. Some researchers believe tektites are actually moon rocks or volcanic material from the moon. Other astronomers think they may be surviving pieces of comets or asteroids that have come through the earth's atmosphere in a fiery shower and then were strewn across fields in different parts of the earth. State Geologist Sam Pickering says tektites definitely are not meteorites or parts of meteorites because the two have little, if anything, in common. "Meteorites are either stony or metallic and, although they may contain small amounts of glass, they are almost entirely crystalline material and they have been crystallized very slowly under great heat and pressure."

The Osierfield specimen created widespread interest and several persons interested in the history and origin of tektites have visited the farm over the years. People are especially interested in the exact field about a mile and a half southwest of Osierfield where the specimen was picked up. I, myself, have spent a good deal of time there, particularly when the field is turned with a bottom plow and then rained on heavily. No luck.

HERBERT L. STODDARD, 1889-1970

I first met Mr. Stoddard at a Georgia Ornithological Society meeting in the north Georgia mountains in 1940. He was, along with Roger Tory Peterson and a handful of Georgia naturalists including Bill Griffen, Dick Parks, George Sciple, Ann Hamilton, Ivan Tomkins and Fred Denton, among the charter members of the Society, which they founded in Atlanta in 1936.

Mr. Stoddard immediately impressed me as being a humble, kind person who went to great lengths to be helpful and considerate. He was full of interesting and useful information and generously shared it with people of all ages if they would but listen. His modesty could deceive those of a pompous nature, but surely they were the losers, for even brief associations with this man left one wiser. He told me in a letter in 1952, "I still find life very exciting with the bird studies we have going on both in Georgia and Florida and, on the average, seem to find a bit more time each year to work with the birds. I greatly hope this trend continues and speeds up, as I love bird work above all else." As I opened his letter, two beautiful wild turkey gobbler feathers floated to the floor. Mr. Stoddard dropped similar feathers in several letters over the years and now, after over fifty years, they retain their magical iridescent sheen.

Modern game management had attempted to mate wild birds with domestic turkeys, producing a semi-wild bird, unacceptable to Mr. Stoddard. He might have accepted the latter day attempts to move wild birds from one locality to another to enlighten the gene pool, but no barnyard turkey blood for him. His forte was the true wild turkey, a wily bird and one of the smartest of the smart and Mr. Stoddard undoubtedly knew more of its habits than anyone.

He has written, "There is abundant evidence that the wild turkey was originally more an inhabitant of the well-drained upland forests and prairie edges than of the river swamps, and that the birds were really returning to a preferred type of habitat when they restocked the upland areas. The species has been forced in the river swamps by man so long that present-day sportsmen consider them birds of extensive swamps rather than of upland forests and prairie edges."

My son about gave up deer hunting several years ago and now considers it a tame sport compared to hunting turkeys. He makes his own calling boxes out of local hardwoods, turning slate box scratchers on a wood lathe, and using various mouth calls to bring twenty-plus pound gobblers from afar. He enters the woods way before daylight and usually gives a pretty good rendition of the barred owl's hooting calls, sometimes eliciting a gobbling sound away off. Bubba has become so adept at calling gobblers that many of his friends, along with their sons, line up to go on a gobbler hunt with him.

While Herbert Stoddard is probably most famous for his monumental work, *The Bobwhite Quail: It's Habits, Preservation, and Increase*, published in 1941 and still referred to as the "Quail Bible," he is equally well remembered for his fight to establish prescribed or controlled burning as an important tool for management of Southern pinelands, and for the benefit of quail.

For years, he was opposed by government forces using veiled threats in an effort to stop his preaching of the many benefits of setting the woods on fire. I believe a self-taught man, as Mr. Stoddard was, holds stronger convictions than many professional foresters, and knows in his heart, and by dint of years of experimentation with woods fires, when he is right.

In 1960 he put forth a great deal of time and effort to outline the salient features of successful controlled burning, all for my benefit. By this time I had heard a lot about his burning theory and had been trying the practice on a small scale. I burned mostly small-acreage plots, back burning against the wind, so that the pace was slow and the flames seldom over two feet high. Fortunately for the timber grower, Mr. Stoddard has been vindicated and his methods largely adopted and recommended by most forestry services. Controlled burning has proved to be the single most valuable tool in Southern pine stand management.

He will be sorely missed from the circle of those dwindling few that lived in this country when our natural resources were plentiful and unspoiled, but he can rest in peace with the thought that he did his part in developing a love and understanding of the natural world. As he said himself, "One can find no greater satisfaction in life."

BUZZARDS

Few folks realize that between 1920 and 1950, buzzards were regularly trapped on southwest Georgia plantations because they were reputed to be predators of quail. Early-day game management intended to eliminate all predators, potential predators and suspected predators. The effort included a bounty on foxes, skunks, coons, possums, buzzards and hawks.

The trap consisted of an approximately twenty by twenty foot pen made of woven or hog wire—very simple and easily constructed. On one side of the pen a fifty-five gallon steel barrel with both ends removed provided an entry at ground level. One-quarter inch metal bars, facing into the pen, were installed midway in the barrel, designed to work on the same principle as a fish basket, allowing the buzzard to get in but not out. The trap was baited with a fat shoat or calf, recently dead if such was available, but sometimes shot for the purpose. Apparently the inert body plus ensuing smells attracted the buzzards—both turkey and black, but predominantly the latter.

Vultures flying high in the sky and seeing the corpse would land, circle the wire pen, find the barrel opening and enter for the meal. It was a one-way street, for once they entered it was impossible to get out against the opposing metal prongs. They gorged on the bait and sought release, to return to the sky, without avail. No water was available so they perished and hence provided more bait. It was self-perpetuating—more buzzards, more bait—and anyone approaching the operation better do it upwind. Buzzards were finally exonerated of their love for quail flesh, but the practice of trapping continued at least until 1951 at the Wildlife Refuge on Gillionville Road in Dougherty County.

On returning to the Osierfield farm in 1951, I duplicated a buzzard trap in a corner of a hog pasture. After its completion I lay down in the middle of the pen, facing skyward and shading my eyes from the sun with sunglasses. Believe it or not, several turkey buzzards appeared overhead (I hadn't noticed any while building the pen) and they began circling lower and lower until they were fifty to one hundred feet above me. I was convinced my inert body had attracted them. Several days later I baited the trap with a dead hog and successfully trapped several buzzards but let them free once the trap was deemed a success.

People have debated for years whether buzzards find carrion by sight or smell. It's probably a combination, but I believe most of their ability to find dead animals lies in their eyesight. They perceive an inert body in the same place for a good while, such as mine lying in the hog pasture, and approach to check it out. People have hidden a carcass under a brush pile and buzzards did eventually find it, but after a spell, probably when the carrion got real ripe.

Nowadays most buzzards find dead-on-the-road (DOR) animals and feast on them, especially savoring armadillos and possums. Occasionally a red-tailed hawk will partake of carrion alongside the buzzards. Apparently, buzzards seem not to care for a dead dog, for I've seen many dead dogs along the road with none attended by the birds. At the approach of a vehicle, buzzards will usually fly off about three or four feet above the ground, make a sharp turn and fly right back across the highway over the dead animal. This habit can lead to unpleasant results for the vehicle driver and the buzzard. In the 1930s my daddy hit one near Valdosta that crashed through the windshield on the passenger's side and went out through the rear window. Many years later in January 1994 we saw a pickup truck parked beside the highway in Coffee County, with an impaled black buzzard stuck in the shattered windshield.

When thinking of buzzards, I always recall Joe David Brown's characterization of a hung rural jury: "as solemn as a row of turkey buzzards holding a post-mortem on a dead horse."

ENCOUNTER WITH A GIANT SNAKE

Growing up in south Georgia I had seen indigo or gopher snakes draped around the neck of a winsome maiden in a carnival pit or hootchy-cootchy side show. The lady usually sat cross-legged on the floor of the tent, reached into a wooden box, and slowly pulled out several feet of shiny blue-black, thick-bodied snake. She would gradually bring it within inches of her face occasionally kissing the snake on its nose—the snake was supposed to be charmed or hypnotized. Then she would drape the snake around her neck, continually stroking and talking to it.

The fact of the matter was that this lady was handling one of the most docile snakes in existence, one almost never known to strike and bite. I found this out some years later, but as a youth I was very much impressed and wanted to get closer and hold the snake myself. It was fitting that I didn't understand the indigo snake's nature at the time for it would have killed a lot of excitement and enthusiasm in me.

In 1962 our family got hold of nearly eight hundred acres of nearly virgin turkey oak, longleaf pine and saw palmetto on the east side of Seventeen Mile Creek in Coffee County. Only a few of the majestic pines were left, but the tract of land had lain idle since the days of WWI and was truly wild and undisturbed. There was no human habitation, the nearest house being four or five miles away. The remnants of two-rut sand roads were barely visible, for encroaching vegetation had taken over from both sides and above. I did a lot of exploring, probably on a good portion that hadn't been walked since the Indians were there. On one of these exploring jaunts I met an octogenarian a couple of miles from any human habitation and greeted him with, "Cap'n, are you lost?"

"Not hardly, young man, are you lost?" he says. "I been wandering these sand hills since the early 1890s. Fact is, I used to cross right along here on my trips to a one-room school house 'bout three miles over yonder."

"Well, tell me what the county looked like seventy years ago."

"It looked about like it does now 'cept there was more long leaf yellow pine than now; not too many though, maybe four or five to the acre and each one of the big trees had two to four cut boxes (for turpentine) in the base of them. This here tract of sand ridge has been a free-for-the-taking woodyard for Douglas and hereabouts. It grows some of the finest red oak in the country though I'll 'low it may take fifty to seventy-five years to grow a good tree. It's the best wood for the fireplace or barbequing meat. In the '30s, ain't no telling how many truck- and wagon-loads of this wood was hauled to Douglas for a dollar a cord, then cut it into stove length and split for a quarter extra. These gophers are mighty fine eating too; you know they don't eat anything but leaves and grass."

For a couple of weeks I had carried Uncle Rob Dixon and Mister Fred Deese down there with bush hacks to clear the roads. Exploring the secluded tract was an exciting adventure. Every day I wandered off several miles in various directions toting a WWI Colt, not knowing what I might encounter. We subsequently located three active moonshine stills on the tract, but luckily I made friends with all the folks running them after telling them my purpose on the land. The thought of turning them in to the High Sheriff never entered my mind. They sold a good safe product, called Coffee County Rye, made from a mash of wheat shorts in copper stills. They were making an honest living without government help or interference.

Sand ridges, on the east sides of most major streams and rivers in the coastal plain of Georgia, have always intrigued me. There's something there I can't put a handle on, something lonely and quiet; all types of grasses, plants, and trees growing in a harsh environment—some of the big bare spots of sand so lacking nutrients that nothing will grow there. One spot in particular had several square acres of bare sand with only a few clumps of deer moss. The sand is so absorptive that only minutes after a two-inch rain, no water can be found standing anywhere. It's such a harsh environment that few birds and animals use it. In the warmest months gopher tortoises feed there at night or in early morn to get the dew on the ground then return to their cool burrows.

The indigo snake is at home on south Georgia sand ridges, along with the diamondback rattlesnakes, coach whips and black racers. The indigo snake usually spends the winter deep in gopher tortoise burrows that slope downwards, often for eighteen to twenty feet, ending in a hollowed-out cavity, sometimes as much as ten feet below the surface. The indigo is an omnivorous reptile and will eat a large variety of food, including other snakes. Once I carried a six-foot specimen back to Osierfield in a cotton collecting sack and the next morning found two three-foot young coach whips the specimen had regurgitated into the sack.

One time I was trying to follow the sand ridge south near where it dropped off eight to ten feet in elevation to the floodplain of Seventeen Mile Creek, whereupon I came in view of a pile of snake that appeared to be enough to fill a #3 washtub. Mind you, this was in January, and the indigo, encouraged by eastern sunlight in the gopher hole, had emerged to soak up warm sunlight and possibly to feed. I was amazed at the snake's size and length, but remembering textbook descriptions of record specimens measuring up to one hundred and five inches, I could accept what I saw piled on the white sand mound in front of the gopher hole.

Large physical size alone in creatures of the wild is intimidating, even though they might not appear aggressive. However, having seen the carnival women handle indigos with apparent abandon, I walked up and knelt down within reaching distance of the huge coil of reptile. I squatted between it and the hole to prevent her from reentering. She put a U-shape in her neck, swelled up and hissed once, rattling her tail on the ground as I reached to put a hand around her midsection. I raised her up to my standing height, and there still remained on the ground a lot more of snake. Her body was a glistening blue-black almost as thick as my forearm.

Being over a mile from the pickup truck, I decided the best way to transport her was drooped over one shoulder, as one would carry a large rope or chain. Her head almost reached the ground in front of me and her tail almost reached the ground behind. I never did weigh the snake but she got to be quite a load and I had to continually shift her from one shoulder to the other.

Uncle Rob and Mister Fred saw me coming, then saw the huge snake and, dropping their bush hacks, made haste over a good bit of sand ridge. They finally began hollering to me from about a hundred yards down the cleared road and, it being late in the afternoon, told me in no uncertain terms that they would walk home (just thirty-five miles) unless I put the snake in the metal tool box on the back of the pickup truck and locked it securely.

I did this and we headed towards the farm at Osierfield. The two men with me began describing "our" snake as about two times actual size. At home I constructed a pine box about two feet square and six inches deep, placed the snake in by coiling its body several times and then locked on the lid with 8D finishing nails, hammered only halfway down. I planned to offer the snake water before shipping it to Professor T.P. Haines of Mercer University.

Lo and behold, the next morning I awoke to find an empty snake box. The huge reptile had forced the pine planks clean off the box and escaped into our home. We turned the house upside down for several days in search of the snake without success. I was certain it had not escaped. Wife Mary had a few-months-old baby girl at the time and wailed, "That huge snake will swallow my baby." I knew this was impossible but couldn't convince her. The other children were eleven and thirteen and thought it good fun to tell their classmates, "We have an eight-foot snake loose in our home." They had both handled the snake at length before I placed it in the box.

One morning early, while we were eating breakfast, my peripheral vision caught a swift darting motion from behind a large upright freezer. Here was our snake. She was coiled in and out of the heat dispensing coils on the back of the freezer which was backed up to a closed window. The freezer had recently been loaded with over six hundred pounds of a beef we had just killed on the farm, and I hated to think of unloading and reloading all that meat. We decided the best method of recapture was to take out the window casing from the outside, remove the lower window and get to the snake. This took some time and effort and I had three pairs of eyes watching from inside the house to be sure the snake didn't move to another hiding place.

She had wound herself around and in and out of the coils of the freezer, probably seeking warmth. We worked gently to get her to turn loose and when this was finally accomplished we put the snake back into her shipping box. This time the lid was securely nailed down.

After affixing the address on the box I added "Live Snake" in big letters. Railway Express agencies prided themselves on shipping anything, but I thought it prudent to leave the snake box in the pickup truck, enter the freight agent's office, and tell him what I wanted to ship. He says loudly "A live snake?"

"Yes, sir." Whereupon he said, "Boy, don't bring that thing any closer in here. Push my scales outside on the loading platform, weigh the box and I'll give you a label to attach to it." He again admonished me not to bring the box inside his office.

T.P. Haines, head of the biology department at Mercer for over forty years, got his snake the next day. He kept a good number of live snakes as a hobby and for teaching purposes. It turned out that the big indigo was a gravid female and subsequently laid eggs, which T.P. hatched. The snake was handled by hundreds of students over a period of years and finally gave a girl a nasty bite on her forearm.

This ends the snake story, except for the Osierfield farm portion. Uncle Rob Dixon and Mister Fred Deese liked to tell snake stories in the turpentine quarters, where over forty families lived. In their version of this story, our snake was as long as a pickup truck and weighed over a hundred pounds!

THE SPEED OF SOFT-SHELLED TURTLES

In south Georgia there are many kinds of turtles, but we classify them into two general groups: the hard-shelled "Baptist" turtles such as the cooter or streaked headed terrapin and the soft-shelled "Methodist" turtle. The latter species is best known for its speed either on land or submerged in a pond or creek. They are the fastest of the fast.

In the 1950s I accompanied John and Nell Crenshaw to several of Florida's clear springs. John was then working on "Turtles of the Southeast," his Ph.D project at the University of Florida. John steered the boat with me in the bow. We'd try to quietly slip up on basking turtles, and as they lunged from their sunning perches on projecting logs or emergent stumps, I was to dive in and pursue them. This worked tolerably well for the slower moving hard-shelled turtles and we secured quite a few, but when a soft-shelled turtle hit the water, it was another story—they all outdistanced me with their swift swimming. They were aided by their shape, nearly flat as a pancake, and their partially webbed feet, and they were fast as greased lightning under water. Perhaps, too, I knew they could stretch their long, tubular necks half-way back their shells and give me a nasty bite.

I had imagined soft-shells were a bit lethargic on land but I was corrected in September 1996. As I was driving east towards Osierfield at a good rate of speed, I met another vehicle also traveling rather fast from the opposite direction. Suddenly a soft-shelled turtle eight or ten inches in length broke from the edge of the highway on my left, got up on its legs and rapidly ran across the highway between the two vehicles. Its plastron, or belly shell, cleared the paving at least four inches as it sped across the road. Very few soft-shells end up dead on the road, while many hard shells draw in their necks and stop, thus getting splattered.

SMELLING FISH BEDS

Many of you have heard of the ability of some folks to smell out fish beds, particularly those of the bluegill bream. Mr. Reeves, late of Fitzgerald, was one of those persons. He was a truck driver for the Railway Express Agency and made a daily trip to Ocilla but nearly always stopped at Minnie's Mill Pond, nowadays known as Lake Beatrice, to fish. He grunted his own bait, driving a one by four inch scantling into the moist earth down to about twelve to fifteen inches below the surface. Then, he took a smooth face brick and rubbed it horizontally back and forth over the top of the stob, producing a grunting sort of sound and sending vibrations through the ground outward from the stob. Within a few minutes, dozens of fat, succulent earthworms, some up to eight inches in length, would begin to emerge from their burrows or tubes and start crawling over the surface. In about ten minutes he would have a #2 tin can full of worms.

A lot of folks around knew of Mr. Reeves' ability to catch as many as fifty nice-sized bream within an hour. He always caught more than his needs, gave some to friends and sold a few. One day the Murray twins and I followed him into the lake. He attempted to lose us several times to no avail so probably said to hell with it and paddled straight to a certain spot where he almost immediately began pulling in huge bream. We tied up to a cypress tree nearby, but not too nearby for fear of his wrath upon us. We fished where we were tied for about ten minutes without even a nibble, then got braver by the minute and paddled closer to Mr. Reeves, who was steadily pulling in three-quarter pound bream. I guess we made too much noise talking and hitting the sides of the boat—he had been sitting silently fishing with three short cane poles—so he pulled in his lines, shook his fist at us and paddled away. We immediately paddled over and tied up at the exact spot Mr. Reeves had been in. We had been fishing with the same bait he was using without luck, up until then.

The fish began biting as soon as our baits sank to the bottom. Before an hour was out we three had a live box (built into one of the middle seats in the boat with holes in it to let the pond water flow in and out) pretty well half full. We all took, or thought we took, an account of our bearings for a return trip but dared not mark the spot conspicuously for fear of others finding it. On the following days we tried to find that spot again and also to smell the fish beds. But none of us could smell beds—the whole frog pond smelled kind of fishy to us—and we never found Mr. Reeves' beds again.

Fish beds are circular pits in the sandy bottoms of most ponds where the male bream fans out sand with strong strokes of his caudal fin, then entices a mama bream to swim in and lay her eggs, whereupon he immediately fertilizes them with his sperm. The males guard their beds ferociously and will try to bite or in some manner drive out competing males. Sometimes the male will even bite and swallow a bare hook in their frenzy to get anything foreign out of their beds. This is why the fishing is so good, since the big, fat old males are usually in their beds.

Fishery biologists say the bluegill bream will deposit fifty thousand eggs in a season, laying as long as the water temperature is over sixty-five degrees Fahrenheit. Probably less than one percent of the hatchlings survive, but even so, most southeastern ponds are way overstocked with small bream who, in the absence of a good largemouth bass population to control their numbers, will just about starve themselves to death, becoming almost transparent.

In the 1960s, I was flying a light aeroplane about two hundred feet over one of the ponds on the Osierfield farm and noticed a conglomeration of washtub-sized white spots below—all in a line and concentrated on the west side of the pond in about two feet of water. I mentioned this to one fellow whereupon he promptly proceeded to the spot and caught a fine mess of bream. Another fellow regularly caught nice strings of shellcrackers under a power line crossing the pond. He attributed this to the habit of our purple, or bee, martin colony adults and fledglings of perching on this line and depositing many droppings in the water.

Neither of these guys could smell beds, but I'm a firm believer that some folks can. Maybe it's an innate ability, not transferable, to smell out fish beds, but it's a fact that some folks can do it and some can't, and apparently it's a closely guarded secret.

POSTSCRIPT
How To Cook Bream, Southern Style

We'd split the fish down the belly, head to tailfin, leaving on the head, after punching out the eyes, scale them, salt and pepper them, and shake them in a brown paper sack full of corn meal. The fish were fried in hog lard, either purchased at the market in fifty-pound cans or prepared at home by those who had pigs. We'd never heard of cholesterol.

I recall one of Lewis Grizzard's bream tales. He was coming north out of Florida when a cafe in Willacoochee caught his eye. It was the No Name Café, still in operation a couple of years ago probably because of the publicity it received from his column. He couldn't resist stopping, going in and looking over the menu. One of the offerings was a hot bream sandwich, a local favorite. He ordered one and thought it delicious. The sandwich was made up of a hand-size bream, redbreast, from the Alapaha River, fried crisp so you could eat bones and all. The bream had been gutted, eyes punched out, salted and peppered, shook in a sack of cornmeal and fried to a golden brown. That was it—just the crisp-fried fish between two slices of white bread and a pint Mason jar of sweetened Luzianne tea.

ROBINS

It's the 18th of November. As I look out the open side door, I see a single robin, *Turdus migratorius*, (the thrush that migrates) hurriedly short-hopping over the lawn, cocking his head first right, then left. I've been told they are listening for underground noises of earthworms.

Stepping outside, I spot at least a dozen in the side yard and going further into the yard I see dozens more. In the pineland adjacent to the yard there are probably a hundred flying back and forth. They weren't here yesterday or even this morning, but now at one in the afternoon they are here in big numbers, apparently just arrived from a long flight. Finding the boondocks of south Georgia to their liking, many will spend their winter here. They are ravenously hungry after the long flight and voracious in their search for food—and large amounts of it. They concentrate on the red fruit of the flowering dogwoods; a few test the new crop of blackgum seeds. Robins also like to hunt for food under chinaberry trees, for they often find the fruit irresistible. After feasting on the overripe, fermented berries the robins will become drunk and staggering, unable to fly far.

Robins have been nesting in west Fitzgerald for many years. They favor neat, close-mowed yards and build their nests in dogwood trees and Japanese magnolias. The nest is sturdily constructed of wet mud, sticks and grasses, well-anchored onto a limb. The young birds will have speckled breasts in the fledgling stage, a throwback to their thrush relations. As adults, males sport a bright orange breast and the females a dull orange breast and paler head.

I wouldn't think of shooting one today, but in my youth they were fair game. An old hand on the Osierfield farm told me a tale about torching, or shining, these birds around the turn of the century.

" 'Bout a hour fo' sunset dem robins would pour into a thick gallberry patch 'hind the house," he said, "and ago to stuffin' demselves on de gallberries. We'd let 'em git a fillin' and just at good dark we'd light up our lightered knots and go after dem. We'd fetch de torch in one han', high over our heads, and 'bout a three foot stick in t'other. Day 'ud jus sot still fo' us, or flutter around a short piece, and us boys 'ud soon have a sackful apiece. One night bro Joe shined a screech owl while we'uns was doin' this and you know whut? He told one t'em other boys it were a pottage (partridge, or quail) and dat boy traded him three robins fer it! I kin still taste them robin pies, but I hain't et one in a mighty long time."

A robin tastes similar to a mourning dove's dark breast meat. If you ask me how I know, I can only reply that maturity comes late for some, never for a few.

This reminds me of a defendant standing before a judge for sentencing in a case where he'd shot and eaten a bald eagle. The judge was curious about the taste and so asked the man about it.

"Your honor, it tastes very near like a whooping crane," the defendant replied.

CANINES IN THE WILD

Dr. McElroy showed me a wolf pit in the mid-1940s. It was on the north side of the Osierfield farm situated on the original mid-lot line about four hundred yards south of the present CSX Railroad line. The wolf population was a threat to the domestic stock of early settlers and farmers sought to exterminate them in any way possible, including digging wolf pits. J.B. Clements in his *History of Irwin County*, describes them:

> A round ditch was dug about six feet wide, several feet deep. In the center the earth was not disturbed. A very high fence was built around this ditch except at one place that was left low enough to allow a wolf to jump over it. In front of this low place the ditch was covered over with light brush, straw, etc. to look very much like the surrounding earth. In front of this low place in the fence and directly in front of the covering of twigs and straw over the ditch, on the ground in the center, was placed the bait for the wolf, which was usually a sheep, calf or some other dead animal. And the wolf would jump the fence not suspecting the ditch he would fall into in attempting to reach the bait and would land upon the straw-covered ditch and fall through and go to the bottom from which he could not escape. When his captors arrived, they would find him confined in the ditch where he was quickly dispatched with a gun.

The wolf pit on our farm was much like what Judge Clements described, but only about four feet deep due to filling in over the years. It was still visible into the 1970s but has since been leveled to prevent a tractor turning over in it.

In the early 1800s, folks thought wolves were eating lambs, calves, piglets, and so forth. Nowadays they claim coyotes are doing the same things but I think both canines were falsely accused. We have seen coyotes eating calves but believe the calves were stillborn. Brood cows and bulls are very protective of their young and would probably fend off coyotes attempting to kill live calves. Sheep, though, are more vulnerable. Lambs, ewes and even rams will stand without bleating and let a dog slowly kill them, usually going for the throat first. In the early 1960s we inherited a flock of thirty-six sheep. We tried to see after them, but within a year's time all were gone except six—feral dogs had done them in.

Coyotes have been in the area for over thirty years. The tale hereabouts is that they were imported from Texas by fox hunters in nearby Turner County. The coyote has spread north as far as Macon and is very common on the farm. On a roadside they often stand and let a vehicle pass, their ears pricked all the while, before they cross the road. When they finally run they quite often pause and look back. I have seen many in my rearview mirror.

Recently a trapper has been catching them in steel traps that have coated teeth, which trap and hold the coyotes. Amazingly, the trappers says it's fairly simple to put them in a dog box when they are caught because they will sull like a possum and not try to bite. The trapped coyotes are sold for seventy-five or eighty dollars apiece to hunters who release them and sick their hounds on them for a little "sport."

Chasing coyotes is a recent trend in south Georgia. Trapped foxes or coyotes are introduced into a fenced field of four or five hundred acres where, for a fee, hunters with their dogs can chase and tree the wild animals. Local hunters tell me of coyotes running their dog packs upward of ten miles, whereas foxes usually run in large circles covering only two to three miles. Foxes, usually "treed" in the ground, are left alive to run again.

Milton N. Hopkins, Jr.

THE LIMEY BIRD RINGER

People have been banding birds since John J. Audubon's time to learn more about the birds' life span, their speeds, and routes and destinations when migrating. Bands are made of lightweight aluminum and have numbers stamped on them. Most bird banders spend a lot of time and effort without any reimbursement, except for the love and excitement of the work. The U.S. Fish and Wildlife Service will furnish the bands only to someone proved competent at bird identification and who has obtained a federal banding permit.

Sometime during the winter of 1967, my friend Hedvig Cater from Warner Robins introduced me to Squadron Leader Philip Murton. Murton had flown Supermarine Spitfires for the Royal Air Force, warding off German Messerschmitt Fighters and Heinkel twin-engine bombers intent on destroying London during the Blitz, an endeavor at which the English pilots were barely successful. He was transferred to Warner Robins Air Force Base for additional training and while he was there, I invited him down to the farm expressly for the purpose of banding or ringing wading birds on their home territories. He turned out to be the most enthusiastic individual I've ever known.

We put Murton up at the Pond House at Osierfield. He was interested in banding any and all North American birds, regardless of species. He banded under a federal permit held by a couple in Pennsylvania, and carried with him an ample supply of band sizes. His first attempts were quite successful; he mist-netted a great number of summer resident species in the area and asked for more.

Murton became particularly interested in the purple martin colony occupying the twenty-one room martin house in the backyard of the Pond House and vowed he'd band every member of the colony before he left. He had had good success with the common dickeybirds but was a miserable failure at mist-netting purple martins.

He meticulously rigged two poles directly in front of the martin houses and stretched the hardly visible mist net between the top poles, barely three feet away from the house. The martins, both male and female, were continually going to and from the house to feed their young. The birds took this net as a challenge and continued coming and going at high rates of speed but adeptly ducked under the net or passed just above it by a few inches. At day's end Murton had banded one or two martins and these accidentally. He was dismayed but enthusiastically continued to try to net the martins, though never with much success.

In Wilcox County, I pointed out to Murton a mixed sand and clay bank, actually a roadcut through a hill. In past times workers built the road around a hill to avoid all the pick-and-shovel work and use of mule-drawn dirt pans, but with steam shovels, dump trucks and a little manpower, hills could more easily be conquered and the resulting roadcuts produced many steep banks. Two species of birds, rough-winged swallow and belted kingfisher, found these roadcut banks to be prime nesting spots. They would claw and peck cavities deep into the banks, sometimes six feet deep. Murton found an ingenious way to band the occupants, especially the swallows. He would take an empty paper towel roller, slip a pantyhose over one end, then push the other end into the round hole after the parent had entered to feed the young. The birds could still see light at the end of the tunnel and would fly out and be caught in the pantyhose. Murton then gingerly removed the bird, recorded the sex if he knew it, put a band on one leg and released the bird.

His greatest show was banding in the waterbird colonies that I had located from a light aeroplane. Most waders nest in trees standing in water and are colonial, their nests often numbering in the thousands in a very small area. In 1968, on fourteen visits from May to August, Murton and I banded 1810 birds including green heron, cattle egret, little blue heron and anhingas. Over the following few years we received returns (banded birds that were recaptured, shot or found dead) on many cattle egrets from Iona, Nova Scotia, Canada, Guatemala, Cuba, Mexico, and Westwego, Louisiana. For the little blue heron, we had returns from Eastman, Georgia and one from Florida. Several years after we banded one cattle egret it turned up in a cow pasture on the

Osierfield farm. I saw a band on at least one more cattle egret in a peanut field later on but was unable to retrieve it.

Bird banding can require some considerable effort. Once we went to band at the Dodge County rookery and discovered there an abandoned leaky boat. We upended it, got the water out and used it as a platform. I stood on the boat to reach for the young birds and then passed them down to Murton, who was standing in waist-deep water. We were selecting only young birds, about two weeks old, who had legs large enough to hold a band. Many hundreds of smaller birds were passed by.

On one occasion Murton pushed me into a black wasp nest as big as a ten-gallon hat. All I remember was a mighty roar when they attacked my face and head, resulting in over twenty bites, which by the following morning had my eyelids swollen almost shut. I can recall seeing the nest, hearing the roar and diving headlong into the muck and holding my breath until I thought my lungs would burst.

Murton apologized, but I imagined I detected a smirk on his face and swore to somehow even the score by wreaking vengeance on him. The occasion presented itself a few moments later when I stepped into a gator hole, much over my head in depth, and went all the way under. Murton hadn't witnessed this so after getting back out, I called for him to come over towards me, for I had a nest of young birds ready for banding and indicated the route, directly over the gator hole.

He followed my directions, fell into the deep hole, and as his head was about to disappear under the surface of the water he yelled, "My God, my notes, my notes." For a few minutes all I could see was a cap floating on the whirlpool he'd created. It read, "British Ornithology Union." He came up sputtering and spitting duckweek and foul heronry water, which ain't too pleasant.

THE GOLDEN MOUSE

Professor Frankie Snow, who teaches science and math at South Georgia College in Douglas, came through the farm this afternoon and showed me a globular nest from a small dead pine in a swampy area of Atkinson County. I immediately identified it as a golden mouse nest. He said it had been collected at the junction of a sand ridge affronting a swamp and was located approximately eight feet above ground. It had one clearly visible entrance, a hole about an inch in diameter on one side. With close examination we found a second opening on the opposite side, probably an escape route. Many mammals do this, fox, for instance; some in fact tunnel not one but several entrances to their nesting sites or breeding abodes.

My first encounter with this beautiful deer mouse, also called a white-footed mouse or red tree rat, came in 1941 when Robert Norris and I were wading in a cattail marsh on the west side of Lake Beatrice in Ben Hill County. We were looking, primarily, for birds and their nests and had already flushed several sora and king rails when we began to see globular nests up in the cattails and in the marsh. The nests were constructed mainly of skinned cypress tree bark and various grasses and had a dome-like covering over the top of them. The nests puzzled us somewhat, so on coming to the next one, we tapped on its supporting vegetation and out ran a small, reddish mouse that unhesitatingly plopped into the waist deep water then rapidly swam to a nearby cypress buttress and climbed up it, squirrel-like. This event took place so fast that we doubted what we had seen, at the time not knowing the mammal and its arboreal nest-building habits. The nest contained a handful of naked mice only a few days old.

Back then they were common—the nests and the species. Nowadays, though not rare, they are often overlooked by modern field trippers. Most mammal guides say the nest is globular and located a foot or so above ground. There is no mention of nestings above water. Francis Harper, in *Mammals of the Okefenokee*, thought it, at first, to be a rare find. During his time in the Okefenokee, Harper was enamored with the largest, most common, and most easily observed of the swamp critters and overlooked the ubiquitous golden mouse. He finally talked to a local who told him that there was a red tree rat that built nests in the trees and ran over water and tree limbs when leaving the nest.

They are one of, if not *the* prettiest of small mammals. Their pellage is truly golden or rich reddish when seen in good light and their prominent, jet black eyes seem almost to protrude from their sockets. Golden mice are nocturnal in habit, avoiding daylight. Some writers even say they will not come out on nights when the moonlight is too bright.

ASAFETIDA

Asafetida is the fetid gum rosin of various Oriental plants (genus Ferula) of the carrot family, used in medicine as an antispasmodic, I learn from a reference. The herb is not listed in the latest *Physician's Desk Reference*, yet it was in common use in the 1940s at Osierfield in the turpentine quarters. I don't know where the folks there got their information but asafetida was thought to ward off mad fits and other sundry ailments.

There was not a child in the quarters that did not wear a small, hand-sewn cotton sack of asafetida around his or her neck, hanging from a dirty, frazzled cotton string. It stunk like hell. Sadly, all the old folks who inflicted this curse on their younguns are long gone but many of their children, in their forties and fifties now, still remember wearing the sacks and figure the preventative brought them safely through childhood.

CATAWBA WORMS

Botanically, it's *Catalpa bignonia* of the family Bignoniaceae, but we always called the big-leafed tree, the one with worms eating on the leaves in the spring and foot-long beans hanging from it in early fall, catawba. The worms were actually a caterpillar of *Ceratomia catalpae*, the catalpa sphinx, commonly called hawk or hummingbird moth. It was termed sphinx because its shape when at rest recalled the sphinx at Thebes.

Moths undergo complete metamorphosis in four distinct stages: egg, larva, pupa and adult. The adult sphinx moth is probably drawn to the catalpa tree by chemical substances given off by the tree. The adult female lays her eggs, numbering from a few to eighteen thousand and less than one millimeter in diameter, on a leaf and attaches them with a gluey secretion. The eggs usually hatch within a week and become our catawba worms. They feed on the leaves, sometimes completely defoliating a tree, and in a few days become one and one-half to two-inch caterpillars, black in color with bright yellow markings.

This is the time to harvest them for fish bait, and it coincides with the season when bluegill bream and redbreasts are on their beds. We helped ourselves to the caterpillars, picking as many as several hundred from a good tree. The surplus was sold for a penny apiece and the rest were carried to the river or creek in something similar to a cricket cage. Then we pulled them out, one at a time, mashed in their heads with a cordwood match and turned them inside out so the succulent juice would smell up the water around the hook. They were prime fishing bait and beat the hell out of digging or grunting earthworms.

One of the beauties of catawba worms was that if you had live ones at quitting time you could put them in the refrigerator where they could live for up to two weeks. If not used as fish bait, the caterpillars, when they gained enough nutrients, dropped onto the ground under the tree and went into the pupal stage for a year.

POSTSCRIPT
Catalpa Tree Pods in the Smoking Room

Catalpa trees not only supplied good fishing bait, but also provided us with "cigars." It was common knowledge among us boys that Indians cut off each end of the seedpods of catalpa trees and smoked them. In emulating some of our elders, we tried smoking a lot of things—coffee, dried corn silks, and rabbit tobacco. We generally did our smoking in the "smoking room" of one of our caves, which we made by digging down two or three feet into the clay and then excavating two feet wide tunnels. The passageways ended in a room about six feet in diameter. We covered the passageways and the room at the end with old roofing tin supported by boards and then piled six or eight inches of dirt on top of the cave. We took care to put a ventilating pipe through the top of the room. It was secure from our elders, for all were too big to get on their hands and knees and follow the labyrinth of passages to our smoking room. Sure, it was a lot of hard work but it beat playing drugstore cowboy downtown and probably kept us out of serious mischief.

SEVENTEEN-YEAR LOCUSTS

We have, in this area of south Georgia, several species of cicadas. The most common one in late summer and early fall is the dog-day cicada or harvest fly, often called lyreman. The insect is about two inches long and the best known of them is probably *Tibicina septendecim*, commonly called seventeen-year locust. The common name is a misnomer since true locusts are members of the order Orthoptera, along with grasshoppers, crickets and cockroaches. The cicada was probably called locust because it appears in great swarms, reminding early settlers of the hordes of migratory locusts or grasshoppers of the Old World.

The cicada has a remarkable life history. The eggs are laid in twigs of various trees and the nymphs hatch in about six weeks, then drop to the ground and bury themselves. They obtain nourishment by sucking juices from roots of forest and fruit trees. Empty pupa-skins, with a split down the backs of the exoskeletons, appear on tree trunks, especially pines, in late summer. I used to gather these pupa-skins—thin, weightless and almost transparent—wondering what strange insect had left them, but not finding out for many years.

Most remarkable is the fact that the nymphs remain underground for seventeen years, through snows, floods and whatever else Mother Nature serves up, and then emerge during the last half of May. There is another variety of cicada that has a development period of thirteen years. It is chiefly a southern form, while the seventeen-year locust broods occur in the north. More than twenty distinct broods have been traced in this country so that one or more broods appear somewhere in the United States nearly every year.

In May 1985 I was enthralled when I found myself in the middle of a hatch out on the Ocmulgee River. My friend, Betty Stewart, and I had been invited to visit a riverboat anchored at Red Bluff on the county line between Ben Hill and Coffee County. We drove in late one afternoon and immediately were dumbfounded by the shrill, raucous calls of millions of periodic cicadas. The male cicada vibrates membranes of special sound organs on the underside of the abdomen producing prolonged shrill notes, the sound filling the air when cicadas are about. That day insects appeared in solid masses on every available type of vegetation for about a square mile and the combined roar was nearly deafening. Although we both had training in the natural sciences, neither of us had witnessed this before and wanted to know more. We secured a boat and proceeded to the opposite, north, side of the river seeking the source of the cacophony. We thought it was dead ahead, a few hundred feet away, but the ventriloquistic quality of the calls puzzled us; it sounded as if the insects were calling from all directions, and truly this was the case.

After this experience it became one of my fondest dreams to hear the cicadas in song again. Counting seventeen years from 1985, I anticipated the opportunity in 2002. But nature fooled me and the hatching happened in 1998. I missed it.

SANDHILL CRANES

They are a magnificent species, standing over five feet high when their necks are extended. These long-legged wading birds were first correctly identified on the Osierfield farm in the middle 1950s, flying south in late November, as they had been wont to do for thousands of years. At this time their numbers had been sadly reduced by hunters, since they were fair game and the old timers relished the meat.

In late February or early March of the following spring they came back over, heading north. Their calls sound something like ber-roo-roo-roo and one must roll the r's to simulate the sound. When they pass over the farm, we usually hear their haunting call sometime before they come into view over the tall pine timber. The calls can readily be heard inside buildings if the doors and window are open.

Old-timers had mistaken the cranes for geese and I had put so much credence in their belief that I'd not been cognizant of their real identity. After observing them closely with powerful binoculars, though, I decided they weren't geese. Yes, of course, geese do migrate through here, both south and north in fair numbers, but usually they fly lower. Also, these birds didn't honk, but instead gave out a loud, guttural, sonorous trumpeting. They fly with necks stretched out in a straight line, whereas herons and egrets fly with their necks in an S-shaped curve.

Now we know sandhill cranes by the thousands. The latest count of individuals leaving southward from Jasper-Pulaski refuge in Indiana was upwards of twenty-six thousand. Most end up in mid-Florida but others stop short of there. They are very smart birds, hence their increase in numbers and survival into the 1990s. They usually put off their departures, both coming and going, until they have the benefit of favorable tail winds. At take-off, they do a lot of flapping to gain altitude and begin riding the heat thermals, then peel off and begin their leisurely circling and sailing.

Their majestic appearance and power of flight, sometimes carrying them above low hanging clouds, is not soon forgotten.

Some flocks fly over two thousand feet above the ground, so high they are out of hearing range. The great birds alternately flap and glide, forming wedge-shaped flight patterns, then long, undulating lines, and back into wedged formations again. They often soar to higher altitudes in circles, drifting or being carried along their northward journey by southerly winds.

Some of our sightings were recorded and described in "The Birds of Ben Hill County and Adjacent Areas." The first recording was on March 5, 1956 when a wedge-shaped flock of twenty-three cranes passed over Osierfield six to eight hundred feet above the ground, flying in a north-northwesterly direction. The species has subsequently been noted almost every spring since then between March 1 and 19 and the birds have always been flying in the same general direction. On March 7, 1969 two flocks numbering eighty-nine and one hundred and fifty individuals flew over, the largest numbers yet seen in one day. This was immediately surpassed the next day when three hundred and ten cranes flew over Osierfield at 12:45 p.m. and less than an hour later, two hundred and fifty more were seen. My only fall sighting was on November 18, 1959, so apparently they usually pass by a little to the east or west of here when migrating south.

Donny Young was familiar with the birds and reported a large number down in an isolated pond about five miles northeast of here on March 13, 1971. Strong winds from the south accompanied by heavy rain and a low ceiling, had forced the high-flying birds down. Mary Hopkins and I joined Donny, watching and listening to the cranes until about midnight. The birds bugled incessantly and flew around in small circles, their calls coming from every direction. It was an unforgettable occasion, and never matched, before or after, in local bird watching. By seven o'clock the following morning all the birds had gone.

The total of migrating cranes must reach into the thousands. Mary and Bubba, both familiar with the bugling call of this species, have seen and heard cranes passing over Fitzgerald in the early spring on the same days that I saw them ten miles away at Osierfield. The migration corridor through here may be as much as seventy-five miles wide, for Tommy Patterson of Dublin, eastward, and people in Albany, westward, tell me of their passing. Recently William Dopson of McRae, while cruising timber near Albany, told me of hearing northbound cranes calling continuously between one and four in the afternoon.

Ken George of Valdosta has often heard them calling and passing over at night, as we have here on the farm, but by and large the greatest number of observations are between eleven in the morning and four in the afternoon. Sometimes the cranes will still be walking around at ten or eleven in the morning, waiting for the ground to heat up, and will not take to wing unless disturbed.

Dr. D. W. Johnston of Gainesville, Florida, has written to say that cranes were leaving the vicinity of Payne's Prairie, south of Gainesville, near the dates that we noted them in this area. It would be interesting to know if these were some of the same birds, or if they are a part of the population in the Okefenokee Swamp. It would be equally, or probably more interesting, to know how many miles they cover in a day.

Our place must be an ancestral stopping point on the birds' trip north and south. We now know they often set down in late afternoon in a large, hundred-acre field about two miles north of here. Granddaughter Amy Sue Hopkins first reported this location, having seen them from a school bus window. She carried me back that way a few minutes after arriving home so that I could witness the sight.

Unfortunately, some people still believe they are geese, especially when they pass over in wedges or V-shapes. In March 1970, I observed two flocks, one of over two hundred cranes and another of thirty-seven, flying north-northwest over the edge of Fitzgerald. A farmer friend of mine was watching these birds with me and said, "Peers they've lost their leader, the way they are wandering around. I sho' believe there's more geeses hearabouts than they used to be." I have heard rapid automatic rifle firing in recent years, and shortly thereafter the cranes calling.

But more and more people, I must report, recognize the birds for what they are, and I get many calls during the spring and fall letting me know the cranes are overhead again.

HUNTING QUAIL

My first experience with the quail, called partridges by Paw Scott, was probably in the early 1930s. We lived on the south side of Fitzgerald where the dirt streets stopped and the woods began. There were patchwork garden spots free for the taking, and lots of folks took advantage of this—mostly locals from the sparsely settled south side of town. It made a very good quail habitat, for safe cover in the woods was only a few fast wing-beats away.

At age ten I began following Mr. Walter Murray and his three sons, Junior and the twins Edward and Edmund, who were my age, on quail hunting jaunts around the southern periphery of Fitzgerald where today houses and shopping centers stand. Mr. Murray was a real sportsman. He kept good dogs— King, a liver-spotted pointer, and Queen, a nondescript long-haired setter. He fed them properly but not too much, made them mind and punished them if they didn't. The hunts started at the Murrays' doorstep and usually covered a four- to five-mile circuit south of the township limits. I remember King, backed by Queen, locating and locking in a covey of partridges every three to four hundred yards. I don't like to exaggerate—this is the God's truth.

Mr. Murray shot only on covey rises and never, never shot a quail on the ground. Back then, hunting out singles was a last resort; you shot covey rises and forgot about singles, for more action was just ahead. The Murray twins and I toted Benjamin pump BB guns or air rifles on the first few trips and Junior shouldered a fine-looking .410-gauge single-barrel with a black painted stock and nickel-plated breech mechanism.

On one particular hunt we had found a big covey of birds. It was a sparse cover situation and we could see birds running on the ground ahead of the creeping dogs. The twins and I begged to pot a single each with the BB guns but Mr. Murray wouldn't buy this. He said, shouldering his Belgian-made Browning automatic unplugged .12 gauge, "Give King some more time. He'll lock in and we'll shoot into the whole covey." I knew what he was thinking: if we jumped the whole covey he could cut down four or five birds with the unplugged gun. He could stand in one place while

Queen would fetch each fallen bird, deposit it at his feet and go look for another.

Mr. Murray would have been pleased to witness an episode that happened when I was hunting alone one day in a fallow broomsedge field on the south side of the farm. When quail go to roost, the covey stands in a circle with tails almost touching and heads pointing out in all directions. I had noticed numerous telltale, circular piles of droppings that indicated a roosting spot so I knew quail were nearby. Standing at the edge of the broomsedge patch overlooking several hundred acres of cotton, I saw four covies fly into the patch from the cotton fields. It was almost dark but I loaded my Ithaca double-barreled 16-gauge shotgun and waded in. On the first covey rise I got a bird with each barrel but then could not find them in the gathering dark. I marked the spot with my handkerchief and returned at sunup the next morning to retrieve the two downed birds.

I had built a reputation of being a crack shot during my first fall tenure at Osierfield. Twelve or thirteen cotton-picking hands were riding on the rear of a pickup truck I was driving back to the quarters. A cock quail darted out between two cotton rows and ran down the middle of the road in front of the truck. I jokingly pulled out the Colt .45 revolver and said, "Watch this." Believe it or not, a single shot, left-handed at that, cleanly knocked off the head of the running partridge. He was promptly retrieved and enhanced some hand's supper table. Tales of my prowess traveled quickly through the quarters endowing me with a reputation that sometimes served for dubious purposes.

Crack shooting doesn't always guarantee good results in the field though. I recall when Jimmy Lester Jinright, Reason Young and I went quail hunting on the north side of the farm following Jimmy Lester's dogs. Both of the other guys toted hip bottles and continually sipped so I tried to stay behind them and only took shots when the birds flew to one side.

A flush suddenly came up from the edge of a cotton field north of the railroad right-of-way. Carver, the dog, pinned them down and we all pushed off safeties. The covey roared into the air, having been caught in the open, and we leveled our guns. The birds were near safe cover but in their panic chose to fly almost straight up, reverse their direction, and then cut back just over our heads. Jimmy Lester and Reason both got off two shots apiece and didn't cut a feather. I followed with a single and got the whole load as it passed overhead. It was not an event to build pride though, for when we went to gather the results we found one wing but no other parts large enough to put in a frying pan.

After this episode, we three were a bit winded, besides being dumbfounded, so stopped at the next fallen pine log and sat down. Naturally the conversation drifted to bird dogs, their training and obedience, and Jimmy Lester 'lowed as how his pointer and setter had been so thoroughly trained that they could not be invited or forced to eat a quail. Every one he shot, he said, they returned, toting it with a tender mouth so as not to bruise it, and dropped it at his feet.

"I ain't never seen a bird dog that on occasion wouldn't eat a quail," says Reason. Along about then, Carver sneaks up to Reason's hunt vest, sticks his snozzle in and with a few quick gulps swallows a quail whole, feathers and all.

Reason guffawed. "See what I told you?" he says. "All bird dogs, if they aren't watched close, will eat quail."

A lot of words passed while I tried to be a non-participant. Pretty soon Les had his loaded pump gun pointed at Reason and Reason did the same with his. It was getting a little hairy so I stepped behind a big pine tree to await the outcome. All of a sudden I heard loud laughing, the guns were lowered and the two decided the situation was good for another drink. They cut wrists and went on hunting, and I decided then and there that drinking and hunting don't mix.

Quail hunting stories abound. I remember the first day of quail season in November 1952. Jimmy Lester and I took his two bird dogs and headed up the railroad tracks toward Prospect Church crossing. We planned to hunt up the right-of-way on the south side during the first half of the morning, and come back along the north side. This was good hunting territory because quail like the edges of railroad right-of-ways; they are kept fairly clean of dense foliage, but safe cover is nearly always nearby.

We had almost reached the crossing when all of a sudden quail started getting up all around us. Lester emptied his unplugged .12-gauge pump, I my Ithaca double-barrel, and though both of us had time to reload, we stood and watched, dumbfounded, as the huge covey of birds took wing. Honestly, nearly a hundred birds went flying off. Their ages ranged from little fellows barely able to clear the grass to full-grown, fast-flying adults.

The combined number had to be a get-together of six or seven sizable coveys, and why they had congregated in an area of a few hundred square feet in size is a puzzle to this day, over forty years later. I recall the hunter-author Nash Buckingham relating a very similar story, but with even more partridges, near the Mississippi River around the turn of the century. I often wish I had noted the weather that day and the prediction of forthcoming weather, for birds and animals do strange things when fast-moving fronts rush down from the north in November. I have never again witnessed such a sight.

Bob Humphries of Marietta, Georgia, has run bird dogs on the Osierfield farm for over thirty years and probably knows the land lines better than anyone else. For the first twenty years there was a fifty-acre tract of almost virgin longleaf and slash pine owned by Miss Sarah Harper, an elderly spinster who lived on her homeplace about a mile southeast of here. Humphries is of the opinion that a large portion of the quail raised in this area, with its stand of scattered longleaf pines and understory of wiregrass and gallberry, used this tract as a nursery and a place to raise their young and repopulate the surrounding area. I think Humphries was on the right track.

Trying to maintain a strong quail population, we have control burned for thirty-five years, observed game laws and left the quail a certain amount of feed in the fields after harvest. Bubba has disked in numerous food patches of bicolor lespedeza, Egyptian wheat, browntop millet, and Sesbania or partridge pea, and he never completely gathers all the corn, but leaves a few patches in the edges of all the fields.

There was, however, a distinct drop in the quail population when the following sad story happened. Sometime in the 1960s

Sarah Harper died intestate, very likely from old age and malnutrition, or at least the lack of a balanced diet. The wooded, park-like land, inherited from her father and which she had resisted selling, passed to a distant nephew. He promptly clearcut the timber and sold the bare land at public auction. All this tale offers is—ain't nothing, even with the best intentions, forever.

POSTSCRIPT
Cooking Quail Eggs

A few years ago son Bubba inadvertently mowed off the top of a ground-level quail nest. It contained fourteen eggs. He told me of the nest and I retrieved the eggs since the mama had been killed by the rotary mower's blades. On breaking one of the eggs I ascertained they hadn't been sat on but for a few days, since the fertilization spot was minuscule. The next morning I put a slop of peanut oil in the cast-iron frying skillet and proceeded to break the remaining thirteen eggs into it.

The albumen immediately cooked and the yolks shortly after, producing a pan of eggs sunny side up. It was a beautiful sight, likened to thirteen human-sized eyes looking up at you from the pan. Along with bacon and hog sausage, this was an epicure's delight.

Milton N. Hopkins, Jr.

THOUGHTS LATE OF AN EVENING—BEING IN ONE PLACE FOR 50 YEARS

April 14, 1997: a thrill today was spotting and observing at least six different species of birds that I hadn't seen on the farm since last August or October. Collectively they'd loved, nested, laid and become promoters of their races, then flown south and returned after a period of quiescence in late fall, the cycle so gradual as to be almost imperceptible.

April 17, 1997: a real jewel of the bird world turned up, the indigo bunting, along with eastern kingbird, great crested flycatcher and blue grosbeak. Palm warblers are still here in good numbers plus a flock of beautiful cedar waxwings. I suppose the latter will hang around till they've stripped the fruit-bearing mulberry trees and it probably will not take many more days for there are forty to fifty birds.

I recall now a time in the spring of 1945 after we sailors on a destroyer coming from Guantanamo Bay, Cuba, rose in the morning. This wasn't a leisurely affair. First came the shrill whistle of the boatswains pipe over the intercom, followed by "Reveille! Reveille!" All hands hit the deck, jumping out of hammocks, and commenced ship's duties, followed shortly by another pipe, "Turn to, sweep down all decks, ladders, and compartments."

We welcomed a new day in Navy life; but this was not an ordinary one. On climbing up to the main deck, we found that hundreds of warblers, thrushes and various other species of land birds had joined us. They had been heading north in the springtime and met a nor'easter so they sought temporary refuge on the destroyer. Most clung to the cable surrounding the main deck and a few perched in the uppermost rigging; some were lying, alive but motionless, on the steel decks. They would rest for a short time and then take wing northwards, often into indeterminable fogs and mist, being driven so by age-old patterns of migration carrying them northward to their ancestral breeding grounds. The speed of the northward migration has been long known to be more rapid than the leisurely flight southward. The number of miles covered increases daily as the birds approach their destination.

Most of this I learned later under the tutelage of Gene Odum, while answering the role call of his ornithology class in the late 1940s, though I could identify most of the birds that sought refuge on the ship because I'd known the same birds during spring around Fitzgerald. As I've continued to observe the passing of birds over the farm I imagine the trials and travail they have gone through to get this far, already having persevered through the worst part of their journey across the Gulf of Mexico.

I'm often asked, "Have you really, really seen all the different birds you tell about right here on the farm?" Yes ma'am, it's the truth. One can be in one place for a long time and see a multitude of different bird species that the uninitiated wouldn't expect. Comes to mind the golden plover, magnificent frigatebird and black skimmer pushed here by hurricane winds on the coast over a hundred miles east of here.

When we lived at the old pondhouse we had a prominent window in the bathroom that looked out over a vast expanse of pond. I've made some of my better bird observations there sitting on the throne. I recall the time the pond was frozen over from the upper end to half way down. A flock of greenwing teal came gliding in, touched down on the ice and skidded along thirty to forty feet, then regained their footing and took to the air. The flock had twenty-five or thirty individuals in it, the largest concentration of greenwing teal I've seen here in my fifty years of birding. I can remember also seeing black terns, herring and ring-billed gulls fly by the window.

I have seen all of these species and more by just sitting in one place long enough and letting the birds come to me. God, what a revelation and classroom this life has been for a farm boy.

— Milton N. Hopkins, Jr.